Digital Play Therapy

Digital Play Therapy focuses on the responsible integration of technology into play therapy.

With a respect for the many different modalities and approaches under the play therapy umbrella, this book incorporates therapist fundamentals, play therapy tenets, and practical information for the responsible integration of digital tools into play therapy treatment. Written in a relatable manner, this book provides both the foundation and practical information for confident use of digital tools and brings play therapy, and therapy in general, forward into the 21st century.

Digital Play Therapy provides a solid grounding both for clinicians who are brand new to the incorporation of digital tools as well as to those who have already begun to witness the powerful therapeutic dynamic of digital play therapy.

Jessica Stone, PhD, RPT-S, is a licensed clinical psychologist, registered play therapist–supervisor, author, innovator, and speaker specializing in the therapeutic use of digital tools in therapy.

Digital Play Therapy

A Clinician's Guide to Comfort
and Competence

Jessica Stone

Routledge
Taylor & Francis Group

NEW YORK AND LONDON

First published 2020
by Routledge
52 Vanderbilt Avenue, New York, NY 10017

and by Routledge
2 Park Square, Milton Park, Abingdon, Oxon, OX14 4RN

Routledge is an imprint of the Taylor & Francis Group, an informa business

Library of Congress Cataloging-in-Publication Data
A catalog record for this book has been requested

ISBN: 978-0-367-00190-2 (hbk)
ISBN: 978-0-367-00192-6 (pbk)
ISBN: 978-0-429-00110-9 (ebk)

Typeset in Times New Roman
by Apex CoVantage, LLC

Contents

vi *Contents*

Foreword

Play therapy has been the treatment of choice for children for more than 60 years. It is the preferred and developmentally appropriate intervention for children who are experiencing behavioral, emotional, and/or developmental difficulties. Play is considered the child's language, as it is through play that children process their world and experiences. Children often use their imagination and create alternate means of dealing with their inner worlds. The source of their imagination influences how they are able to create the play that helps them manage whatever situations they encounter.

Play therapy began in a different era and therefore children's play has changed over time. Now, children speak through different mediums in their play. In their day-to-day lives, children use digital tools for playing, learning, exploring, and creating. Therefore, play therapy needs to expand and incorporate digital play therapy (DPT) to understand and use the current therapeutic language of children's play.

Activating the therapeutic powers of play helps children manage their internal world. These therapeutic powers of play refer to the specific change agents in which play initiates, facilitates, and strengthens their therapeutic effect (Schaefer & Drewes, 2003). It is important to emphasize that the play actually produces the change and is not just a medium for applying other change agents. One of the most powerful aspects of play is the ability of children to express themselves through playing. Play creates the safe emotional climate that enables children to express a wider range of internal experiences. Their expressions will be largely dependent on safety, their worldview, honoring their culture, and the medium(s) provided.

Dr. Stone's focus on the 4 Cs toward which a play therapist should strive – competency, culture, comfort, and capability – gives depth and understanding to what a qualified therapist should achieve and aspire to, especially in play therapy where the clients are children. Certainly, children's culture influences their play and self-expression. Being culturally aware of the children's environment and interests is a necessity in order to help and understand how children psychologically heal. Although play therapists would agree with cultural awareness as well as cultural competency, the definition of culture has broadened over time (Zimmerman, 2017). It is important that play therapists honor the multifaceted scope of today's cultures.

Now there is a new influence that has a powerful impact on children's play: digital tools and technology. Children's use of digital tools impacts how or what they will play, and it is the clinician's responsibility to be able to use these tools to help children. Through the inclusion of digital play therapy, the clinician can treat the whole child. The DPT interventions allow for the inclusion and understanding of children's additional new language.

Play therapists may use a directive, nondirective, or integrated approach in working with children. It is very important that the therapist respond to children in a way that facilitates self-expression. The language that the therapist uses can be integral to allow children to feel safe in expressing themselves. Therefore, knowing the language of the child will include knowing the digital world. Play therapists can provide children assistance through digital tools to access whatever they need for psychological healing. As most play therapists agree that play is the language of the child and toys are the words, there is a more expansive vocabulary that is needed now to promote expression and psychological healing.

In a world of digital technology, it has become a necessity to include electronic games, systems, and/or platforms as part of anyone's play therapy treatment. The language of the child is still play, but now it has a different source of input which play therapists have to understand and include in treatment. We must be able to know more about what can be done and seen digitally than many have previously known.

Dr. Stone has put together a hands-on, easily followed teaching of how digital technology can be integrated into play therapy treatment. Certainly, most play therapists are aware that digital tools exist, but questions still exist as to the application of the tools and how to utilize them in therapeutic way. The understanding of research to support what the play therapist will use and why is also a major focus of this book. Learning about the research is of utmost importance in order to use empirically supported treatment for children. And so the birth of this book by Dr. Stone has come at a time when all play therapists can benefit from her expansive knowledge on this subject.

This all-encompassing text explores the very basic nature of the use of therapeutic digital tools and Dr. Stone's own journey of discovery of the same. In her own words, "The chapters are intended to emphasize for the reader the importance of a solid foundation of theory and play therapy principles, an education about the materials involved, and then onto practical application". By being one of the pioneers of DPT through her creation and implementation of Virtual Sandtray®©, Dr. Stone has seen that the use of digital tools can enhance the play therapist's ability to know more about the new language of children and help these clients through the use of electronic games or apps in the play therapy setting. Children can feel immediately familiar and safe when the play therapist has digital tools in the playroom, such as an iPad, computer, or Nintendo Switch. The language barrier that exists when children are asked questions directly would immediately be dissolved, especially if the therapist asks for help learning one of the games on the platform presented. Children love feeling like the expert, and that can be established during the intake or soon thereafter. The use of the digital tools enhances the relationship between the therapist and children, and it can also be very useful as the medium (i.e., Minecraft) for helping children with executive functioning difficulties. Many of the popular games that exist currently can be used in play therapy to facilitate not only self-expression but also training of self-control and social skills as well. There are many games and apps that facilitate the therapy process, and Dr. Stone has given us a book to know how, when, and what to use for children in therapy.

Dr. Stone's passionate approach to this topic, and especially to this book, is evident in every chapter that you will read. This book can easily help enhance any play therapist's repertoire of treating psychological difficulties in children with the most up-to-date information written in a user-friendly manner. What a wonderful way to fully engage in the modern child's world. Therapists will be encouraged to return to this book from time to time to get grounded again in how to keep DPT alive in their practice and further their own knowledge as the field continues to expand while still keeping the belief of the therapeutic powers of play.

– Heidi Kaduson

References

Schaefer, C. E., & Drewes, A. (2003). *The therapeutic powers of play: 20 core agents of change*. Wiley.
Zimmerman, K. A. (2017, July 13). What is culture? *Live Science*. www.livescience.com/21478-what-is-culture-definition-of-culture.html

Author's Note: Minecraft Matters

There are moments, when researching books, articles, and more, in which an author comes across something that is just fantastic. Perhaps it is a phrase or a sentence where the writer stated something so eloquently that it does not do the meaning justice to paraphrase when incorporating the information into the new text. In these instances, we place it in quotations and cite it properly, so the reader knows they are someone else's words. Sometimes there are larger portions that are included but not the main author's words; for instance, in this book you will find the entire chapter of interventions is written by other play therapists. This allows the reader to have the voice of multiple professionals and perspectives when thinking about different digital tool possibilities.

I came across a link to a blog on Facebook. I was casually perusing the posts. I clicked on the link and I became so energized and ecstatic. This mother was beautifully and eloquently illustrating so many points I have been trying to make clear. I immediately reached out to her and requested permission to use her blog post in this book. She granted the permission and I am pleased to provide it for you here, in full. I thought I would pull out excerpts, but frankly, it is better to read all she had to say. After my brief exchange with her, I discovered that she holds a doctorate and works with and advocates for people with autism.

I believe the salient points in this blog apply both to neurotypical and neurodiverse populations. I believe this applies to us all. To all parents who experience value for their children, for their loved ones. Again, this is not to say balance is not important. It is to say that consideration of the value for some people is valid and powerful and should not be dismissed. It is with gratitude and honor that I publish this blog post within my book.

Minecraft Matters

May 28, 2018

> A few months ago, one of my youngest son's therapists and I were discussing the pre-planning I had done for his NDIS* funding. As some of you will know, the NDIS requires you to recount, in detail, the rhythm and flow of your child's daily life and activities. My little guy is happiest just being in

the safe, predictable environment of home, where I home-school him and his two older autistic brothers, and he prefers playing with children much older than his age-peers. Our family narrative reflects this reality.

As the therapist glanced through my day-to-day recount, she looked at me and asked, gently but with clear censure, 'so just how much screen does he have each day?' Argh. I cringed internally with guilt and shame but squared my shoulders to justify his iPad usage . . . only to shy away from that confrontation to reply vaguely, 'um, not that much'. She gave me that look – you know the one that's part doubtful, part disapproving judgement, part reminder that your failures are seen and noted – and dropped the matter. But even months later, it's still bothering me: the question itself, and my own lacklustre, totally inadequate, evasive response.

We all know what the question behind her question was. Or, more properly, what the intent behind the question was. It was a reprimand, a reminder, that by allowing my son so much iPad I was somehow damaging him, enabling his social isolation, coddling him, exacerbating his autism. I've heard it all before, and it's rhetoric to which we're exposed often as parents: technology is damaging, it's isolating, it's anti-social. And when it comes to technology, I spend my life consumed by paroxysms of guilt: if I take my sons' iPads (or other miscellaneous gaming devices) away, I know I do my children a disservice; if I give it to them, society shames me for it and my already shaky feelings of self-efficacy as a mother waver even further.

And there's the rub. I know that I know my children and their needs best. But I can't help being bullied by external expectations, and social pressures. So, I've decided it's time to rectify that wrong. Now, months later, I've finally formulated the answer I wish I'd have delivered to my son's therapist when the issue arose.

In order to understand the importance technology – specifically Minecraft – has in our house, you need to know more about my youngest boy, Mr Z. Mr Z undermines most assumptions people have about autistic kids, not least because he has the most amazing, complex and vivid imagination. This is a little boy whose internal world is vast and deep and profound.

Mr Z has certain ways of experiencing his imagination which are both visceral and uplifting for him, but he has neither the expressive language nor the fine motor to share his imaginative visions with us, his family. Mr Z is verbal, and generally he has a precocious vocabulary, but the complexity of his internal imagination is so great that he can't always access the right words to describe what's inside his head. As he begins to learn that we aren't inside his head with him, that we can't automatically see what he sees, he desperately wants to share his internal world with us; he wants to make the internal, external.

But when a child's words simply don't suffice, and when they struggle to draw, and they're too young to type or write (even if they could access the right words), how can that child share – communicate – what they so *deeply desire to share? How can they give their family a way of seeing what they see, in their special, awesome, intensely detailed way?*

Well, for us, and for Mr Z, the answer is Minecraft: Mr Z recreates his internal worlds in the Minecraft universe so that we can see, we can experience, what he does. Minecraft is Mr Z's AAC if you like. For most people, Minecraft is a highly motivating 'sandbox game', an open-ended virtual world, which encourages building and creation with few game-directed goals and requirements. For Mr Z, it's a way to augment and complement his current verbal capacity when that capacity isn't sufficient for him to communicate what he wants to communicate. It alleviates communication frustrations and gives us access to a world that would otherwise be confined to Mr Z's head.

Minecraft gives Mr Z a way to express himself that is natural and appropriate for him, that he enjoys, and that he can share. How liberating for him, to have a tool that enables him to share and communicate all the amazing ideas he wants to share and communicate! Minecraft, then, is a cornerstone to Mr Z's interaction with his family; it is an interface between us and Mr Z.

But the benefits of games like Minecraft go beyond Mr Z's very specific use of it to help him represent and recreate his imaginative workings. The potential of Minecraft, and games like it, is located in its social currency: Minecraft is the second-highest selling computer game of all time, with a monthly player base of 55 million, and although it has special appeal to the autistic community (as witnessed by the player base of autistic servers like Autcraft), it is equally treasured and beloved within mainstream communities.

Now, research tells us that the most successful social encounters for neurodivergent children have their foundations in activities based around shared interests and passions. Scaffolding socialising through shared interests is effective not only in promoting social engagement for our children, but equally in supporting such engagement. Research also shows us that collaborative virtual environments offer unique opportunities for autistic children to engage socially, and to collaborate and communicate with their peers, with fewer risks and challenges than socialising solely face-to-face: these environments facilitate communication, interaction, socialisation, collaboration, and the formation of meaningful relationships. They allow our children to socialise authentically autistically, rather than holding them to ransom with neurotypical norms.

In our house then, many of our play-dates – whether they are with neurodivergent or neurotypical peers – are Minecraft play-dates. Since Minecraft is an environment in which players can join together to play virtually in a unique, shared world, it allows my boys to socialise with their peers in the context of their passions, respectful of their neurology, and without the stresses and challenges of traditional play. Their play on Minecraft is usually collaborative, cooperative, interactive, and prolonged. And they are hugely competent in it. Within Minecraft, my boys are set up to be socially successful, because they excel at something with universal appeal and popularity in both the neurotypical and neurodivergent populations.

For my boys, as for many others like them, Minecraft actively encourages and supports them to form authentic, respectful peer relationships, grounded in reciprocal passions and shared interests, humour, enthusiasm, appreciation, and playful competition. Virtual environments, such as Minecraft, respect a neurodivergent way of socialising and offer alternative avenues for social expression and communication. For our family, Minecraft has helped the boys foster quality friendships, based in mutual support, trust, humour, reliability and reciprocity, which are then developed and maintained both within and without virtual environments.

It's interesting . . . when my boys have play-dates that don't include a virtual element, when they are forced into a traditional, neurotypical pattern of socialisation (which admittedly I don't allow often), I can almost guarantee two results. Firstly, the play is parallel and limited; we can manage perhaps fifteen to twenty minutes of side-by-side play that is rarely cooperative and is often frustrated by the nuances and subtleties of neurotypical expectations. Secondly, after the playdate, one (or more likely all) of my boys will be absolutely exhausted and usually on the brink of meltdown. Minecraft (and indeed gaming more generally), on the other hand, provides them with a feeling of social competence (this is something they're good at, something they excel at, and something they enjoy), as well as social stamina.

So, next time you go to judge someone else's use of technology, next time you feel a tut-tut emerging because someone proposes a Minecraft play-date, or because you feel that their children have Too Much Screen . . . Stop, and think of this.

And, next time someone challenges your child's technology usage – next time you experience that heavy feeling of guilt as some well-meaning aunt or grandparent or friend or professional looks askance at your child absorbed in a virtual world – remind yourself of the importance of this tool, of its potential to boost your child's social self-esteem, of its communicative benefits. And calm that guilt. It's OK.

(Heyworth, 2018)

Reprinted with permission from the author, Dr. Melanie Heyworth (via *Reframing Autism*).

*National Disability Insurance Scheme (NDIS)

Reference

Heyworth, M. (2018, May 28). Mindcraft matters. *Reframing Autism*. www.reframingautism.com.au/resources/minecraft-matters?fbclid=IwAR1Pm08wD2Y2v vTqNj-nBLTiQ4H22GnehkapWBTHm9HqGC7DotKQnUNmOR8

Acknowledgments

A very special thank you to:

- My family, who endured the late nights, absent-mom moments, and eating out that completing this book required;
- My friends, who encouraged me to keep going;
- My colleagues, who have supported the importance of a digital play therapy text;
- The organizations who have supported my message, cause, and presentations; and
- Kristyn Buchanan, who literally made the completion of this book possible.

I am humbly in debt to all of you.

1 Introduction

To Begin

Play therapists understand play. Of any group of psychologically focused professionals, play therapists know more about the intricacies, nuances, fundamentals, and processes of play than anyone else. The therapeutic powers of play, fueled and guided by a trained professional, can drastically alter a child's understanding of themselves, their place in this world, and aspects of interpersonal interactions.

A significant portion of the play therapy process is understanding what the client's language is. What is it about their vernacular, cadence, vocabulary, and content that really illustrates who they are? Who they want to be? Who they have been? How does the play therapist incorporate what is understood about the client into the treatment progression? Speaking the client's language through play therapy allows a window through which these important questions can be answered. The use of digital tools in play therapy is a way for therapists to honor and incorporate client's current language. This book intends to provide a solid foundation for the appropriate, therapeutic use of digital tools in play therapy.

This author echoes sentiments written by Paul Abney and Cleborne Maddux in 2004: "We should avoid pointless and destructive polarization of the counseling field such as that which took place years ago in psychology as a consequence of disagreement between behaviorists and cognitivists" (p. 19) and "tolerance of dual approaches to applying technology in counseling will best permit the counseling field to progress" (p. 2). Concerns about a divide in play therapy was also raised by Snow et al. (2012). The approach for this book is focused on the responsible integration of technology into play therapy. There is no intent for division or controversy, rather, an acknowledgement that there is room for many different modalities and approaches under the play therapy umbrella. There is room for us all.

Author's Journey

As an undergraduate student searching for a doctorate program, I knew I wanted to work with children and earn a Ph.D. in psychology. I was not exactly sure what type of programs to look for and the task was daunting. The California School of Professional Psychology (CSPP) had a program in Fresno, California that looked promising. This program had an emphasis in Ecosystemic Clinical Child Psychology, led by Dr. Kevin O'Connor. Honestly, I had never heard of the program, Dr. O'Connor, or play therapy, but it seemed to fit the criteria I had at the time. I applied, was accepted, and moved to Fresno, California, to begin my first Fall semester as a G1 (Graduate Level 1) student.

The Association for Play Therapy was relatively new at that time and the office was housed in my graduate school. I worked there as a helper, an "envelope stuffer" if you will, and volunteered at a few conferences. The board meetings were held locally, and I was able to be exposed to many of our play therapy pioneers. Throughout my time at CSPP I was fortunate enough to be exposed to and trained by some of the most prominent play therapists and psychologists of the time. I am very thankful for my education and believe the program was ultimately the right fit for me.

I have had a few areas of interest and focus over my almost three-decade-long career. An overarching focus has been the importance of incorporating and, in a way, capitalizing on the interests of a client. "Capitalizing" is the chosen word because the information gained by understanding these interests are invaluable in the therapeutic process and utilizing them to better the treatment process is important. Speaking the client's language is a powerful and necessary tool when working with clients of all ages, and particularly children. It is a way to honor and understand the client. What is it that interests them? What topics or activities bring cohesion to their experiences and beliefs? How can I, as a therapist, understand my clients better, see into their world view, and help them improve their lives through speaking their language?

Over the decades different trends have been brought into play therapy sessions by clients. I have always seen it as my job to explore these trends and interests and see what therapeutic value might lurk within. For example, when Pokémon cards were first extremely popular many play therapists were expressing their dislike. I would teach a class and bring up Pokémon and there would be a collective groan in the room as play therapists were tired of hearing about this fad. Because of my speaking-the-client's-language-viewpoint, I did not feel that way. I saw these cards and their characters as a gold mine of information about the client. What character was the client attracted to? What were the strengths and weaknesses of the character? What did it evolve into? It seemed very natural to me to wonder about these aspects. I also noticed that the clients enjoyed my genuine interest. I recognized that the clients felt seen, heard, understood, and important. This is a fundamental human desire.

An expertise in using board games in therapy was developed through work with Dr. Charles Schaefer. This relationship and common interest recently led to a co-edited work, *Game Play, 3rd Edition*, 2019, and a chapter in the *Handbook of Play Therapy*, 2016, on Board Game Play Therapy. The work which has included the underpinnings of using board games in play therapy has been an important foundation for the work with digital tools in play therapy.

An expertise in working with gifted people arose from the desire to be educated in the area due to the needs of numerous family members. This culminated in a variety of writings, including a chapter focusing on the gifted in my edited book, *Integrating Technology into Modern Therapies* (Stone, 2019). Although the overall gifted population is small, a portion of my private practice clients have been of higher-than-typical intelligence. The education and readings in this area have certainly been beneficial, but the focus on speaking the client's language has been key in working with gifted people as well. Again, it is the focus on what is important to the client that fuels a strong rapport whatever the population, whatever the diagnosis, whatever the level, and whatever the interest.

Interest in Digital Tools

There is an irony in my current area of focus that is not lost on me. I am not an inherently tech-savvy or even tech-interested person. I fought against the trend of getting a cellular/mobile phone in the early 2000s. I vividly remember saying "I don't need to be that connected and available all the time". I did not allow my older children, now in their 20's, to get a PlayStation console when they were little. At the time it was so new, and I did not really understand very much about it all. I have not been a person who wants to have the newest technology, or learn to code, or need a lot of gadgets. Until . . .

There are many spokes to this wheel for sure. If we place digital items in the center and have the spokes coming out in all directions, there would be personal, parental, and professional arenas. I was wrong in the early 1990's – I *do* want to be connected with others and I want to have the option to be very connected or minimally connected. There was a day when I was scheduled to provide psychological testing of a child for a local psychologist. I was on my way and my car broke down on the busy California freeway. Thankfully I was safe and not harmed, but I was frantic because I had no way to tell this family what had happened. It was a Saturday and the office building was locked without me there. I could only imagine what they were experiencing: prepping their child to attend the appointment, dedicating their Saturday, driving to the building, only to find that it was empty. The door was locked, lights off, and no way to get in contact with the person they were to meet. I really, really wished I had had a cell phone. I got one as soon as I could after that.

There are many areas of our lives that benefit greatly from the current digital technologies. In speaking with a colleague recently, it was said that the current shifts are the biggest technological advancements since the Industrial Revolution. The direct and indirect effects of the current advancements are creating ripple effects in many directions. I believe we are only seeing the very beginnings of what is to come. With great change comes a host of pros and cons. It is inevitable. As Jeffrey J. Magnavita stated in his 2018 book, *Using Technology in Mental Health Practice*, "What is familiar to us is comfortable and feels secure, but the disruptive nature of change is unavoidable. Rather than fearing that our work will be subsumed by technology, we need to be adaptive and open to new ways of providing care. Our work is still relevant" (p. xiv). There are certainly concerns along the way and these are not to be ignored, however, the reality is that digital tools are here to stay and utilizing them to benefit our clients therapeutically is of utmost importance.

Runescape and the Importance of Joining Their World

During the years leading up to 2011, I began to adopt more types of digital technology into my day-to-day life. My children became interested in different types of video games and consoles and, yes, we ended up with a PlayStation. I saw their interest and decided I needed to learn more. I often give this example of wanting to join them in what they were playing. I wanted to understand what they were doing and, as much as I could, why they were doing it. I asked about an online game my older children really enjoyed called Runescape. Runescape is an action–adventure game (more about that in subsequent chapters) in which your character explores the land and various maps to accomplish a whole host of tasks and quests. I decided I would make an account in this game and enter my children's world. The funny thing is, I am not really very good at these games. I am a bit directionally challenged and I would get lost in the maps all the time. I would wander into places and get my character into trouble. I felt like I was really going to fail at this attempt. One day when I was logged in and feeling determined, I came upon a village. I saw people gathering feathers, bones, and meat from the chickens in an area of the village. It was a safe section of the Runescape world and other characters were wandering around collecting, cooking, and selling a variety of items. This was much more my speed!

I camped out in the chicken coop area and began collecting feathers, bones, and meat. I soon realized that these items were needed for particular quests and players needed them in great quantities. I decided to set up a business. I would log in and camp out in this area. I was known as the "chicken lady" in the game and eventually people would ask when I would be playing. The community of online players knew me as a person from whom to get these items and they would seek me out specifically to buy them. They did not want to waste their playing time gathering the large quantities needed for certain quests and I had the supplies readily available to sell. It really was a win-win. My children thought I was a pretty cool mom and I was seriously rich in the game currency. I believe it brought my children and I even closer together. I took interest in something they were playing. They could see when I was online because we were friends within the game. They could come and chat with me and see what I was doing and then go off and do what they wanted in the game, which was always much, much more advanced than what I was doing. I am so glad that I decided to make that account, even if I never ventured terribly far past my role as the chicken lady.

Personally, I felt pretty darned accomplished in the little Runescape role I carved out for myself. The initial fear and feeling of failure while playing was not something I wanted to continue feeling. I could have decided the game was not for me and deleted my account. The problems with that approach were that 1) I do not like giving up and 2) I really wanted to understand more about what my children were doing. I knew I had to work through my frustration to find a way to make this workable. Once I had my role as the chicken lady figured out, I really felt a sense of belonging and community. I do understand how odd that sounds to those who do not play these types of games; however, it is true. It was an unexpected artifact of the gameplay. I contributed something to this society, and I earned a place of importance, albeit minimal. I made friends with people within the game. They only knew my username and my role and reputation as the chicken lady to identify me, but we would chat online within the game and check in with each other. There were certainly people with whom I felt a camaraderie. No wonder my children enjoyed this game. They could explore, achieve, attempt, fail, connect, and so much more. They could try and try again, without tremendous risk, until they were successful.

I remember one day when my oldest son came to me devastated because he had been attacked and many of his valuables had been taken. There may have even been some trickery involved. I know he remembers this vividly as well. He was in such pain. Thing is, without having played the game myself, I would have seen my son in pain and tried to comfort him without really understanding what had really happened. However, because I had entered his world and I understood what he meant when he explained what had happened, there was a whole new level of connection and comfort I was able to provide.

I learned so much about connection through my experience as the chicken lady and I am forever grateful.

I decided that I had a whole new area of life to understand and learn about. I needed to learn more so I could understand and connect with my children, but also to understand and connect with my clients. This is their language and it is our job as play therapists to speak it. I started to research and ask my children about all sorts of games and programs available. I fumbled a bit and more than a few clients and I giggled about my feeble attempts, but I believe they appreciated my interest and efforts. All of this was the foundation for my next professional focus, unbeknownst to me.

In 2011, a tsunami hit Japan and a dear friend, Dr. Akiko Ohnogi, published a plea online for play items to be sent to Japan. She and her colleagues were working with families in the midst of the destruction without many play materials. Our local news station interviewed me about the need for materials and people donated some amazing things. I went to Target and bought as many things as I could afford. Federal Express donated the shipping of four large boxes to Japan. It was what we could do from afar.

The Birth of the Virtual Sandtray

I began to wonder, though, given the popularity of sandtray therapy in Japan, how on earth would that be possible? Even portable trays and sand are bulky, heavy, and cumbersome. How would that work in the crisis situation they were faced with? I said to my husband, Chris, that we need a more portable sandtray. It needs to be truly portable. It needs to be on an iPad. I had just gotten my first iPad as a Mother's Day gift. Truth be told, it had really been taken over by the kids and seemed more like a gift for them. By this point I had four children and all of them exceeded my technological abilities, even the small ones. However, knowing what the iPad was capable of and how portable it was let me know that it was the perfect medium.

Chris has long been my go-to tech person. He has had a long-standing interest in computers and coding. When I spoke with him about my idea, he was unable to help because of other commitments. My older sons and I purchased books to attempt the project and I did the "poor man's patent" of mailing myself the idea through the U.S. Postal Service. I was not sure what good that would do, but I thought it was a place to start. I called around and the least expensive bid I received to *start* the project – not for a completed project – was $35,000. I knew that figure would double or triple if I moved ahead and I quickly put the phone down in disbelief and sadness. It looked like the iPad sandtray idea would not come to be a reality.

Sometime later, Chris began the project. His work has been above and beyond what I had ever imagined. The Virtual Sandtray was born. This has been a family passion project for over eight years. We continue to expand upon the original ideas and have programs for iPad and the Vive and Rift S virtual reality systems. I am so very proud of our family and thankful for Chris' dedication to something he originally did not even fully understand (sandtray). So, I disclose to you that I have a financial tie to the Virtual Sandtray, if you want to call it that; we have financed the project all on our own and our debt far, far exceeds any proceeds. The patent application alone has cost more than $15,000 to date and it is still "pending". This is a project born out of a need and fueled by beliefs that 1) accessibility matters, and we are contributing our small part, and 2) speaking the client's language is of utmost importance and adapting tried and true methods to current language(s) is imperative.

This book has been quite a journey for me. Initially I proposed it as a basic introduction and guide to the concepts and therapeutic uses of DPT. It seemed quite reasonable to start at the beginning and work through important concepts so one can 1) determine what the therapeutic value of these tools are or can be; 2) understand the basic therapeutic underpinnings; 3) receive some information and direction regarding set-up within the play therapy office; and 4) explore ways to write notes, speak with parents, and speak with collateral contacts about the work. As the writing continued, and frankly at the publisher's due date witching hour, I decided the book needed more. There is no way this volume will cover every aspect (and that is something I remind myself of every day), but it must give the play therapy practitioner a solid foundation of how and why the use of digital tools in play therapy is not only an "okay" thing to do, but that it is valuable and important. In and of itself, the rapport building, information gathering, and intervention implementation that using these tools can provide is more than I would have ever imagined. The power available to play therapists through the use of digital tools is something we are just beginning to understand.

"What does the future hold?", you might ask. There are certainly a lot of valid questions regarding the future. It is clear that well-constructed, rigorous research is necessary. This is a fast-paced industry with new hardware and software on the horizon at all times. Exploration of all of the different possibilities is an ongoing process. Play therapists should proceed with an open mind and a skeptic's analysis. Clients are our number-one priority. Growth and change are inevitable. The inclusion of digital tools is happening slowly now, but will move forward quickly in the next generation for several of reasons: 1) clients we have now are digital natives and they have never known life without the inclusion of these items; 2) the parents of the digital natives either were brought up using these items or knew people who did, so the concepts either are well-known or, at a minimum, not foreign or different; 3) digital natives will become clients and, ultimately, the parents of clients and will have a lot of confusion regarding the *lack of* inclusion of these items in therapy (not the confusion about the inclusion as we might experience now); and 4) the clinicians who are graduating now do not feel these items are foreign since these tools have been an integral part of their lives too. The question will be "why are we not including these tools?" as opposed to "why would we?". Play therapy should be prepared with a well thought through approach.

Terminology Confusion

Sometimes I get caught up in words. When I hear a concept or terminology, I want to understand the fundamentals so that I can have the best opportunity to grasp the meaning. I search for the definitions of words all the time, whether I am reading them or writing them. I am teased about this frequently. Sometimes I believe I know the definition, but I want to confirm that I am using it properly. I will often read multiple definitions to make sure they are consistent and agreed upon. Therefore, when definitions do not yield the same or very similar meanings, I find myself unsettled and I want to investigate further. This has happened many times in my quest to understand more about the use of digital tools. You will find this approach illustrated numerous times within this text.

I also have confusion about words like "technology". It might seem simple to label all technology together under one umbrella. Using the term technology in this way is confusing to me because humans have utilized "technology/technologies" for hundreds of years. What about paper, Electricity, everything within the Industrial Revolution, and so much more? We have experienced so many changes and developments because of different technologies over the time humans have occupied this earth that it seems strange to lump what is happening now with all that has come before.

Really, there are a number of things that confuse me. For instance, what really is "screen time"? How is screen time all lumped together when it can mean many very different things? And, accordingly, how can research findings about this so-called screen time concept be useful to organizations, parents, therapists, and more when the basic terminologies mean different things to different people including researchers? When uses of these many different products serve very different needs and purposes? How do we make any sound decisions or form solid knowledge-based opinions when it really is all a swirl of confusion and, in many cases, fear? There is a significant lack of consensus and standardization. In addition, the research world is experiencing some much-needed upheaval, with scholars questioning the very process of research, publishing, and transparency. Between the lack of solid definitions, the wide variety of variables, and the identified pitfalls in research practices, it can become overwhelming very quickly.

It also confuses me to speak of the overweight, singularly focused, socially daft, young, pale white, male "gamer" sitting in his mother's basement in ratty, dirty clothes with no future prospects. What even is this description and where did it come from? I personally know many highly educated, multicultural, well-rounded, thoughtful, intelligent, socially capable, high-striving men AND women who enjoy a variety of activities, including video games. I have had passionate, informed conversations about a variety of things people have witnessed, experienced, created, and learned through the use of all kinds of digital tools. I have presented numerous times for conferences which are geared toward people who enjoy a whole host of activities, including, but not limited to, "gaming". Gaming is in quotation marks because it too is an insufficient umbrella term to me. There are so many different types of hardware that can be used to play hundreds and hundreds of different types of software. So if we do not even really know what the terms "gamer" or "gaming" identify, how are we having such simplistic conversations – or, better yet, sensationalistic proclamations – that gamers are rotting their minds and that gaming is bad? Nothing is simplistic in this matter, yet the boiled-down version is often: technology is bad, screens are bad, our youth and future society is doomed, and we (as a society) will all sit around stating how bad it all is while we read about it on our screens.

Fingers are pointed at teens routinely for their use of their phones and social media. Not long ago a photo of a group of teenagers sitting in a museum all starting at their phone screens went viral on numerous social media sites. The comments were typically negative and revolved around these "oblivious young people" who were so caught up in their phones they would not engage with the magnificence of the masters that surrounded them. This did not sit well with me. This is not what I witness when I see large groups of teenagers together who are assembled for a purpose. There are always outliers in any group who will do something like defy a situation or expectations for a variety of reasons, but the whole group of young people in a museum doing this? That did not make logical sense. So I researched further. What I discovered was that this was a class who was accessing information through their phones as they were *instructed to do* by their teacher. However, the majority of people who shared and commented on this photograph through social media were quite pleased with themselves to assume that this was proof that there was X, Y, and/or Z wrong with the youth of today. Why? Why is this the default? Why is it not more commonplace to question what is really happening?

When I come out of the swirl that surrounds all these topics for me and I dig my way out of the many rabbit holes, I am left with two major concepts: 1) we have a lot to discover about all of this and 2) the therapeutic possibilities to expand psychology in ways we previously could only formulate with words are now here. It is an amazing time. This book intends to further the explorations and uses of these important topics.

I certainly do not have all these answers. Concerns should be explored and discussed. What I do have is a great thirst to explore further and to learn all that I possibly can along the way – from the research, the literature, and my clients. What I also have had is the privilege and honor of witnessing profound change, relief, understanding, and breakthroughs of my clients using digital tools in play therapy. This has led me to my current position, and I have every confidence that it can and will do the same for you and your clients. As Michael Rosen stated in his book, *Michael Rosen's Book of PLAY!*, "there are many parts of the digital world that have really become new play spaces" (2019, p. 224).

One Valuable Rabbit Hole Find

Clive Thompson authored a book entitled *Smarter Than You Think: How Technology Is Changing Our Minds For the Better* (2014). I found myself enthralled with the history of the game of chess and how the advent of computer chess programs changed the game. I had no idea what the chess players, who were chosen to learn grand-master-level chess in the 1970's, experienced. If a player was deemed to be at a high enough level in the Soviet Union, the player would be flown to Moscow and brought to the "elite chess library" where one would have access to paper records of the world's best games (p. 17). The process even to retrieve the records was arduous: the player would identify a possible first move, look through a catalog to find what games began with that historically, then the librarians would retrieve the files using "long sticks like knitting needles" and the moves of the game would be studied (p. 17). This amazing collection of games and moves gave those with access phenomenal advantages, however, the storage and retrieval was laborious and fragile, and only available to a select few. Strategies would be researched, and new moves would be analyzed for weeks or months. Players rarely veered from their identified strategies (Thompson, 2014).

Computers and CDs opened a whole new world for chess players (and many other groups of course). A CD could store and allow quick access to thousands of chess games and moves. These moves were available to everyone and the result was an evolution of the game of chess. The players and the game became more daring, more creative (attributed to Frederic Friedel, Thompson, 2014, p. 17). The result of the accessibility of the data and the analyzing abilities of the computer programs has been an explosion of new moves and gameplay. People are currently reaching grand master chess player status younger and more often. The game has been elevated. The digital tools available allowed knowledge to become more accessible; the knowledge gained allowed for the exploration of new moves; the strategic analysis of the software discovered new possible moves; all of this allowed the chess player's minds to work less on the access and retention of the material, and more on the application of the gained knowledge. These digital tools did not reduce their abilities, they allowed the entire process to reach new heights – augmented by digital tools and implemented by the powerful human mind.

A part of me romanticizes the process of an elite few gaining access to these delicate documents. I can picture the young chess masters, wide-eyed, pouring over the ancient texts, studying and working to absorb every detail and commit as much to memory as possible. I have no idea what it all looked like, but in my mind I envision a Harry Potter–type environment, with people peering over texts by candlelight.

In a strange way it makes me think of SPSS, or the Statistical Package for Social Sciences (1968) hardware and the process of learning this in graduate school (Sigma Plus Statistiek, 2019). I remember having to work through horrifically long mathematical equations by hand and being told it was important for me to understand the math behind the statistical analyses. This sounds important and like a task that is difficult but critical for really understanding the intricacies of the math involved in statistics, and therefore research analysis. This is what Ph.D. students must endure, right? Once we were able to work through the equations by hand, we were able to use the SPSS software. After a bit of data input and some box-checking, the user could choose an analysis and within moments it was complete. The only mistakes would be born of human error in data entry or statistical choices. The SPSS equations were solid, the math was calculated properly, and the data was presented in an organized manner. I promise you that the length of time taken to perform the analyses by hand, the fear of making even the simplest of mistakes (which would affect all the findings and therefore the conclusions, etc.), has absolutely no romanticization in my mind. It was hell and stressful and I am happy to say I have never had to go through that again.

This brings to mind a proposed concept in the Clive Thompson book: centaurs. Once computers came onto the chess scene, some important discoveries became clear – humans and machines "think" differently. Humans learn to play chess by studying and committing strategies and knowledge to memory while experiencing intuition and analyzing the psychological state of the opponent. Machines inspect the board, calculate the options, and chooses the most optimal plays after analyzing many moves past the initial. The computer has speed, memory, and does not make mistakes if the information is inputted properly. There is no intuition, no psychological analysis; the process is very different from the human mind. The human mind cannot hold as much information as a computer can all at once. However, a combination of both is optimal in chess. The information holding and calculating is superior in the computer and allows the human mind to concentrate on other critical parts of the game interaction. This realization of the power of collaboration, formed by world chess champion

Garry Kasparov, gave birth to the concept of a centaur: "A hybrid beast endowed with the strengths of each" (p. 3). Players considered what moves the computer recommended, examined historical databases, and then decided whether or not to follow the computer's advice. Kasparov dubbed this "advanced chess" (p. 3) and his experience of this type of play was described as "freed from the need to rely exclusively on his memory, he was able to focus more on the creative texture of his play" (p. 4).

Perhaps digital play therapists are centaurs, utilizing the best of both worlds and the strengths of each.

Either, Or, And

My mind exploded with interest and excitement while reading this portion of the book. It is an interesting story of the evolution of a time-honored game; however, when one breaks it down and looks into it further, the implications are far-reaching. One main concept that stands out for me is the importance of not looking at the advancements of digital tools as "either-or", but rather "and". The exploration should be more about the strengths and weaknesses of the human mind, the human being, and so on; the strengths and weaknesses of the digital tool; and how they might come together. If the digital tool can provide information, analytics, strategy, options, and other abilities so that the human can use their brain and body power in other ways, could the result be an acknowledgement of differences, a meeting of needs, and an amalgamation of skills?

The centaur approach created a dynamic which allowed for the exploration of what a human could explore, understand, realize, experience, and even feel if some of the more taxing and brain power consuming tasks were handled by the digital tool. Another important concept here is the "and". Instead of polarizing views of good or bad, additive or depleting, perhaps there are so many more components to understand and the evaluative answer most likely has pros and cons AND depends on a number of variables regarding the people, the situation, the needs, the history, the present, the future, and so much more. This means we cannot have a singular answer or recommendation which ends up being good and not-so-simple news. The good news is that there can be a spectacular tailoring of uses, concepts, and interventions when utilizing digital play therapy. The not-so-simple news is that the use and usefulness of therapeutic digital tools use are really determined on a case by case basis. The use of digital play therapy is absolutely therapeutic; the what, where, when, how, what, and why all come together to determine the appropriateness of the use of digital tools within play therapy for each client.

Digital Play Therapy

So, I give you this book, another passion project born out of a need and fueled by a desire to do more, give more, learn more. The chapters are intended to emphasize for the reader the importance of a solid foundation of theory and play therapy principles, an education about the materials involved, and then onto practical application. It is critical that play therapists, who are the most knowledgeable professionals with regards to the importance of play, embrace this language, seek knowledge about the therapeutic components, and enter their client's worlds for a holistic, competent treatment standard. If we deny these portions of our client's lives, we are not treating the whole client. We are excluding part of who they are, their culture, their identity. Congratulations for reading this book and honoring your clients and your profession of play therapy. I sincerely hope you find many gems in the following pages.

References

Abney, P. C., & Maddux, C. D. (2004). Counseling and technology: Some thoughts about controversy. *Journal of Technology in Human Services, 22*(3), 1–24.

Magnavita, J. J. (2018). Preface. In J. Magnavita (Ed.), *Using technology in mental health practice* (pp. xiii–xiv). Washington, DC: American Psychological Association.

Rosen, M. (2019). *Michael Rosen's book of PLAY!* Profile Books.

Sigma Plus Statistiek (2019). *SPSS: What is it?* www.spss-tutorials.com/spss-what-is-it/

Snow, M. S., Winburn, A., Crumrine, L., & Jackson, E. (2012). *The iPad playroom a therapeutic technique.* www.mlppubsonline.com/display_article.php?id=1141251

Stone, J. (2019). *Integrating technology into modern therapies: A clinician's guide to developments and interventions.* New York, NY: Routledge.

Thompson, C. (2014). *Smarter than you think: How technology is changing our minds for the better.* New York: Penguin Books.

2   What Is Digital Play Therapy?

Many play therapists have incorporated digital tools into their play therapy practice. For some, the incorporation is as simple as engaging in conversations regarding the client's digital interests. Others have begun to utilize their cell phone to take photos, search for information, listen to music, or view something at a client's request. For a third group, the incorporation includes the purchase and use of hardware and software specifically to provide the client with highly engaging, highly motivating, increasingly accessible play therapy tool options. All of these options fit under the digital play therapy umbrella.

The key importance regarding any level of digital tool use incorporation in play therapy is that the clinician understands how and why the use of digital tools in play therapy is appropriate. The inclusion of DPT in a therapist's repertoire is not suggested merely as a trendy response to client's interests, rather, it is a component of a fundamental belief system regarding the respect and acceptance of clients combined with solid play therapy tenets. Further in this book we will discuss the therapist components of these underpinnings, that is, the therapist 4 Cs and the therapeutic powers of play, which are activated in the many different interventions and interactions we employ. The therapeutic powers of play provide a structure and language for play therapists to understand and communicate what the play therapy session entails.

Balance

A clinician who incorporates DPT into their sessions is not endorsing an acceptance of all and everything digital, nor are they suggesting that there are no concerns about the use by the client or society as a whole. A digital play therapist is acknowledging the interests of the client, the culture of the client (more about that in the 4 Cs chapter), and the wealth of understandings and information a clinician can glean from digitally based interactions. The digital play therapist is utilizing this tool to access the experiences and information necessary to move forward in the treatment plan.

Balance is an incredibly important concept. Fundamentally, I believe balance is important in every aspect of our lives. It is not always possible, but it is an important goal to aspire toward. Balance is one of the most important words in this entire book and applies to DPT just as it applies to everything else. We need balance in all aspects of life. Humans do not function well when imbalanced whether that be regarding food, work, school, sleeping, running, or anything else. Internal balance is achieved when the activities and interests of a person do not cause other aspects of life to become under- or over- inflated.

When thinking about the digital revolution the world is experiencing and the common view of trends that concern us – such as infants being handed a device in lieu of direct social interaction with a loved one – it can be difficult to think of incorporating such tools in a therapeutic interaction. However, there are a few fundamental differences we must address.

First, our society as a whole must come into a balance regarding the use of digital tools and the other aspects of our lives. That is not to say that all humans have difficulty with the balance, but a quick internet search will highlight numerous areas where the imbalance of the use of such devices has negatively impacted one or more areas of people's lives. These areas often include families, parenting, marriage, and work.

Interestingly, research regarding the use of a laptop in the presence of a partner without engaging with each other was associated with a couple's negative perception of the relationship, but not when a cell phone, television, or computer was used (Leggett, 2014). If the couple used technology together, the perception of the relationship was positive, particularly with television use. This is an interesting concept; the use of a technological tool together with a person with whom there is a relationship alters the perception of the relationship and quite likely the interaction in general. A positive impact was also found in families who co-play video games or apps (Chambers, 2012; Leggett, 2014). Wang, et al., concluded that "playing video games together with family members can bring family members closer and enhance family satisfaction, especially for those with little communication opportunities" (2018, p. 4088).

Having researched other times in human history when advancements have caused imbalance, I am optimistic that a balance will be achieved within society in this area. The concern, then, is regarding the impacts of the current imbalance and what the effects of this will have on the generations it is currently affecting before the balance is achieved. What will the generational impacts be? Perhaps mental health providers are in a key position to assist families in finding their own balance in these areas to minimize the impact while the rest of society works toward balance. The goal would be to assist families achieve a customized balance which incorporates their needs, values, and beliefs with the most positive outcome possible, particularly for the children involved. Our jobs as play therapists is not to impart our values on our clients and their lives, but to respect their values and identify the areas of imbalance, in all aspects, including those effected by anything technology-related.

Second, the research and writings about technology is fraught with folk devils and moral panic which societies have seen numerous times over many centuries. These concepts will be explored further in their own chapter later in the book, but for now the key elements lie in the importance of balanced, transparent, well-constructed, and well-conducted research that allows us to truly investigate and evaluate the effects that the use of technology is having on humans. This is not merely about looking into overarching umbrella concerns but also in dissecting the many variables involved, combining and separating them in numerous ways and producing reputable and replicable results. These solid results can then assist us in shaping the necessary re-balancing that is so needed.

Third, the inclusion of digital tools in play therapy does not mean a forfeiture of any concerns regarding such imbalances. It does not signal an overarching acceptance or inclusion of any and all hardware and software. It does signify a play therapist's inclusion of the tools available to us at this time. The rich and powerful aspects of some of today's technology can greatly enhance the therapeutic process. The highly motivating and attention retaining stimuli allows the clinician to gather the information and experiences needed for a successful play therapy process. Horne-Meyer et al. found that recent research indicated that "electronic methods are often equivalent to more traditional treatments and may be more enjoyable or acceptable, at least to some consumers" (p. 1). For some clients, the inclusion of digital tools is exactly what is needed.

> The digital tool is merely a medium for the expression, creation, communication, relationship, understanding, assessment, and intervention within the therapy, just as any other tool in the playroom would be.
>
> (Stone, 2019)

Digital Play Therapy

> *Digital play therapy is a modality that utilizes highly motivating, immersive activities to incorporate areas of client interest into the play therapy process to deepen relationships, gather information, implement interventions, and advance the treatment plan forward.*

I began this digital play therapy path by including an iPad in my office along with the many other items in my well-stocked playroom. Having been a play therapist since early 1994, I have had plenty of time and experience to carefully choose what will be included in the room. I believe all items should be carefully analyzed for their therapeutic value. The therapeutic powers of play structure is a fantastic guide to use when evaluating items. Discovering what core agents of change within the powers of play are activated by each item informs the choices regarding the contents of the room. If core agents of change are not activated, the item should not be included in the playroom.

The iPad was initially included for the use of the Virtual Sandtray program. After realizing the power of this tool, both in the Virtual Sandtray specifically and in the use of the iPad, I began exploring other apps and programs to evaluate them for possible therapeutic inclusion. As I continued to teach about these tools, course participants would also share their experiences with different apps and my own clinical offerings began to grow.

The Nintendo Switch was the next tool to be evaluated for inclusion in the therapy room. The excitement about the removable controllers sparked the interest, but the actual use and available games proved the tool to be worthy. The ability to engage a client, while each held a controller and had to communicate in some way to be successful, brought some aspects of the play therapy interaction to a whole new level. Having a selectively mute client suddenly shout, "RUN OVER THERE!" while playing the Legend of Zelda was a highlight of my career. Other tools in my playroom did not elicit this response from this particular client, but this tool did, and I am forever grateful.

After the Virtual Sandtray iPad program was complete, it became clear that a virtual-reality version must be created. The powerful, immersive world of virtual reality adds many layers of benefit to the therapeutic experience. Therefore, the next and final (to date) addition to my office's play therapy digital tools has been virtual reality. I currently have an HTC Vive tethered head mounted display unit and the computer to power the programs and two Oculus Quest free standing head mounted display units. Different clients benefit from different programs and hardware, but the use of these tools has provided numerous positive results. Some of these results were not occurring with other tools available in the playroom.

Important Aspects of Use

I have not had the experience of kids hyper-focusing on these items or having any more trouble transitioning within or out of session, compared with using other items. With a focus on mutual respect in the room, one of my jobs is to balance what they are doing with the parameters at play (time, space, noise, etc.). The more I understand about the client, their needs, their abilities, and their styles, the better I can structure the session for success. This is true with any tool they use in session, including the digital ones.

So much really depends on how the tools are used, what is made available to the client within session, what the expectations are of the client, the therapist, and the caregivers. The solid foundation of the underpinnings of the therapeutic value, whatever the tool, allows the therapist to apply their knowledge to the process. This is how a therapist who plays basketball in session gleans therapeutic value – it is about the unfolding process, the interactions, the reactions, the connection, and the understandings. These are the cornerstones of the conversation regarding the therapeutic benefit, not the fact that the activity was basketball. These activated core agents of change define the interactions, not the basketball or the app played, or the dolls played with; this is the difference between "just playing" and play therapy.

Digital play therapy includes tools of a digital nature. The therapist properly vets the tool to determine if inclusion is appropriate, the tool is made available within the playroom, the use activates the core agents of change, and the therapist continues with the treatment plan. Ultimately, digital items are just another tool in the playroom, and they can be very powerful when used properly. If you have attended to the foundational aspects, both within yourself as a therapist and within the therapeutic process, then the use of the digital tools remains in the therapeutic realm.

Co-Playing

The concept of co-playing is most commonly associated with playing while occupying the same physical space. Research has offered significant support for parents co-playing video games with their children. Aarsand found that co-playing reduces the digital divide and brings generations together (2007). Parents, mothers in particular, reported that their participation in a five-week video game co-play study was the only time they got uninterrupted quality time together. Children in the same study said co-play taught them how to help people (Siyahhan et al., 2010). They found that an "intergenerational play space provided a valuable way to engage with their children's thinking, character development, and learning" (Siyahhan et al., 2010, p. 429).

Given the powerful and positive impacts the adults and children experienced in these co-playing situations, it seems reasonable to conclude that co-playing video games between a therapist and client would have the same or similar results. Perhaps the results would yield an even more powerful impact due to the nature of the therapeutic space, time, and rapport. Our clients rarely have the opportunity to spend 45 to 60 minutes of focused, uninterrupted time with a trusted adult even once a month, never mind once a week. Research which focuses on exploring theses dynamics between client and therapist would be very beneficial.

What Play Therapists Want to Know

Having presented about these topics for some years now, I can share a bit of what I have learned about what therapists want to know regarding the use of digital tools. Play therapists want to know, understand, and experience the following aspects of the use of digital tools in play therapy.

1) Safe
   a. There are solid therapeutic underpinnings.
   b. There is solid research, even if within other disciplines while play therapy specific research is being done, to indicate the support for such use.
   c. The therapeutic process will not be hindered by the inclusion of digital tools in play therapy.

2) Guidelines and ethics
   a. Play therapists want to know that there are guidelines for the inclusion of such tools.

    b.   To date, many regulatory bodies have provided guidelines, including but not limited to

        i.   The Association for Play Therapy,
        ii.   The British Association for Play Therapy,
        iii. The American Psychological Association,
        iv. The National Association of Social Workers,
        v.   The American Academy of Pediatrics, and
        vi. The Royal College of Pediatrics and Child Health.

3) Competence

    a.   They can be competent in the use of digital tools in play therapy. Play therapists will become competent through

        i.   Education,
        ii.   Supervision,
        iii. Consultation, and
        iv. Use/experience.

4) Comfort

    a.   They can be comfortable in the use of digital tools in play therapy. Play therapists will become comfortable through

        i.   Education,
        ii.   Supervision,
        iii. Consultation, and
        iv. Use/experience.

5) Capable

    a.   They can become capable in the use of digital tools in play therapy. Play therapists will become comfortable through

        i.   Education,
        ii.   Supervision,
        iii. Consultation, and
        iv. Use/experience.

6) Clinically important and relevant

    a.   Play therapists want to understand how digital use is clinically important and relevant.

        i.   Through connection/rapport
        ii.   By speaking their language
        iii. By entering their world
        iv. By accepting their culture
        v.   By understanding/hearing/seeing/importance in their interests and all aspects who they are

7) Types

    a.   Play therapists will benefit from understanding different types of digital tools.

        i.   Different hardware
        ii. Different software

8) Uses

    a.   Play therapists will benefit from exploring and understanding many different uses for digital tools in play therapy.

        i.   Different populations
        ii.   Different ages
        iii. Different abilities
        iv. Different needs
        v.   Different goals

Populations

It is best for play therapists to determine for themselves which populations DPT is best suited for. These answers are directly shaped by the theoretical foundations of the therapist. Based on my foundations I have discovered that, as with the other items in my playroom, clients self-select very well. Their selections appear to be a direct reflection of how they approach many things in their lives. If a client who is drawn to the use of something typically out of their range (age, ability, etc.) they are probably doing this in other areas of their lives as well. If the out-of-range intervention can be tailored to their needs to have a successful result, then the alteration should be presented. If the intervention results in frustration tolerance or otherwise, then address the concept in a therapeutic way.

The interactional styles of a person who acts before thinking would probably display such tendencies in their board game play, block building, and digital play. If the client chooses a digital tool for use, my prescriptive play therapy focus might tailor the program used toward the known needs of the client. This would include the identification of the client's needs so the interventions or interactions could be most beneficial, whatever the client chose to use. All the aspects are interwoven: what is in the playroom supports the interests and needs of the client, how the therapist interacts with the client and the tools supports the relationship, the relationship supports the process, the process supports the treatment plan, the treatment plan supports the needs of the client, and so forth.

The edited book *Integrating Technology into Modern Therapies* begins the discussion of a number of populations and environments within which digital tools are used (Stone, 2019). Supervision and competency-based mentoring, therapeutic texting, virtual reality use in therapy, and video game use in therapy are all discussed. Supervision and mentoring can really benefit from the use of digital tools in so many ways, including but not limited to the ability for the supervisee to seek out dynamics (specialties, frameworks, etc.), which may or may not be available in one's geographical area. The world suddenly becomes a lot smaller. Therapeutic texting is a way to connect with clients, especially adolescents, who are often very comfortable with fast-paced, abbreviation- and emoji-filled interactions. Virtual reality and video games are used primarily for immersive experiences to address a number of presenting concerns and learn about the approaches, skills, and styles of the client.

Special populations include, but are not limited to, those who have experienced trauma, those who are neurodiverse, including autism spectrum disorder, attention-deficit hyperactivity disorder, and more, and those who are gifted. Each of these special populations present with needs and tendencies which can be addressed through the use of digital tools and interventions. Including digital tools in the playroom can afford clients flexibility regarding their chosen activities within their sessions.

Pediatric patients within medical settings, those in speech therapy, and those in vulnerable populations can also benefit from the use of therapeutic technology. Regarding vulnerable populations, digital tools can greatly enhance access for those who have difficulties accessing services, whether that is due to physical differences, financial constraints, rural settings, crisis settings, or otherwise.

Addiction Conversation

The conversation regarding addiction is currently premature. The research is not only conflicting, but downright convoluted. It is not merely that camps on either end of the concern spectrum do not agree, it is more that the research is lacking in many ways regarding definitions; included, excluded, and marginalized variables; and more. Instead of focusing on the concept of addiction, let us focus on therapeutic dynamics which could lead to a more balanced existence when addressed.

A trending focus of concern is about "brain structure changes" due to technology use. Let us look at this more closely and recognize a need for more information. For example, a current longitudinal study by the National Institutes of Health is looking at the effects of technology on children. They have noticed that children who play some type of digital device for more than seven hours per day have thinning cortexes. Headlines across the internet blasted these preliminary results as proof of the evils of technology; however, the lead researcher Dr. Dowling even stated, "We don't know if it's being caused by the screen time. We don't know yet if it's a bad thing. It won't be until we follow them over time that we will see if there are outcomes that are associated with the differences we are seeing in this single snapshot" (Cooper, 2018, p. 13). Dr. Dowling further cautioned against drawing conclusions from the preliminary findings (Bloomberg, 2018; Cooper, 2018). Even the very recent JAMA Pediatrics article regarding screen-based media use and white matter integrity concluded, "Meaning: These findings suggest a need for further study into the association between screen-based media use and the developing brain, particularly during early childhood" (Hutton et al., 2019, para 1). The issue with this topic is *not a lack of concern* regarding brain changes. The issue is that everything effects our brain structure – trauma, depression, anxiety, smelling a beautiful flower, and even reading these words. Everything affects us in some way. We must dissect these concepts further to really understand the implications. We need more information.

In an effort to identify a way to address these use concerns clinically, Stone discussed the importance of asking about the whys and whats regarding unbalanced behaviors (2019). The questions were as follows*:

1) What dynamics led to the behaviors/situations?
2) What is the person's support system? What role does the use take in the person's day to day life?
3) Is the person well-supported and -connected by the other people in the activity?
4) Does the person's self-esteem, self-worth, and/or social skills benefit from these interactions?
5) Is the person avoiding certain components of his or her life?
6) Is the person escaping abusive dynamics?

*reprinted with permission

Understanding the underlying dynamics of any difficult situation in our client's lives allows us to tailor the conversation and recommendations to the specific scenario. Boiler plate responses or categorizations will not serve the client's day to day life. Blanket recommendations based on an "expert's" opinion may or may not apply to the client's needs or situation and ultimately will not be followed through with.

Conversations With Caregivers

Just as with many other play therapy interventions, it is very important to communicate well with the client's caregiver(s). Within the necessary paperwork and conversations every therapist must have with their clients, informed consent regarding the use of digital tools should be included. The presentation is dependent upon the ethical guidelines of your discipline (which are paramount) and the conceptualization of the tools (which is critical, but secondary to the ethical requirements).

If the digital tools are conceptualized as "just another tool" then they would be discussed as other tools in the playroom are discussed. The digital tool use would fall into the category of the toys or other interventions that could be utilized and the core agents of change would be the focus of the conversation. Meaning, the focus would be on the ways the tool enhanced the components of facilitating communication, and not on the defense of the use of the tool(s). The therapist could explain how the tool facilitated the process.

If the digital tools are conceptualized as a different-enough type of tool, then specialized discussions and paperwork would accompany the use. For instance, disclaimers and specifics would be presented verbally and in writing to obtain the explicit consent for the use of the digital tools in session. For me, this approach transmits a position and message I am not comfortable with. Each clinician must decide for themselves what is important for the caregivers to know about the work we do. An emphasis on the process, such as the change agents activated within the interactions, rather than the specific items used to achieve these, is most important to me.

This does not mean that I do not discuss the interventions used. To make sure bases are covered, my informed consent paperwork includes a line regarding the inclusion of digital tools in the therapy. It is a line among others, not a head-line. More importantly for clinical reasons, caregivers are offered a tour of the playroom during the initial intake appointment. This tour includes discussions regarding the various tools within the playroom and their therapeutic benefits. The digital tools are included and discussed within these conversations.

Front loading the conversation with caregivers regarding the therapeutic bene-fits of play therapy and the interventions within will open the lines of communica-tion regarding the treatment. Not only might this reduce any confusion regarding why they "brought their child in so they could play checkers" or anything else, it can enhance the investment and support the caregiver has toward the treatment.

Notes and Collateral Contacts

Having a solid understanding of what you are doing and why you are doing it will strengthen your case note writeups and your discussions with collateral contacts. How you conceptualize the work, your role, the goals, and the meth-ods will be conveyed in your demeanor and presentation of the information. The more you explore, understand, and formulate your theoretical underpin-nings, the more you will understand the tools you use and the more congruent (internally and externally) your work will become.

Potential Limitations

The use of DPT is predominantly limited by the therapist's competence and com-fort. Clients of all ages and abilities are commonly interested in and/or familiar with, and want to engage in, the medium. Understanding the foundation of the therapeutic value of play will strengthen the therapist's competence and comfort. Additional limitations are more logistic in nature, such as space for additional equipment, time and money for training and supervision, and/or the cost of the materials.

Conclusion

The inclusion of DPT as a modality among others can benefit clients of many ages and needs. Balance is a key concept within the client's life and in play therapy sessions. The appropriate usage of digital interventions along with many others can greatly enhance the therapeutic process. The competent, capable, comfortable play therapist who incorporates a variety of tools that activate the core agents of change is meeting the needs of their clients. The play therapist who includes digital tools, for those with interest, in their repertoire is honoring their whole client and culture while providing the medium for therapeutic change.

References

Aarsand, P. A. (2007). Computer and video games in family life: The digital divide as a resource in intergenerational interactions. *Childhood: A Global Journal of Child Research, 14*(2), 235–256.

Bloomberg, L. L. (2018). NIH study probes impact of heavy screen time on young brains. *Information Management*. www.information-management.com/articles/nih-study-probes-impact-of-heavy-screen-time-on-young-brains

Chambers, D. (2012). "Wii play as a family": The rise in family-centered video gaming. *Leisure Studies, 31*(1), 69–82.

Cooper, A. (2018). Groundbreaking study examines effects of screen time on kids. *60-Minutes*. www.cbsnews.com/news/groundbreaking-study-examines-effects-of-screen-time-on-kids-60-minutes/

Horne-Meyer, H. L., Meyer, B. H., Messer, D. C., & Messer, E. S. (2014). *The use of electronic games in therapy: A review with clinical implications*. www.ncbi.nlm.nih.gov/pmc/articles/PMC4196027/

Hutton, J. S., Dudley, J., & Horowitz-Kraus, T. (2019, November 4). *Associations between screen-based media use and brain white matter integrity in preschool-aged children*. https://jamanetwork.com/journals/jamapediatrics/article-abstract/2754101

Leggett, C. (2014). The impact of technology use on couple relationships: A neuropsychological perspective. *International Journal of Neuropsychotherapy, 2*(1), 44–99.

Siyahhan, S., Barab, S. A., & Downton, M. P. (2010). Using activity theory to understand intergenerational play: The case of family quest. *International Journal of Computer-Supported Collaborative Learning, 5*(4), 415–432.

Stone, J. (2019). Digital games. In J. Stone & C. E. Schaefer (Eds.), *Game play: Therapeutic use of games with children and adolescents* (3rd ed., pp. 99–120). Wiley.

Wang, B., Taylor, L., & Sun, Q. (2018). Families that play together stay together: Investigating family bonding through video games. *New Media & Society, 20*(11), 4074–4094.

3 The 4 Cs of a Therapist
Competency, Culture, Comfort, and Capability

Play therapists are in such an honored position. We understand the importance and power of play and possess the skills to help children communicate and heal through this medium. In thinking about some of the essential components of a well-rounded, well-trained, ethical play therapist, some key elements emerge. This chapter continues the important theme of foundation. Before we can understand any new concept, we must understand the fundamentals which support it.

Professional ethics and guidelines dictate many things about our day to day therapeutic work with clients. The structure of our practices, the required training, and the way we conduct ourselves are all guided by these frameworks. Although each discipline within the overarching umbrella of play therapy has their own requirements, the common thread includes bringing no harm to the client. We must "do no harm while doing good" and strive to improve our client's lives dramatically.

Under this umbrella of play therapy are four important Cs for therapists of any discipline and degree: Competency, Culture, Comfort, and Capability. This chapter will focus on expanding each concept as it pertains to the fundamental qualities of the therapist. Guiding frameworks from multiple disciplines will be introduced, along with the knowledge and desire for further guidelines, as more is understood about the integration of technology into modern play therapy.

Competency

What Is Competency?

Although competency and competence appear to be common, fundamental, often-used terms, perhaps it is best to begin with some definitions. Establishing the basics allows for a firm foundation from which to build. Merriam-Webster defines competence as "the quality or state of having sufficient knowledge, judgment, skill, or strength (as for a particular duty or in a particular respect)" and "the knowledge that enables a person to speak and understand a language" (2019a, para. 1). Since the main topic of this book is defined as the importance of skilled play therapists speaking the client's digital language, these definitions fit particularly well.

Given that ethical guidelines require competence to provide mental health services, we can explore this term with great interest. A key word in Merriam Webster's first definition is "sufficient". It is not clear who would determine what level of knowledge, judgment, skill, or strength would be sufficient, however, this is most likely determined by our educational institutions, supervisors, and licensure governing bodies.

The business world offers some solid information regarding these concepts for clarification. According to Julia Penny, "skills" refer to the skills required for the job and "knowledge" refers to one's education and experience (2019). Judgement refers to one's ability to apply the skills and knowledge to make beneficial decisions.

Penny lists "12 Core Competencies for Job Success": decision making, teamwork, work standards, motivation, reliability, problem solving, adaptability, planning and organization, communication, integrity, initiative, and stress tolerance.

Table 3.1 12 Core Competencies

Decision making	• Sound judgment to make good decisions • Commits
Teamwork	• Effective interactions • Supports group decisions and is able to place group goals ahead of one's own
Work standards	• High performance standards • Follows up
Motivation	• Energetic and enthusiastic
Reliability	• Assumes personal responsibility • Completes work timely and consistently
Problem solving	• Gathers and organizes relevant information to make decisions • Finds appropriate solutions
Adaptability	• Adapts to change, priorities organizational needs, and diversity
Planning and organization	• Achieves objectives through planning and organization • Allocates resources properly
Communication	• Expresses, organizes, listens, and delivers
Integrity	• Shares information • Adheres to policies and procedures
Initiative	• Takes action • Does more than required
Stress tolerance	• Emotionally resilient • Uses appropriate coping techniques

Adapted from Penny (2019)

When conceptualizing these components for a play therapy focus, we can see that being a competent play therapist includes similar items. A competent play therapist must apply each of these to the work, some inside and some outside of the playroom. One additional caveat would be the assumption of a solid knowledge base and adherence to and application of the competency components in accordance with one's professional licensure standards.

American Psychological Association

The American Psychological Association (APA) dictates such standards for psychologists and often sets the tone for other organizations (American Psychological Association, 2006, 2015). A primary emphasis is for the practitioner's competency to focus on the safety of the client. According to the 2006 APA Task Force on the Assessment of Competence in Professional Psychology, APA states: "We have a responsibility to ensure via education, training, and ongoing life-long assessment that practicing psychologists and future generations of psychologists provide quality and safe psychological services" (American Psychological Association, 2006, p. 3).

The APA paper "Competencies for Psychology Practice in Primary Care" defines six cluster areas of competence: science (research and evaluation), systems (administration and advocacy), professionalism (values and diversity), relationships (inter-professionalism), application (management, assessment, intervention, and consultation), and education (teaching and supervision) (APA, 2015). Further distinction can be made between minimal and aspirational competencies. Minimal competencies are those required to function within the job. Aspirational competencies are "those for which we strive to achieve and those who achieve them often are considered experts or masters" (APA, 2006, p. 12).

Association for Play Therapy

The Association for Play Therapy (APT) is a 501(c)(6) professional organization established in 1982 (Association for Play Therapy, n.d.a). APT has outlined competency standards for play therapists based on a belief in the "educational/ developmental model of how psychotherapists develop knowledge, skills, and personal capacities" (Association for Play Therapy, n.d.a, para. 7). In short, APT requires that registered play therapists, a certification obtained through the organization, receive direct instruction, followed by supervised direct clinical work (Association for Play Therapy, n.d.b). In an effort to deepen the knowledge, and integration of such knowledge into therapeutic work, APT requires that play therapists understand the therapeutic powers of play (Schaefer, 1993) and their influence on play therapy practice. These therapeutic powers are to be a basis for understanding play therapy theory, models, skills, instruction, and supervision.

Play Therapy

McNary, Mason, and Tobin, 2018, address components of DPT competency in an article entitled *The Unexpected Purpose of Technology in the Playroom:*

Catharsis. This has been expanded upon by Stone as recommendations for therapists using digital tools in play therapy.

Recommendations for the competent use of DPT:

1) Engage in training.
2) Consult with other play therapists who are trained in using digital tools in play therapy.
3) Learn what digital tools clients are using at home and at school.
4) Invite clients to teach you about their favorite games, programs, etc.
5) Add physical items in the playroom which represent figures in the digital world.
6) Discuss the potential benefits of digital tool use with parents.
7) Monitor client progress when using digital tools in play therapy.
8) Seek supervision from a play therapist who is knowledgeable about incorporating digital tools into play therapy.
9) Watch YouTube videos regarding specific digital game play.
10) Play games introduced by the therapist before inclusion in the play therapy process.
11) Play games introduced by the client initially in session, but also research and learn more about the game outside of the session.[1]

Summary of General Competency

Competency is, at its core, a necessity for play therapists to obtain, maintain, and exhibit solid clinical skills, knowledge, and judgement. Over the course of a play therapist's career, the drive is to achieve higher levels of competency and to continuously aspire to the highest level of professionalism, integrity, and knowledge. On a practical level, this includes continuing education, research, supervision, and an ability and willingness to expand one's repertoire along the way. This competent play therapy professional provides the highest level of mental health care to their clients. Competency in DPT allows the play therapist to appropriately incorporate the therapeutic aspects of the client's digital interests and utilize digital tools to assess, process, understand, and intervene within play therapy sessions.

Culture

Culture is another frequently used term which should be defined for the ease of communication. What is culture? According to Zimmerman, who explored this concept in 2017, culture is a very broad term. "Culture is the characteristics and knowledge of a particular group of people, encompassing language, religion, cuisine, social habits, music and arts" (Zimmerman, 2017, para. 1). The concept of culture moves beyond a particular region or religion and includes interests. Cristina De Rossi, an anthropologist in London, added: "Culture encompasses religion, food, what we wear, how we wear it, our language, marriage, music, what we believe is right or wrong, how we sit at the table, how we greet visitors, how we behave with loved ones, and a million other things" (para. 3). Stemming from French and Latin terms meaning to tend to the earth and grow, cultivate, or nurture, culture "shares its etymology with a number of other words related to actively fostering growth" (para. 4).

National Association of Social Workers

If we are to have a professional focus of respecting cultural diversity, we must understand these expanded definitions of the concept. All professional organizations have intentionally focused on diversity over the past three decades. One mental health discipline which has a particular focus on cultural diversity, is social work. The National Association of Social Workers (NASW), includes cultural competence as a primary standard. "Clinical social workers shall have, and continue to develop, specialized knowledge and understanding about history, traditions, values, and family systems as they relate to clinical practice with individuals, families, and groups" (National Association of Social Workers, 2005, p. 20). The NASW standards expand the concept further to include: "In addition, clinical social workers need to be knowledgeable about the deleterious effects of racism, sexism, ageism, heterosexism or homophobia, anti-Semitism, ethnocentrism, classism, and disability-based discrimination on clients' behavior, mental and emotional well-being, and course of treatment. Clinical social workers must also recognize racial, ethnic, and cultural differences that maybe interpreted as barriers to treatment and develop skills to ameliorate such barriers" (National Association of Social Workers, 2005, p. 20).

NASW (2005) guidelines continue even further to require that clinical social workers do the following:

1) Establish and maintain a relationship of mutual respect, acceptance, and trust.
2) Gather and interpret social, personal, environmental, and health information.
3) Evaluate and treat problems within their scope of practice.
4) Establish achievable treatment goals with the client.
5) Facilitate cognitive, affective, and behavioral changes consistent with treatment goals.
6) Evaluate the effectiveness of treatment services provided to the client.
7) Identify appropriate resources and assessment instruments, as needed.
8) Advocate for client services.
9) Collaborate effectively with other social work or allied professionals, when appropriate.

(NASW, 2005, p. 13)

It is clear that the NASW really has a focus of understanding the client, speaking their language, and working to connect with the client in ways that facilitate the therapeutic process and assist with achieving treatment goals. Addressing both issues of culture and comfort, NASW (2005) continues: "When additional knowledge and skills are required to address clients' needs, the clinical social worker shall seek appropriate training, supervision, or consultation, or refer the client to a professional with the appropriate expertise. Clinical social workers shall limit the scope of their practice to those clients for whom they have the knowledge, skill, and resources to serve. They shall be accountable for all aspects of their professional judgment, behavior, and decisions" (p. 13).

Additional Types of Culture

As indicated previously, the definition of culture has expanded. With a professional shift to acknowledge that culture includes location, religion, beliefs, interests, and more, it is important to recognize other lesser known cultures. Some of these apply to this conversation of digital inclusive play therapy. We now have "geek culture", "nerd culture", "gaming culture", and more. We have terms such as "technophile" (enthusiast) (Merriam Webster, 2019c, para.1), "technologist" (a person who specializes) (Dictionary.com, 2019), and "techno-skeptic" (one who has skeptical interest) (The Technoskeptic, 2019). Thousands of people flock to conventions, trainings, competitions, and more each year to join together as a variety of cultures or a singular culture within the technology realm. I consider myself a "techno-neccessist"; I am not particularly tech savvy; I am not a technophile nor a purist technoskeptic. I see the importance of technology in our lives and our work and I think it is necessary to honor and enter our client's culture.

Cultural Competency

As a profession, mental health standards dictate that we are to acknowledge and respect cultural diversity. Culture is broad in scope and includes people who have similar interests and beliefs. Many interests and beliefs will be different than that of the mental health professional, however, we have been trained in the importance of education and acceptance of such differences. It is very important to acknowledge and understand one's personal biases and beliefs. A play therapist should seek education and supervision to ensure that these differences do not affect the therapeutic process as much as humanly possible. The definition of cultural competency must expand to include cultures such as those of the technologically interested technophiles and more, and therapists must be open to learning about their clients' cultures despite personal biases. For therapists, this includes any culture identified and included by the client. Play therapists do not have to work with every person who presents in the office for therapeutic work; however, they do have a responsibility to explore their own biases and beliefs, increase their knowledge and training, and refer when therapeutically appropriate. Referrals are necessary when it becomes clear that even with supervision, education, and training, the therapist is unable to participate in the therapeutic process without their own biases and beliefs effecting the treatment of the client.

Comfort

Therapist comfort will be defined here in terms of what is comfortable, or free from vexation or doubt; stress or tension (Merriam Webster, 2019b). When a therapist achieves a level of comfort, or is comfortable professionally, it is palpable to the therapist, client, family, and any collateral contacts. Moving forward without doubt, stress, or tension, allows the clinician to focus on the important aspects of the play dynamic.

Dr. Carl Rogers wrote extensively about person-centered therapy, also known as client-centered or Rogerian therapy. Along with many other tenets and components, person centered therapy has a focus on the importance of congruence between the actual and ideal self. With regards to the therapist, this importance of congruence manifests in the therapist presentation, approach, and essentially comfort within themselves and in session. In stark contrast to the psychoanalytic blank-slate emphasis at the time, Rogers spoke of therapists removing any façade, being genuine and real. He felt that the therapist must be congruent within themselves and the client to allow the client to change, grow, and achieve self-actualization.

Congruence within a therapist is a bit of a balancing feat. The therapist must continually attend to their own biases, attitudes, opinions, and desires. To be self-aware, one will frequently ask themselves (internally, in session) if a question they thought to ask the client benefitted the therapist or the client. Any topic guidance or activities included in session are thought of in terms of the benefit to the client. The balance needs to happen between the therapist's own comfort and belief systems and the needs of the client. If these are incongruent, the relationship between the therapist and client, and therefore the therapeutic process, will be negatively affected.

The question then becomes one of identifying how a therapist achieves comfort and if they do not, what the next steps should be. A bit of soul searching is important when the incongruencies between the therapist's comfort and the client's needs arise. Traditional routes dictate education, consultation, supervision, and research will assist the therapist with achieving a new level of comfort and congruence when an incongruence is realized.

Some play therapists experience this incongruence regarding the use of digital tools in play therapy. Their own comfort level is potentially low and yet their clients are bringing in stories and experiences which include their digital interests. Not only do people worry about the inclusion of something new because it is unknown, but also because clinicians do not want to do anything wrong. Therapists do not want to harm their clients and that concern is expected and necessary. So, when a client wants to discuss the game they love to play or even want to play it in session, the uncomfortable therapist's unease increases the incongruence between the therapist and client. This incongruence results in obstacles for the client's growth and healing. Comfort, then, becomes a critical aspect in DPT.

In the play therapy room, comfort will be recognized by the client in terms of a feeling of safety. Disruptions in congruence equal disruptions in perceived safety. Without safety in the playroom, the play will be altered in ways that will hinder the therapeutic process. Therefore, congruence and comfort are fundamental.

As previously mentioned, one way therapists can increase their comfort is through education. When structures are in place that give voice and guidance to a process, the comfort level typically rises. With increased comfort, the play therapist can focus on the underlying dynamics. With increased familiarity regarding any given activity and an underlying understanding of the therapeutic powers of play, (Schaefer, 1993; Schaefer & Drewes, 2014) therapists can reduce the incongruencies in the relationship. The therapeutic powers of play (TPP) provide a structure for the play therapist within which to recognize therapeutic components of all types of play. These powers will be further explored in Chapter 3; however, in general, the TPP include 20 core agents of change and are critical identifications for play therapy interactions. Understanding what you are doing in the therapy session and why you are doing it provides a necessary level of comfort and confidence (Stone, 2016a).

Entering a client's culture, or speaking their language, is another way to achieve comfort through cohesion. Even if interests and beliefs differ, the willingness of the therapist to learn about the client's culture is very powerful. Humans relax and connect when they feel seen, heard, and understood (Stone, 2019). When working toward comfort with speaking a client's digital language, seeking further knowledge can be very helpful. For example, if the interest is in video game play, therapists can learn a lot from watching YouTube videos of actual game play. Internet searches about the type of game can also assist with finding therapeutic value. There are numerous genres of video games and many of them have fundamental therapeutic underpinnings, such as adventure games. An adventure video game relies and builds on a story and the player makes choices along the way which alters the narrative. This type of game is ripe with therapeutic value. The play therapist who understands these therapeutic underpinnings will be able to focus less on the specific tool chosen (the video game) and more on the narrative being developed. This therapist comfort and acceptance will breed comfort in the client and benefit the play therapy significantly. The video game genres chapter will discuss this further.

One of the ways therapists gain professional comfort is through the application of structured guidelines. A number of professional groups have begun the process of outlining the ethics and guiding principles of the use of digital tools in mental health treatment. Over time these will be altered and updated, but it is fantastic to see their presence as we further incorporate such tools.

Formal Guidelines for the Use of Digital Tools in Therapy

To date there are a few solid documents available, predominantly regarding client's confidential information. APT has released a set of best practices for using digital tools, Stanford Libraries has released a "Statement of Guiding Principles" (2018), and the World Economic Forum released "Eight Actions" and "Five Ethical Challenges", all regarding the use of technology in mental health (2019a). The forward-thinking individuals involved in each have realized that the inclusion of digital tools into clinical settings is inevitable and already happening, and as such, guidelines need to be adopted and adapted to ensure appropriate client care.

Association for Play Therapy

Along with supporting the guidelines of a variety of disciplines, APT has established several "best practices" and the use of technology in play therapy is included (Association for Play Therapy, 2016). Practice management and ethical conduct in general is discussed within the use of technology section, however, Section J4 (p. 18) specifically addresses the use of technology within play therapy sessions. This portion of the chapter will provide a brief synopsis of the guidelines. Please refer to the original document for a full description.

APT recommends that a play therapist review any technology that is planned for use and to "become fully aware of the potential benefits and limitations" (Association for Play Therapy, 2016, p. 18). Of great importance is a focus on the client's abilities, needs, and protection. Chosen technology is to be properly vetted, explained prior to use to the client and the guardian, and be deemed appropriate for the treatment goals. Client's identifying information should be protected and steps should be taken to ensure the appropriateness of what they view in terms of unintended internet content such as pop-up ads and the like (Association for Play Therapy, 2016).

Stanford Libraries

In 2018, more than 30 professionals participated in a seminar at the Stanford Libraries to discuss the important balance between the individual's need for privacy and the societal need to protect public health. The document has a distinct focus on the ethical use of products and services and the protection of the personal information collected and generated. Stanford librarian Michael A. Keller wrote: "Given the exponential rate of developments occurring in the digital health space, we offered to initiate the conversation and report out on results of the seminar" (Karempelas, 2019, para. 3).

The ten principles born from this meeting aim to be a starting point for the ethics-in-digital-health conversation. Per Keller, "This is only a first step at addressing the ethical questions looming in digital health. We must start somewhere, so let these principles serve as the conversation starter". Further, he hopes the following: "We want this first set of ten statements to spur conversations in board rooms, classrooms and community centers around the country and ultimately be refined and adopted widely" (Karempelas, 2019, para. 8).

A distinction between "digital health product" and "digital health information" was made for clarity. A digital health product, per the Stanford group, is considered a commercially available product "that is promoted based on claims to improve human health outcomes, and which collects and generates digital health information" (Stanford Libraries, 2018, para. 1). It is important to recognize that some programs will collect personal and usage data, and some will not. Just as most websites collect "cookies", or bits of information regarding an individual's use of the site, such as Amazon, other programs, including the Virtual Sandtray®© (a program developed for use in therapeutic sessions), do not collect any data whatsoever besides the login information (Stone, 2016b). However, one defines a digital health product, and whether the information is collected or not, decisions must be made regarding safeguards within one's practice.

These safeguards can vary dependent on the hardware and software used; however, some general rules can apply. For instance, if a game requires a profile be created, the therapist can create the profile in advance using cryptic information such as false names and birthdates. The client and therapist can also create this together within the session, sparking conversations and modeling of the importance of online safety. All information used should be documented within the client's records for clarity and future access.

The Stanford position regarding digital health information includes "all information collected and generated by a digital health product that is connected to the Internet" (Stanford Libraries, 2019, para. 1) and an emphasis on the balance between protecting private information and benefitting public health. The "benefit to public health" refers to utilizing sanitized information to assist in "controlling disease outbreaks and discovering cures to conditions without adequate treatments" (para. 2). Technology affords an unprecedented ability to gather information. This information, *used properly*, stands to address areas previously unknown or have had difficulties due to a lack of robust information.

To this end, the Stanford Libraries group offers the following initial ethical guidelines regarding the use of digital health technology. Note that many of these principles are focused on the products and use of information, and not on the direct clinical use.

Statement of Guiding Principles for Ethics in Digital Health

1) The products of digital health companies should always work in patients' interests.
2) Sharing digital health information should always be to improve a patient's outcomes and those of others.
3) "Do no harm" should apply to the use and sharing of all digital health information.
4) Patients should never be forced to use digital health products against their wishes.
5) Patients should be able to decide whether their information is shared, and to know how a digital health company uses information to generate revenues.
6) Digital health information should be accurate.
7) Digital health information should be protected with strong security tools.
8) Security violations should be reported promptly along with what is being done to fix them.
9) Digital health products should allow patients to be more connected to their care givers.

10) Patients should be actively engaged in the community that is shaping digital health products.

(Stanford Libraries, 2018, para. 5–14)

World Economic Forum

The World Economic Forum (WEF) is a not-for-profit organization established in 1971 in Switzerland (World Economic Forum, 2019b). The WEF mission statement includes a focus on supporting businesses while upholding the "highest standards of governance" (World Economic Forum, 2019b, para. 2). The key components of the WEF's 2019 White Paper include the clarification: "We are not advocating that machines should replace psychotherapists; our wish is for the adoption of technology as a supplement, in a fair, empathetic and evidence-based manner, to ensure that everyone everywhere facing a serious mental health challenge can get the help they seek" (World Economic Forum, 2019a, p. 5). Some of the components of the Stanford Guidelines can be found expanded upon in the WEF paper.

The WEF White Paper includes eight actions regarding the use of technology in mental health (See Table 3.2) and five ethical challenges to be addressed

Table 3.2 Eight Actions Regarding the Use of Technology in Mental Health

1) Groups (developers, government, and mental health practitioners) should come together to work to create new programs and "include the voices and views of those with mental health concerns" (p 22). This shall include the direct use of technology in sessions and the handling of client's personal information.

2) Create regulations which allow for flexibility to encourage innovation and adjustment and ensuring client safety through the collaboration of governmental bodies, medical experts, and technology-led mental health care providers.

3) Include responsible practice when designing technology. Developments happen very quickly and have great potential to help many; however, it is difficult to keep up with research, therefore responsible practice in each step will help safeguard those the technology is intended to help.

4) With any new technology-led mental health services, include a test, learn, and adapt approach. Protocols will need to be established and regulated, particularly programs with potential risk for clients.

5) Entities, private and governmental, should work together to continue to move forward and "maximize funds and minimize effort and duplication" (p 22). Working together will help coordinate mental health strategies to provide services beyond a country's borders.

6) Agreement regarding unified metrics and measurement design will contribute to more standardized analyses. A focus on cost effectiveness and ensuring that inequalities are not introduced or perpetuated by the use of the technology should be held. The inclusion of those affected by mental health is imperative.

7) Collaborations between private and governmental agencies will work to yield sustainable projects and more simple projects will not be discounted.

8) The need for mental health support in low-income communities and countries and a focus on these populations should be maintained.

Adapted from WEF White Paper (2019b).

Table 3.3 Five Ethical Challenges to be Addressed With Urgency

Trust	Mental health practitioners will work hard to build trust and value regarding technological tools in therapy and software companies must embrace ethical practices.
Big Data	Personal data regarding experiences assists with further understanding in assessment, diagnosis, and intervention. Sharing this information is delicate and must be handled carefully. Engage with individuals, respect their information, and create ways to appropriately share such information.
Intervention	Work to reduce the stigma regarding mental health and place it on equal footing to physical health in both discussion and intervention.
Equal Access	Prioritize the development of therapies which will equalize populations and not further contribute to the divide (socio-economic, etc.)
Pragmatic Progress	Higher-risk technologies (those which make diagnoses, etc.) and lower risk technologies (monitor symptoms, etc.) should be distinguished. With the speed of technological development and the length of time necessary for research, the benefits of lower risk technologies outweigh the risks when used to provide support and/or the ability to seek out advice.

Adapted from WEF White Paper (2019a).

with urgency (See Table 3.3) (World Economic Forum, 2019a) In general, this WEF White Paper is an exploration of the importance of technology to address the large portion of the population who are unable to access mental health services for a variety of reasons, along with the focus on including input from people with mental health concerns, collaborations between entities, and a balance between protecting and sharing personal information. This White Paper acknowledges the importance for research, the pragmatic difficulties regarding the speed at which technology develops and the length of time needed to complete research, and the importance of moving forward in areas where the benefits outweigh the risks (low-personal-information risk technological programs). Technology can allow access to support, advice, and interventions to a wider, more diverse population.

It is certain that over the next few years well conducted research will further dictate and guide clinicians when using digital tools in therapy. The areas which need to be addressed include:

1) The clinician's knowledge of the therapeutic components of the tools used.
2) The therapist's knowledge of the non-therapeutic components of the tools used.
3) The therapist's knowledge of the use of the digital tools (i.e., specific game play and use).

4) How the therapist handles client's confidential personal information when utilizing digital mental health tools.

   a. Within the direct use of such tools (i.e., client login and account information)
   b. As collected by the play therapist (pictures, screenshots, stories, etc.)
   c. As potentially collected by the software company (cookies, data forms, etc.)

5) What collected information would be beneficial for society.

   a. How informed consent should be addressed
   b. How such information should be ethically handled

6) How public and private entities should work together.

   a. To increase accessibility
   b. Decrease duplication of effort
   c. Increase client/patient benefit

Although the ethical guidelines and requirements will change over time, the importance of mental health providers working to form and follow such structures as we navigate this relatively new realm is paramount. As a field, the exploration of the appropriate use of digital tools in therapy allows us all to remain current and meet the needs and interests of our clients. Guidelines and requirements will certainly continue to evolve as we learn more about the pros, cons, and possibilities of the inclusion of digital tools in mental health treatment.

Capability

According to Fraser & Greenhalgh, capability is the "extent to which individuals can adapt to change, generate new knowledge, and continue to improve their performance (2001, p. 1). Capability is an extension of competence and includes adaptation of existing skills and the ability to generate new knowledge to improve their performance (Fraser & Greenhalgh, 2001). In the APA's task force document, capability is referred to as much more than competence, rather it is the enhancement of competence which is "generally achieved through feedback on one's performance and coping with unfamiliar contexts and challenges to one's competencies" (American Psychological Association, 2006, p. 13).

People who are considered experts in a topic or field are considered to have taken competence to this higher level of capability. Perhaps it is that capability is a realization of the aspirational competence discussed earlier in the chapter. The expert is distinguished by one "noticing features and meaningful patterns of information, have considerable content knowledge that is organized in a fashion indicative of a deep understanding of the material, possess knowledge reflective of contexts of applicability rather than isolated facts, flexibly retrieve salient knowledge with minimal attention effort, know their discipline thoroughly, and demonstrate varying levels of flexibility in dealing with novel situations" (American Psychological Association, 2006, p. 13). Experts set themselves apart as capable professionals.

Play therapists who grow beyond competence and achieve the status of capability are those who enquire, explore, and learn with more depth and breadth than minimally required. Capability encompasses the potential of the competent therapist and brings it into fruition. Play therapists will benefit their clients and themselves most when they strive for capability.

Conclusion

Play therapists are poised in a position of great honor and importance. The role is unique. Our play therapy (and any other) professional guidelines dictate that we achieve and maintain a number of professional components to best serve our clients. Seeking education (training, research, etc.), supervision (guidance), and expansion (depth and breadth) will result in a play therapist with great competence, culture, comfort, and capability.

The application of these important concepts to the use of a variety of play therapy materials and modalities is imperative. When speaking of digital tools in these ways, we are addressing the inherent professional importance of speaking our client's language and respecting their culture, thereby achieving competence, comfort and capability, to best serve our clients. These concepts build an important portion of the foundational conceptualization for the appropriate use of digital tools in play therapy, or DPT. Chapter 4 will continue this foundation building.

Note

1. Excerpt from Stone (2019); adapted from McNary, Mason, & Tobin, 2018. Reprinted with permission.

References

American Psychological Association (APA) (2006). *APA task force on the assessment of competence in professional practice: Final report.* www.apa.org/ed/resources/competency-revised.pdf

American Psychological Association (APA) (2015). *Competencies for psychology practice in primary care.* www.apa.org/ed/resources/competencies-practice.pdf

Association for Play Therapy (APT) (n.d.a). *About APT.* www.a4pt.org/page/AboutAPT

Association for Play Therapy (APT) (n.d.b). *Important credentialing announcement: Registered Play Therapist (RPT) & Supervisor (RPT-S).* www.a4pt.org/page/SpecialAnnouncement?&hhsearchterms=%22competenc%22

Association for Play Therapy (APT) (2016). *Play therapy best practices.* https://cdn.ymaws.com/www.a4pt.org/resource/resmgr/publications/Best_Practices__-_Sept_2016.pdf

Dictionary.com (2019). *Technologist.* www.dictionary.com/browse/technologist

Fraser, S. W., & Greenhalgh, T. (2001). Coping with complexity: Educating for capability. *British Medical Journal, 323*, 799–803.

Karempelas, G. (2019, February). *Guiding principles on ethics in digital health produced during a seminar at Stanford Libraries.* https://library.stanford.edu/digitalhealthethics/press-release

Merriam Webster (2019a, August). *Competence.* www.merriam-webster.com/dictionary/competence

Merriam Webster (2019b). *Comfortable.* www.merriam-webster.com/dictionary/comfortable

Merriam Webster (2019c). *Technophile.* www.merriam-webster.com/dictionary/technophile

National Association of Social Workers (NASW) (2005). *NASW standards for cultural competence in social work practice.* http://catholiccharitiesla.org/wp-content/uploads/NASW-Cultural-Competence-in-Social-Work-Practice.pdf

Penny, J. (2019). *What are the 12 core competencies?* www.best-job-interview.com/12-core-competencies.html

Schaefer, C. E. (1993). What is play and why is it therapeutic? In C. Schaefer (Ed.), *Therapeutic powers of play* (pp. 1–16). Jason Aronson.

Schaefer, C. E., & Drewes, A. A. (2013). *The therapeutic powers of play: 20 core agents of change.* Wiley.

Stanford Libraries (2018). *Statement of guiding principles for ethics in digital health.* https://hitconsultant.net/wp-content/uploads/2019/02/Stanford-Seminar-Digital-Health-Guiding-Principles_2018.pdf?fbclid=IwAR11e0piPMZeMfbQvjy8YnSIiefZ_ukLotqLuH66jutOtoI9CwY6gnj1GPw

Stone, J. (2016a). Board games in play therapy. In K. J. O'Connor, C. E. Schaefer, & L. Braverman (Eds.), *The handbook of play therapy* (2nd ed., pp. 309–323). Wiley.

Stone, J. (2016b). *Virtual Sandtray.* www.sandtrayplay.com/Press/VirtualSandtrayArticle01.pdf

Stone, J. (2019). Digital games. In J. Stone & C. Schaefer (Eds.), *Game play* (3rd ed.). Wiley.

The Technoskeptic (2019). https://thetechnoskeptic.com/about/

World Economic Forum (WEF) (2019a). *White paper: Technology and innovation for the future of production: Accelerating value creation.* www3.weforum.org/docs/WEF_White_Paper_Technology_Innovation_Future_of_Production_2017.pdf

World Economic Forum (WEF) (2019b). *Our mission: World economic forum.* www.weforum.org/about/world-economic-forum

Zimmerman, K. A. (2017, July 13). What is culture? *Live Science.* www.livescience.com/21478-what-is-culture-definition-of-culture.html

4 Speaking the Client's Language, Prescriptive Play Therapy, and the Therapeutic Powers of Play

The concept of speaking the client's language, or entering and honoring their culture, was introduced in Chapter 3. In this chapter we will expand upon those concepts, discuss prescriptive play therapy, and introduce the therapeutic powers of play (Schaefer, 1993; Schaefer & Drewes, 2014). Each of these topics continue to lay the groundwork for DPT and the incorporation of our client's interests in therapeutically appropriate ways.

Speaking the Client's Language

The importance of speaking the client's language and honoring their culture was initially presented to this author during a play therapy graduate school class. The professor was focused on topics such as vernacular, cadence, and colloquialisms. He would further explain that when a client swore, then the therapist would swear; if the client did not swear, the therapist would not swear, and so forth. These concepts were based off of a tabula rasa: that the therapist would be a blank slate and mirror the client's actions, verbalizations, and so on. As with anything in a course, some of the concepts will be congruent and integrated into one's day to day conceptualization and practice, and some will not. Of all the time spent in that course with him, two key components stood out: 1) speak your client's language, even if his meaning of that was ultimately a bit different from this author's conceptualization; and 2) know your materials; play, play, and play some more until you know it so well that when you're in a play therapy session, you are no longer thinking about the mechanics of the gameplay but rather of the interactions and dynamics at hand. We will concentrate on the first concept in this chapter and the second one later in the book.

When a client presents for play therapy, many things are likely going through his or her mind. The client commonly wonders what play therapy will be like, what the therapist will be like, and what will be done within the session. Other important topics include questions about what the therapist might know about the client, what will be acceptable to the therapist, and how the therapist will react and/or respond to anything and everything about the client. As these queries are addressed, the therapeutic relationship will build. Fundamentally, many therapeutic theories discuss the importance of relationship and rapport.

Rapport and Relationship

As mentioned in Chapter 3, definitions can be critical to the true understanding of concepts. Many terms we frequently use include assumptions. They have meanings which morph over time in different situations, generations, and cultures. Sometimes they retain their historical meaning and sometimes they do not. Let us examine these terms more closely with some basic definitions.

Merriam-Webster defines rapport as "a friendly, harmonious relationship; especially a relationship characterized by agreement, mutual understanding, or empathy that makes communication possible or easy" (2019e, para 1). Rapport, then, includes the term "relationship" and describes the relationship as mutual, empathetic, harmonious and friendly. A relationship is defined by Merriam Webster in terms of a relation. A relationship is the relation connecting or binding participants (Merriam Webster, 2019d, para 1) or it can be defined as a "connection, association, or involvement" and/or "an emotional or other connection between people" (Dictionary.com, 2002). Relation is defined as the "state of being mutually or reciprocally interested" (Merriam Webster, 2019c, para 1).

Defining the basic terminology allows for greater dissection of concepts when evaluating the meaning(s) and assigning value. At its core, play therapy has a tremendous focus and emphasis on the importance of the relationship and rapport between the therapist and the client. At this point we have established that *rapport* is a mutual, empathetic, harmonious, and friendly relationship. A *relationship* is the mutual interest that connects, associates, or involves the participants. Therefore, rapport is ultimately a mutual, empathetic, harmonious, and friendly connection of participants based on mutual interest.

In non-therapeutic relationships, mutual interests often would bring two or more people together and form the basis of the relationship. In therapeutic relationships, two (or more) people, a client and a therapist, are brought together by needs and desires. The needs and desires can include a wide range of items and topics; however, they are not always mutual. If a child is brought to play therapy without an internal desire to attend, the mutuality is between the caregiver and the therapist, not the client and the therapist. It is then the critically important role of the therapist to create an environment, both physical and emotional, which fosters the rapport – the mutual, empathetic, harmonious, friendly connection based on mutual interest – between the client and therapist.

If the client then brings the components, characteristics, styles, skills, abilities, qualities, and interests of him/herself to the play therapy room, these will be the basis of the rapport. The connection is fundamentally who the client is and what they bring into the room. The therapist's job is to understand these qualities as best they can in an effort to connect and form the relationship between the client and therapist.

The therapist certainly brings their own qualities into the room. It is essential that the 4 Cs listed in Chapter 2 have been met or are something that one strives toward: competency, culture, comfort, and capability through education and supervision so the therapist can be very self-aware and self-confident with what the therapist is bringing into the room. If what the client brings into the room is fundamentally incongruent with the beliefs and level of acceptance for the therapist, supervision and/or consultation should be utilized to determine if the rapport can even be established and if the answer is no, then a referral would be most appropriate.

If a therapist proceeds with the attempts to build the therapeutic relationship and the components, characteristics, styles, skills, abilities, qualities, and interests of the client are not acceptable to the therapist, then negative judgment becomes a facet. Judgment is part of being human and it is a facet in everything. We judge people's appearance, behavior, and decisions. We judge people known and unknown to us. It is human nature and therapists will not be immune to this behavior. However, therapists must be aware of these tendencies and the etiology and basis of the judgment.

In its purest form, judgment is "the process of forming an opinion or evaluation by discerning and comparing" (Merriam Webster, 2019a, para 1). Play therapists will be faced with many things within the therapeutic relationship and sessions that will spark judgment. According to this definition, the judgment within a therapeutic relationship would be warranted and part of the role of the therapist. If a child is known to have social difficulties, and during a game of *Uno* she celebrates every time she has a good card play *and* every time the therapist has a not-so-good card play, then hoots and hollers when she wins, some therapist judgment would happen. The judgment would most likely include an evaluation of these behavioral interaction styles and a judgment of whether or not these styles encourage or prohibit positive social interactions. Based on the presenting difficulties for the client, the therapist would use these judgments to benefit the client by assisting him/her with the understandings and skills necessary for more satisfactory interpersonal interactions. Basically, if the child desires better social interactions and the historical behaviors are turning away peers, the need and desire to improve the relationships might result in behavior change at the will of the client. There might be a client-driven internal desire for change which could be practiced and then reinforced through future peer interactions. The judgment, or comparison and discernment, by the therapist was used in a positive way to help the client meet his/her needs and desires.

Conversely, judgment can have negative implications when made by a therapist according to his/her own needs and desires. By definition, to establish a therapeutic rapport, the components, characteristics, styles, skills, abilities, qualities, and interests of the client would be presented for the therapist to understand, accept, and incorporate into the sessions. If the client brings a topic, belief, behavior, interest, or other component into the session and the judgment is according to the therapist's own needs and desires, the rapport cannot be established. This is very fundamental and very important to the play therapy process.

If a client brings in a story about an interaction regarding a video game they were playing online the night before and the therapist is not fulfilling the important steps of competency, cultural (diversity), comfort, and capability (aspiration), the judgment might be a negative one. If the result of the negative judgment is to dismiss the story based on the therapist's dislike or discomfort of the video game example, the result becomes that the client has now had a significant dismissal of their interest, and potentially even more. The client is now going to be less connected; significantly less connected; or, at worst, disconnected from the therapist. At best, the client now understands that the "whole them" is not acceptable and therefore should not be brought into the session. The scenario of not accepting the whole client is not 4 C–congruent.

We want the "whole them" in the session. Would we not, as play therapists, want to afford them the safe environment within which they can display their whole self, interact and share regarding all the parts, and therefore allow the most robust psychological interactive process possible? If the answer is yes, then it supports and highlights the importance of the competency, culture, comfort, and capability components, and the establishment of therapeutic rapport OR the appropriateness of a referral. Play therapists do not need to be everything to everybody, but we do need to understand what our own "whole self" is, what type of judgment is employed, and how each effects the therapeutic process.

If the therapist's whole self is self-understood and congruent enough with the components the client brings in, then the rapport can be established, and the work will be based on the client's needs and desires as determined by the treatment plan process. The task will be to find therapeutic value in the interactions and tools used within session. This applies to any and all therapeutic tools.

The Search for Foundation

Psychological Theory

Psychological theory is often thought of as the underpinnings of the mental health professional's approach and belief system. In general, a theory is a fact-based testable framework, based on hypotheses, used to describe a phenomenon (Cherry, 2019, para 2). Theories can be tested to gain support or be discredited. A confusion exists regarding the word "theory", most likely because of the difference in the layperson's term and the scientific term. The layperson's term typically refers to an idea someone has (Ghose, 2013, para 11). In scientific terms, the key differentiating components include the framework of the theory and that it has been tested repeatedly.

Typically, these scientific term underpinnings provide a model or structure for the professional to understand behaviors, thoughts, and emotions and provide explanations and predictions regarding behaviors. Currently there are many different psychological theory types. These include developmental (explaining human development either over all or of specific portions), grand (seeking to comprehensively explain behavior; are often insufficient, i.e., founding theorists), mini (explaining particular aspects of behavior and development), and emergent (relatively new theories often formed by combining mini theories) (Cherry, 2019, para 11).

The true meaning of psychological theory is quite complicated to define, as most do not fit into the typical scientific schema. It is questionable how well we can test the framework of many psychological theories. People are complex; there are millions of variables within the client and what they bring to the session, the therapist and what s/he brings to the session, and the interaction of all. How does one account for all of them in general? Even a phenomenological study structure would not account for all the variables, but at least this approach personalizes the investigation to the particular "subject" (person being studied within the theory's framework). Larger research studies include a much larger N (number of participants) and therefore only certain variables can be included or the study risks becoming convoluted. In addition, each session, each interaction, each person, and each set of topics introduces new variables and excludes others. It is quite a daunting endeavor to properly test psychological theories.

Perhaps it is more that theories are structures from which one would investigate further. This investigation includes education (formal and on one's own), experience, and supervision. The structure, then, becomes the key foundation, and in turn, the necessary element for internal and external justification (showing a good reason why something has been done, Merriam Webster, 2019b, para 1). Psychological theory is absolutely important for the clinician to understand what is and is not working in the client's life, how to assist him/her with desired and/or necessary changes, and how the changes will be recognized internally and externally. The conceptualization of what happens in the therapeutic interaction creates space for the "who, what, why, how, where, and when" questions regarding the therapeutic process (Stone, 2016). These must be answered for a therapist to know what it is they are doing and why they are doing anything in the therapeutic room.

Play therapists O'Connor and Braverman address the concept of play therapy theories in their book *Play Therapy Theory and Practice* (1997). The book's stated purpose is to allow readers to compare major existing theories and newly emerging ones alongside one another. They state: "It is our belief that to become a competent play therapist one must find a theoretical model that meshes well with both one's personality and the needs of one's particular client base" (O'Connor & Braverman, 1997, p. 1).

Prescriptive Psychotherapy and Systematic Treatment Selection

The quest to understand psychological theory or theories is not unique to the 21st century. More than half a century ago, clinicians were discussing the complexities of treatment evaluation, clinician components, and client contributions (Cole & Magnussen, 1966). The explorations attempted to evaluate if the strict adherence to a theoretical foundation and/or intervention benefitted the client.

Strict adherence was found to be more a reflection of the therapist and his/her training and beliefs than to scientific validity (Beutler, 1979; Beutler & Harwood, 2000; Beutler et al., 2007).

Prescriptive psychotherapy and systematic treatment selection were born of these explorations. Larry Beutler has written extensively about these topics in an effort to define both clinician and client contributors to the therapeutic process. The importance of client factors is paramount; diagnoses, experiences, views, and the like can greatly affect the therapeutic process. In order to best serve the client within prescriptive psychotherapy, the clinician must be competent in many modalities so as to appropriately tailor the treatment to the client's needs. These concepts have morphed over the years, but the questions still remain:

- Is it that the theory provides the foundation for the therapist's conceptualization and the client brings in the material, which leads to a structure within which the therapist can help the client?
- Is the process more collaborative with the theoretical foundation effecting both the therapist and client through its tenets and agents of change?
- Does the theory need to align more with the client needs and beliefs?
- Does the therapist offer one type of treatment and select clients carefully?
- Does the therapist become competent in multiple theories and apply relevant approaches as deemed appropriate?

Beutler's work is worthy of further investigation and thought as it raises questions many do not ponder frequently. His conclusions (and those of his colleagues over the many publications) may not fit your needs, but the questions he poses and elicits inform the therapist's approach. Beutler and Harwood state that "<prescriptive psychotherapy> works from a set of general, empirically informed principles that can be transferred across different theories, rather than from one or another theoretical model or from a finite list of techniques. These principles inform therapists in the use of strategies and allow them to select techniques from their own particular experience and training" (2000, p. v).

Many educational institutions focus on one theory and do not address these questions in depth. Thankfully, this author was introduced not only to a large assortment of theories of general psychology and play therapy, but also a mechanism through which one can evaluate theories. Introduced by O'Connor (1991), this allows for a thorough investigation of the components of a play therapy theory's theoretical structure. His list includes philosophy, personality theory, pathology, goal/cure, curative elements, therapist behaviors, population, play materials, role of play, and course of treatment. For each theory one would like to understand and/or incorporate, completing this worksheet would be a place to begin (refer to Table 4.1). These components also help distinguish theory from belief systems.

Table 4.1 Play Therapy Theory Investigation Worksheet

Name of theory
Underlying philosophy
Underlying personality theory
Conceptualization of pathology
Ultimate goal/cure of the therapy
Curative elements of the therapy*
How the therapist acts/interacts
Populations the theory is best suited for
Play materials included
Role of play in the interactions
Course of treatment components

Adapted from O'Connor, K. (1991). Comparing Play Therapy Theories.
*(i.e., core agents of change – discussed later in the chapter)

Prescriptive Play Therapy

Prescriptive play therapy is an approach characterized by the concept of prescribing the appropriate theory and/or technique for the individual client. Prescriptive play therapy is considered transtheoretical, eclectic, integrative, and evidence-informed (Schaefer & Drewes, 2016). As with prescriptive psychotherapy, this customized approach allows the play therapist to meet the specific and diverse needs of the client. Whereas subscribing to one theory will exclude certain clients, difficulties, or needs, prescriptive play therapy aims toward inclusion.

The prescriptive play therapist must have a well-rounded repertoire in both education and experience. Per Schaefer and Drewes (2016), "Prescriptive play therapists draw from a number of therapeutic approaches so as to have a wealth of change agents at their disposal. They then tailor their therapeutic interventions to the needs of the individual client by utilizing four sources of information: empirical evidence, clinical experience/expertise, client preferences/context, and likely causes(s) of the presenting problem" (p. 236).

Six core principles, or tenets, are associated with prescriptive play therapy. They include individualized treatment, differential therapeutics, transtheoretical approach, integrative psychotherapy, prescriptive matching, and comprehensive assessment. These tenets are fundamental cornerstones of the approach (Schaefer & Drewes, 2016).

A prescriptive play therapist must attain high levels of competency and capability to continue to add new things to his/her professional play repertoire, apply various components of different theories to different needs within the case, and be able to assess and formulate multiple facets into appropriate treatment plans. A simpler path would be to maintain treatment perspectives within one theoretical foundation and focus either on a one-size-fits-all approach where all clients receive the same treatment, or an exclusionary one where only certain clients

Table 4.2 Six Tenets of Prescriptive Play Therapy

Tenet 1	Individualized treatment	Tailor the intervention to the individual needs, characteristics, and situation of the client
Tenet 2	Differential therapeutics	Some interventions are more effective for certain disorders and personalities
Tenet 3	Transtheoretical approach	Select theories and techniques based on the best therapeutic agents of change for the client
Tenet 4	Integrative psychotherapy	Multimodal approach (combining 2 or more theories) utilizing an integrated intervention
Tenet 5	Prescriptive matching	Match the intervention with the client and the specific disorder
Tenet 6	Comprehensive assessment	Initial assessment including multiple informants, methods, and ongoing assessments to track progress

Adapted from Schaefer and Drewes (2016) Prescriptive Play Therapy.

are deemed appropriate for the treatment. The more comprehensive path is to pursue a prescriptive play therapy foundation and continue to seek knowledge and experience that will benefit a wide variety of clients.

With the focus of speaking the client's language in mind, one can see how the flexibility and broad range of treatment options available within the prescriptive play therapy tenets is a preferred approach. If the language of the client includes digital tools, the prescriptive play therapist would naturally seek out information which would allow for the inclusion and customization of the treatment plan, conceptualization, and play.

As stated by Stone regarding the use of digital tools in therapy (2020, in press), "By systematically applying a structure, in addition to a fundamental theory, by which the therapist can evaluate the therapeutic value of the digital tool and language, client interests can be incorporated into sessions appropriately. This structure can assist with fundamental conceptualization, communication with collateral contacts, and writing of clinical notes." Such a structure can be found through the 20 Core Agents of Change within the therapeutic powers of play (Schaefer, 1993; Schaefer & Drewes, 2014).

The Therapeutic Powers of Play

A seasoned play therapist will speak highly of the efficacy of play therapy based on experience. They have witnessed the power of play and continue to hone their work to benefit clients. A difficulty can lie in the communication with those who have not seen the transformations. Additionally, how does this power get communicated and explained to students of play therapy? How is play therapy really distinguished from "just play"?

Dr. Charles Schaefer aimed to answer the "why" and "how" questions regarding play therapy. He set out to discover "the overt and covert activities various theoretical systems use to produce change in a client" (Drewes & Schaefer, 2016, p. 35). The result is the *Therapeutic Powers of Play* and *20 Core Agents of Change* (Schaefer, 1993). Play therapists can utilize this structure as a way to define what is being experienced within the session. The 20 core agents of change provide nomenclature for the therapist to understand what is happening in the session and to be able to explain such things to others. Session notes also benefit from these core agents by providing more succinct explanations of the dynamics and interpersonal process, rather than a focus on the intervention and any justification.

In play therapy, play is not merely the medium which allows an environment for the true change agents to occur. Play is essential to the play therapy process and change agents are inherent in the play interactions. These are complex concepts which are simply stated. The game, doll, console, or art materials are not the icebreaker or intended rapport-building activity so the "real work" can begin. Those materials facilitate interactions within which the therapeutic powers of play are enacted. "Play initiates, facilitates, or strengthens their <therapeutic powers of play> effect (Drewes & Schaefer, 2016, p. 38; Schaefer, 2013).

Therapeutic Powers of Play and the 20 Core Agents of Change

The therapeutic powers are organized into four major categories: facilitate communication, foster emotional wellness, enhance social relationships, and increase personal strengths. These four categories are then described in more detail through the core agents of change as they are assigned to each category. A play therapist could recognize that a dynamic within the play interaction (client–tool, client–therapist, client–therapist–tool) enhanced social relationships, for example. To further describe this dynamic, the therapist could choose from the core agents under that therapeutic power of play heading. As an example, the discussions and/or notes would then explain that the play therapy session met the goal of enhanced social relationships and the appropriate core agents were enacted through the play.

To further understand these powers for conceptualization and integration into play therapy practice, each of the four categories of therapeutic powers and their underlying core agents of change will be discussed. The core agents of change are the mechanisms that bring about change within the therapy. When conceptualizing how a therapeutic power was activated within a session, these core agents can provide the structure needed to define and communicate the process within session notes and communications with others. Please refer to Figure 4.1 for a representation of the therapeutic powers of play and core agents. There may be great value in creating a sheet with categories, change agents, and any desired details to use as a reference when formulating case notes or preparing for a variety of communication. It is important to note that not all categories or core agents will be activated in every play therapy session.

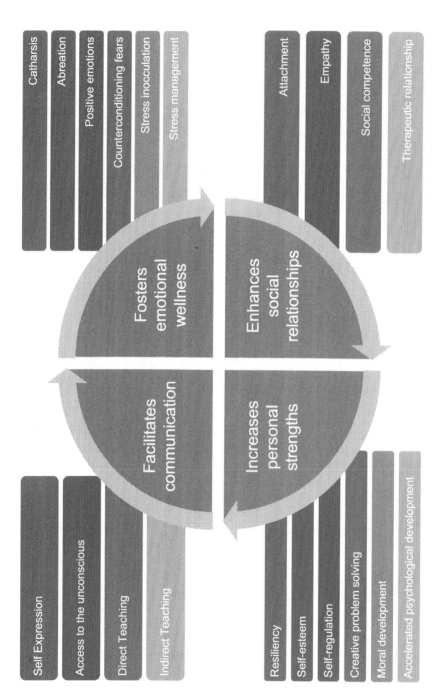

Figure 4.1 Adapted from Schaefer, C. E., & Drewes, A. A. (2013). *The therapeutic powers of play: 20 core agents of change*. Wiley and from Parson, J. (2017) Puppet Play Therapy – Integrating Theory, Evidence and Action (ITEA) presented at International Play Therapy Study Group. Champneys at Forest Mere, England. June 18, 2017.

Facilitate Communication

The first therapeutic power is to *Facilitate Communication*. Fundamentally, communication is a cornerstone of any kind of therapy. This communication can be verbal or non-verbal. The important components include a client who has the ability to communicate their truth and the appropriate environment in which to do so, and a therapist who is able to receive the communication, appropriately respond, and incorporate the information or experience into the treatment conceptualization. A hope is that all play therapy will achieve this therapeutic power and if it does not, the rapport, approach, and environment should all be re-evaluated.

The core agents of change further define the therapeutic process in play therapy. Here again, the definitions are important for the proper understanding of the concepts. All of the following are adapted from Schaefer and Drewes (2016).

1) Self-expression:

    a. Expressing one's thoughts, beliefs, emotions, experiences, views, and opinions in a safe environment and relationship allows for acknowledgment and the potential for personal growth.

    b. Natural language: Play is a natural form of expression and language for children, particularly young children. Play therapists witness children who have a limited vocabulary and/or emotional identification knowledge, exhibit complex concepts through play.

    c. Talking in the third person: Through the use of puppets, dolls, and other characters, children can often give voice to feelings, thoughts and behaviors which are overwhelming, difficult, or threatening for them to verbalize. This play allows for indirect expression.

    d. An "as if" or not-real-life quality: Play can have a make-believe component which allows emotions, thoughts, and experiences to be played out within a more objective presentation.

    e. Indescribable: Sometimes words are not sufficient or possible when communicating and play allows for expression without words.

    f. Engrossment: Being engrossed in play can allow for defense reduction and the revelation of inner beliefs, worlds, and experiences.

    g. Doing while talking: Often, children feel more comfortable when they are doing something, and verbalizations become easier and more free-flowing.

2) Access to the unconscious:

    a. Projection: This process is either conscious or unconscious and includes the attribution of thoughts, feelings, desires, and more to an "other". This could be a play object, drawing, or person.

    b. Displacement: Acting out one's frustrations and feelings onto a play object can allow for a less-threatening expression experience.

    c. Symbolization: Representation is very important in play therapy and is often used by identifying a symbol to represent an abstract concept.

　　　d.　Sublimation: The process of channeling drives and emotions into other activities, such as sports or art.

　　　e.　Fantasy compensation: Fantasy allows a person to take on another role, play out a different scenario, or create that which might not be possible.

3)　Direct teaching:

　　　a.　Attention is captured: Play materials hold the attention of the client and allow space and time to impart information.

　　　b.　Sensory input: Sensory or experiential experiences can allow for increased retention of information.

　　　c.　Safe environment: The play therapy room does not include mechanisms for evaluation, such as grades, and therefore reduces the threat and/or fear of failure.

　　　d.　Active involvement: Play allows for exploration, involvement, and self-initiated learning experiences.

　　　e.　Consolidation of skills: The repetitive practice of skills through play can lead to a reinforcement of said skills.

　　　f.　Learning by example: Use of toy models as teachers and students to teach different skills.

4)　Indirect teaching:

　　　a.　Stories and metaphors: Often used to illustrate or demonstrate concepts; narratives.

Foster Emotional Wellness

Fostering emotional wellness is accomplished through the process of catharsis, abreaction, positive emotions, counterconditioning fears, stress inoculation, and stress management. The ability to release, work through, process, and apply lessons learned allows the client to gain experiences and skills to integrate into their life conceptualizations and day-to-day situations.

5)　Catharsis:

　　　a.　The release of affect such as anger or sadness.

　　　b.　The role of play:

　　　　　i.　The playroom provides a safe and supportive environment.

　　　　　ii.　Symbolic play provides psychological distance.

　　　　　iii.　The positive emotions elicited by play help to balance the negative emotions.

6)　Abreaction:

　　　a.　Repressed memories of a traumatic event are made conscious and expressed.

　　　b.　The role of play:

      i.   Cognitive assimilation and emotional release are achieved through:

        1.   Miniaturization of experiences: Using small toys to represent experiences.

        2.   Active control and mastery: Take on a role of control in a scenario.

        3.   Piecemeal assimilation by repetition: Through distance and repetition, scenarios can gain cohesion and resolution.

7) Positive emotions:

    a.   Balance negative emotions.
    b.   Can have healing qualities.

8) Counterconditioning of fears:

    a.   Replacing undesirable fear responses with desirable, compatible responses through exposure.

9) Stress inoculation:

    a.   Preparation for handling stressful situations.
    b.   The role of play:

      i.   An unfamiliar experience becomes less scary and more known.
      ii.   Learns and practices coping skills.
     iii.   Negative emotion activation is lessened because of the fun and enjoyment of the play.

10) Stress management:

    a.   Antidote for stressful situations by working through situations by playing.
    b.   The role of play includes:

      i.   Humor therapy.
      ii.   Fantasy compensation.
     iii.   Adaptive doll play.
     iv.   Self-soothing play.
      v.   Fantasy escape.

Enhance Social Relationships

Social relationships are desired by human beings. We all crave positive relationships on some level and the types and quantity desired can vary greatly from person to person. Experiencing the therapeutic relationship, understanding healthy attachment, gaining or strengthening a sense of self, and experiencing and understanding empathy can drastically improve one's social relationships.

11) Therapeutic relationship:

  a.   Without rapport, technique and strategy are likely to be ineffective.
  b.   The role of play:

    i.   Play helps build rapport.
    ii.   A fun therapist is found to be more trustworthy and relatable.
    iii. The relationship is experienced as more equal and not hierarchical.

12) Attachment:

  a.   Effects relationship functioning and affect regulation.

13) Sense of self:

  a.   Personal identity.
  b.   The role of play:

    i.   Freedom.
    ii.   Imagination.
    iii. Primary process thinking: symbolic, metaphoric, emotionally laden.

14) Empathy:

  a.   Ability to take the perspective of others.
  b.   Key factor in socio-emotional development.
  c.   Role of play:

    i.   Role play.
    ii.   Storytelling.

Increase Personal Strengths

Personal strengths allow a person to withstand difficult situations, have a healthy sense of self, and have positive social and societal interactions. Creative problem solving, resiliency, moral development, accelerated psychological development, self-regulation, and self-esteem all contribute to a solid personal foundation. These skills help people of all ages navigate day-to-day difficulties.

15) Creative problem solving:

  a.   Symptom reduction.
  b.   Use of insight, divergent thinking abilities.
  c.   Flexibility.
  d.   Alternative coping strategies.
  e.   Empathetic responses.

16) Resiliency:

  a.   Adaptation skills.
  b.   The role of play:

     i. Creative problem solving.
     ii. Training for the unexpected.
     iii. Positive emotions.
     iv. Humor.

17) Moral development:

    a. Understanding the expectations of the social group(s).
    b. Conforming to the expectations of the social group(s).

18) Accelerated psychological development:

    a. Play can make accomplishing a developmental task fun.
    b. Developmental accomplishments can result in achieving an age-appropriate developmental level.

19) Self-regulation:

    a. Ability to moderate one's physical and emotional responses.
    b. Role of play:

     i. Pretend play.
     ii. Sociodramatic play.
     iii. Game play.
     iv. Self-soothing play.
     v. Rough and tumble play.

20) Self-esteem:

    a. Sense of self-worth and personal value.
    b. Role of play.

     i. Ability to feel in control.
      1. Body actions.
      2. Ideas.
      3. Objects.
      4. Relationships.

Conclusion

Speaking the client's language, prescriptive play therapy, and the therapeutic powers of play all contribute to the foundational aspects of being a play therapist. The importance of clients being seen, heard, and understood, having mental health treatment tailored to the needs of the client, and the ability to identify the core agents of change within play therapy, allow the play therapist a very solid and unique position in a client's life. Whatever the theoretical foundation of the play therapist, answering the "who, what, why, how, where, and when" questions about the therapeutic process and understanding the key concepts within a theory or theories will provide a well thought through approach to play therapy.

References

Beutler, L. E. (1979). Toward specific psychological therapies for specific conditions. *Journal of Consulting and Clinical Psychology, 47*(5), 882–897.

Beutler, L. E., & Harwood, T. M. (2000). *Prescriptive psychotherapy: A practical guide to systematic treatment selection.* Oxford: Oxford University Press.

Beutler, L. E., Harwood, T. M., Bertoni, M., & Thomann, J. (2007). *Systematic treatment selection and prescriptive therapy.* www.apa.org/pubs/databases/psyccases/4317107-chapter3.pdf

Cherry, K. (2019, July). *10 types of psychological theories.* www.verywellmind.com/what-is-a-theory-2795970

Cole, J. K., & Magnussen, M. G. (1966). Where the action is. *Journal of Consulting Psychology, 30*(6), 539–543.

Dictionary.com (2002). *Relationship.* www.dictionary.com/browse/relationship

Drewes, A. A., & Schaefer, C. E. (2016). The therapeutic powers of play. In K. O'Connor, C. Schaefer, & L. Braverman (Eds.), *Handbook of play therapy* (pp. 35–60). Wiley.

Ghose, T. (2013, April). "Just a theory": 7 misused science words. *Scientific American.* www.scientificamerican.com/article/just-a-theory-7-misused-science-words/

Merriam Webster (2019a). *Judgment.* www.merriam-webster.com/dictionary/judgment

Merriam Webster (2019b). *Justification.* www.merriam-webster.com/dictionary/justification

Merriam Webster (2019c). *Rapport.* www.merriam-webster.com/dictionary/rapport

Merriam Webster (2019d). *Relationship.* www.merriam-webster.com/dictionary/relationship

Merriam Webster (2019e). *Relation.* www.merriam-webster.com/dictionary/relation

O'Connor, K. (1991). *Comparing play therapy theories.* Fresno, CA: Course Worksheet.

O'Connor, K., & Braverman, L. D. (1997). *Play therapy theory and practice* (2nd ed.). Wiley.

Schaefer, C. E. (1993). What is play and why is it therapeutic? In C. Schaefer (Ed.), *The therapeutic powers of play* (pp. 1–15). Jason Aaronson.

Schaefer, C. E., & Drewes, A. A. (2014). *The therapeutic powers of play: 20 core agents of change* (2nd ed.). Wiley.

Schaefer, C. E., & Drewes, A. A. (2016). Prescriptive play therapy. In K. O'Connor, C. Schaefer, & L. Braverman (Eds.), *Handbook of play therapy* (pp. 227–240). Wiley.

Stone, J. (2016). Board games in play therapy. In K. O'Connor, C. Schaefer, & L. Braverman (Eds.), *Handbook of play therapy* (pp. 309–323). Wiley.

Stone, J. (2020, in press). Video games in therapy. In A. Bean (Ed.), *Integrating geek culture into therapeutic practice: A clinician's guide to geek therapy.* Leyline.

5　Modalities

Some of the current terminology can become confusing for even the most sea-soned play therapist. What is really meant by terms such as theory, approach, modality, technique, certification, or credentialing? I have had some of these conversations with influential play therapists and there do not seem to be simple answers. Play therapy is in a growth period with so many new directions being spoken about, written about, and explored. It will be important to understand the distinctions of the terms presented earlier as a field so we can organize and integrate the growth ahead.

Modalities and Techniques

We will focus on the terms "modality" and "technique" for our purposes here, as they appear to be the best fit for DPT. Lexico, of Oxford Dictionary, defines "modality" as "a particular mode in which something exists or is experienced or expressed; a particular method or procedure" (2019a). Mode, which is in the modality definition but not clearly defined, is "a way or manner in which some-thing occurs or is experienced, expressed, or done" (Lexico, 2019b). Therefore, we can think of a modality as a particular way something is expressed or done, one that exists through a particular method or procedure. DPT is a modality in which play therapy is expressed or executed and exists through particular digitally delivered methods or procedures.

"Techniques" are the particular methods or procedures a play therapist uses to employ the modality. Merriam-Webster defines technique as "a body of technical methods (as in a craft or in scientific research)" (2019, para. 2). The techniques of DPT include the use of various hardware and software, discussion about one's interests and/or use, and research into a variety of interests/use. The techniques included in the modality of DPT activate the therapeutic powers of play when used by a trained play therapist within a therapeutic session.

Play Therapy Modalities

Kaduson and Schaefer have identified 15 major play therapy modalities and pose that play modalities inform how we implement the therapeutic powers of play. Modalities are what we do in the room; they are the actual practice of play therapy. They include storytelling, sand play, block play, sensory play, board game play, guided imagery play, music play, drawings, doll play, drama play, bibliotherapy, clay play, music/movement play, virtual reality play, and electronic game play. According to Kaduson and Schaefer, these modalities were conceptualized as classic or trending (with the intention of becoming classics in the future) and all include the key characteristics of play, that is, positive affect, active engagement, process over outcome, non-literality, and intrinsic motivation (in press).

DPT encompasses a number of the previously listed modalities. Virtual reality and electronic game play are the most obvious; however, others such as storytelling, sand play, guided imagery play, music play, drawings, board game play, and movement play can also be considered under the DPT heading. This is one of the most exciting components of DPT: the enormous breadth of available programs (software, i.e., apps, games, etc.) and units (hardware, i.e., tablets, consoles, etc.) allows many techniques to be used and many topics to be included. Include the accessibility features for those who are unable or uninterested in accessing traditional modalities and techniques, and DPT becomes a very well-rounded, accessible way to enter a client's world; respect their culture; and facilitate understanding, acceptance, and change.

Under the DPT Umbrella

It might be confusing for some play therapists, particularly those for whom the use of therapeutic digital tools is new, to understand how storytelling, sand play, guided imagery play, music play, drawings, board game play, and movement play can be considered under the DPT umbrella. The programs available now can provide numerous experiences that activate therapeutic powers of play and incorporate the fundamental tenets of play therapy. It is not unreasonable to believe that even more modalities will be applicable under DPT in the future. Mobile apps alone have been reported to have an average of 1,434 AppStore new releases *per day* (Clement, 2019). Some of these programs will be quite suitable for other play therapy modality application. Play therapists can, and should, be part of the development of programs to come.

Modalities

Digital Play/Electronic Play

Video games have been incorporated into mental health therapies since the late 1980's (Farrell, 1989; Gardner, 1991; Resnick & Sherer, 1995; Clarke & Schoech, 1994). Farrel provides a glimpse of the history prior to his 1989 article stating that APA had released a list of 150 software programs for use in psychology, amongst other listings, indicating the blossoming interest in incorporating such tools. The uses for technology spanned from assessment to rural access to participation in research from afar. Farrell set out to discover information about the impact of technology on psychology. Much of the work was focused on clerical and practice management–type software and use; however, he also queried psychologists regarding their clinical use. Clinical use categories included: test administration assistance, assigning diagnoses, gathering client data, biofeedback, and cognitive retraining. He stated that the top three reasons psychologists (more than 30% of participants) did not use technology were: lack of time, lack of training or experience, and having a small practice which did not justify the expense of the integration of a computer (Farrell, 1989). These findings were corroborated by Altvater et al. (2017). It is amazing to realize that the attitudes of mental health professionals regarding the use of technology in mental health practices have not really changed tremendously in over 30 years.

Different types of digital or electronic play have been categorized by complexity in the software chapter within this book to attempt to ease any anxiety for new users, however, there are other ways to categorize them as well. One could categorize them by hardware categories, modality focus, type of play, or more. Snow, et al., determined that apps used in play therapy could be organized into five categories, as defined initially by Terry Kottman: nurturing, fantasy, expressive, aggressive, and scary (p. 90–91) (Kottman, 2011; Snow et al., 2012). The categorization can help the play therapist tailor the use of the program to the needs and interests of the client.

The use of video games in psychotherapy was explored by Ceranoglu in 2010. His experiences and research have shown the following: 1) "the therapeutic relationship emerged more quickly when video games were used, in contrast with traditional therapy with children" (p. 143); 2) can be used in the evaluation of visuospatial skills and executive functions; 3) evaluation of frustration tolerance; and 4) the evaluation of affective regulation. He continued: "Observing a child's play style and content choice may offer significant clues to intrapsychic conflicts and may provide material needed to elaborate on those conflicts" (p. 143). Video games are powerful tools to assist with building a relationship, evaluating the client's cognitive processing style, and elaborating upon and clarification of internal conflicts (Ceranoglu, 2010). Hull also spoke of the benefits of using technology in the playroom: 1) the playroom is more inviting, 2) initial bonding between the therapist and client, and 3) "imagination and creativity" (p. 616) offered by digital tools (Hull, 2016; Snow et al., 2012). The use of digital play as a modality is very powerful and useful in clinical settings.

There are many articles available regarding the positive impacts of using video games and other digital tools in therapy. For ease of access and reference, I will provide a list of titles here and you may find the additional information in the reference section of this chapter. The word count of this edition will not allow for the review of each article, but I highly recommend you look into each one and all the articles to which these lead you.

Table 5.1 Positive Articles Regarding the Use of Digital Tools in Therapy

Article Title	Author(s)
Screens, teens, and psychological well-being: Evidence from three time-use diary studies	Amy Orben & Andrew K. Przybylski
The ideal self at play: The appeal of video games that let you be all you can be	Andrew K. Przybylski, et al.
What kids learn that's POSITIVE from playing video games	Mark Prensky
Role-playing games used as educational and therapeutic tools for youth and adults	William Hawkes Robinson
Video games as a complementary therapy tool in mental health disorders: PlayMancer, a European multicenter study	Fernando Fernández-Aranda, et al.
Using popular commercial video games in therapy with children and adolescents	Jason Steadman
Online video game therapy for mental health concerns: A review	Nathan Wilkinson, et al.
Video games in therapy: A therapist's perspective	Jan-Henk Annema, et al.
Technologies of inclusive well-being: Serious games, alternative realities, and play therapy	Anthony Lewis Brooks, et al. (Eds.)
Game-based digital interventions for depression therapy: A systematic review and meta-analysis	Jinhul Li, et al.
Two innovative healthcare technologies at the intersection of serious games, alternative realities, and play therapy	Sheryl Brahnam & Anthony Lewis Brooks
Enhancing the therapy experience using principles of video game design	John W. Folkins, et al.
Clinical psychologists see positive potential in video games as therapy	Alex Barasch
The use of electronic games in therapy: A review with clinical implications	Horne-Meyer, et al.
Video games in psychotherapy	T. Atilla Ceranoglu

Virtual Reality Play

Virtual reality has been experiencing an explosion of growth, research, and multidisciplinary uses. From use with general populations (Stone, in press) to people with motor difficulties (Ortíz-Catalan et al., 2014) to people with autism (Strickland, 1998; Musser, 2018) to those with anxiety disorders (Maples-Keller et al., 2017) and so much more. The immersive, creative, sensory experience of virtual reality (VR) affords a unique and powerful therapeutic experience (Lamb & Etopio, in press).

Historically, psychological treatments such as exposure therapies required in-vivo treatments. A person with a fear of heights would be brought to a building to ride in the elevator, peer down from the top of a building, and so on. With VR, the person can remain in the therapist's office physically but can be transformed to another environment through the VR head-mounted display unit. The possibilities are only limited by the software available at any given time. Worlds can be created artistically and interacted with, as "the world of three-dimensional graphics has neither borders nor constraints and can be created and manipulated by ourselves as we wish – we can enhance it by a fourth dimension: the dimension of our imagination" (Mazuryk & Gervautz, n.d., p. 1). As stated in the hardware chapter, virtual reality has the potential to completely revolutionize the experiences our clients have within mental health treatment. These technologies do not replace the therapist, rather, they expand the abilities of the therapist to deepen, expand, and customize the experience for the client within the therapist–client experience. It is the DPT centaur.

In play therapy specifically, VR really shines in its ability to allow tremendous creativity. With numerous art programs available, the client can create what they imagine and then interact with the world, the characters, the items, and more. Whether it is a Virtual Sandtray–VR creation or a Tilt Brush artist's paradise, the client experiences inclusion and interaction as desired within the world in a way no other medium can provide. The five categories of play identified by Kottman and Snow, et al. – nurturing, fantasy, expressive, aggressive, and scary – can all be realized within VR, either by creating them, finding programs that meet the needs, or both. I simply cannot wait to discover what the future of mental health virtual reality, or tVR (therapeutic vr) (Lamb & Etopio, in press) holds for people of all ages.

Storytelling Play

Storytelling has a rich and vast history. The concept of humans telling stories to one another and over time is intrinsic (Mendoza, 2015). Storytelling has evolved over time with an original focus on visual stories (cave drawings), to oral traditions (word of mouth), then on to narratives (written, printed, etc.). The recent technological trends have allowed us to incorporate all of these storytelling techniques through social media, video, photographs, blogs, articles, and more. (Mendoza, 2015).

In play therapy, clients tell their stories in numerous verbal and non-verbal ways and frequently employ the use of metaphors (Pernicano, 2016). A client can come in with an agenda to tell a story of an experience, a dream, a concern, or many other possibilities. These can be actual occurrences, wishful thinking, or metaphorical. Stories can be spoken, acted out, played out, danced, drawn, created, or avoided. It is important for clients to have the opportunity, safety, and tools with which to tell their story. Regarding the interplay between play and storytelling, British play therapist Sonia Murray (in press) states: "The play facilitates the story, the story facilitates the play" (para. 2).

In DPT we have multiple layers of storytelling available. A person can be drawn to a game narrative, characters, game play, music, lyrics, movement, art medium, and/or any theme that speaks to them regarding the story they need to share. It is important that the therapist understands the digital medium of choice to fully allow the therapist to receive this intention, understand it within the context of the client, and integrate it into the play therapy work.

A variety of apps allow for these types of expressions. Basic word processing can be used to type out a story, incorporate pictures and other graphics, and more. For a more robust experience, the *Storytelling* app, and others like it, allow for the literal creating of a story. Various art programs allow the user to create many different types of art which can depict one's story literally or metaphorically. Sharing posts, updates, memes, *YouTube* videos, *TikTok* posts, and more from social media can also allow a therapist to stitch together the story being presented. There are so many ways to tell stories with digital tools.

Virtual reality brings storytelling to yet another level. Most programs require movement along with the game play or creation. This allows for whole body engagement. Art programs such as *Tilt Brush* and *SculptVR* allow the user to create intricate, detailed, three-dimensional works of art for literal or abstract storytelling. Music and dance programs on a variety of platforms allow for movement and music and lyric storytelling.

Sand Play

Sand play (any type of play in sand for therapeutic purposes) encompasses a number of play therapy modalities. Sandtray, sandplay, and sand play all have therapeutic value with their own set of tenets and principles. Within the traditional modes of all types, sand play can be the tactile experience of touching the sand, running one's fingers through it, pouring it, moving it, and so on. For many, this sensory experience is creative and healing; it is a significant part of the therapeutic experience. However, for others, the experience of touching the sand is disruptive and even traumatizing. The sensory experience of touching the sand can be overwhelming and can create an overload and dysregulation. For some others, accessing the sand is difficult or impossible due to physical limitations, location difficulties, contact allergies, or immunocompromised systems. Sweeney stated that although many reap amazing benefits from the traditional sandtray experience, some "find the sensory experience of sand and related materials to be overwhelming", they "may love sandtray or be repulsed by it", "can also be overwhelmed", and/or can "be devastated by the very tactile quality that makes sandtray so beneficial for others" (in press, clinical applications section). For people with sensory, accessibility, or other concerns, finding different avenues for experiencing sand play is necessary. DPT can provide these other avenues.

This author is not specifically trained in sandplay therapy. Therefore, the focus of this chapter will be on sandtray therapy. Sweeney offers the following regarding sandtray therapy: it is an "expressive and projective therapy that has remarkable and adaptable qualities as a therapeutic intervention" (in press, introduction section). A cross-theoretical intervention, sandtray techniques have the flexibility to be highly verbal or non-verbal, or anywhere in between, directive or non-directive, or anywhere in between, and it can incorporate fundamentals from a variety of theoretical foundations (Sweeney, in press; Homeyer & Sweeney, 2017).

The creation of the "World" is a primary aspect of the sandtray experience, whereby the client is "invited to make 'whatever comes into his head'" (Lowenfeld, 1997, p. 5) For those who would benefit from creating their "World", but are unable for any of a number of reasons, alternate ways to create the worlds should be sought. This powerful creative and projective tool should be available to all who would benefit, regardless of their ability to access the traditional materials. Lowenfeld wrote of her World technique: "An apparatus, therefore, which will give a child power to express his ideas and feelings, must be independent of knowledge or skill, must be capable of the representation of thought simultaneously in several planes at once, must allow of representation of movement and yet be sufficiently circumscribed to make a complete whole, must combine elements of touch and sensation, as well as of sight, and be entirely free from a necessary relation to reality" (p. 4).

Many apps and programs are available which can provide the user with different experiences. The play therapist might refer to the previous paragraph regarding the elements of touch and sensation and question the ability to use alternative methods of sandtray, such as digital. However, it is important to remember that there is an element of touch, albeit different, with a touch screen tablet, phone, or computer. There is also an element of touch with the haptic responses (vibration response felt by the user which is received as touch/ pressure/motion by the brain) of the VR controllers, and even more so with haptic gloves and bodysuits. Some programs allow the user to draw in the sand as one would on the beach, others allow for the creation of sandtrays with items, such as fire, volcanoes, floating planets, and other light effects and more, that would not be possible in the traditional technique, along with the ability to save and revisit previously created trays. Please refer to the software chapter for more information about some of the available apps and programs.

Guided Imagery Play

The mind–body connection of guided imagery has been acknowledged and used for centuries, possibly even as far back as Tibetan monks in the 13th century (Guided imagery, 2013). "Guided imagery is a gentle but powerful technique that focuses the imagination in proactive, positive ways. It has the built-in capacity to deliver multiple layers of complex, encoded messages deep inside – positive, healing, motivating messages – through simple images, sensations, symbols and metaphors, received in an altered or trance-like state" (Health Journeys, n.d., para. 8). "Guided imagery is a mind–body practice that uses the imagination and sensory memory to induce a state of relaxation and physiological, emotional and attitudinal responses" (Jonas, n.d., para. 2). Used in mental health, medical, personal, and many other settings, guided imagery aims to regulate and center a person.

Considered to be housed under the meditation umbrella, guided imagery (also called guided meditation) can help a person achieve a state of relaxation and tranquility (Mayo, 2020). The Mayo Clinic reports that meditation can assist with emotional needs in the following ways: 1) new perspectives, 2) stress management skills, 3) self-awareness, 4) present focus, 5) a reduction in negative emotions, 6) an increase in creativity and imagination, and 7) an increase in tolerance and patience (2020) along with a number of medical difficulties. These techniques are traditionally utilized with another person present to guide the imagery, however, technology has broadened the possibilities and allowed an increase in who will use the techniques and where they are able to use them.

Carris (2019), states that mindfulness can be formally or informally performed, with a focus on breathing, body sensations, walking, sitting, and so on. Being mindful can assist people in dealing with day-to-day stressors and improve our well-being. "When we are mindful, we tune attention to our thoughts, emotions, bodily sensations, and behaviors in a dispassionate way, like a scientist observing them. This process provides us a healthy distance from an overwhelming immersion in our experience; improved awareness highlights how habitual ways of functioning can lead to struggles and creates the conditions for healing" (Carris, 2019, p. 167). Guided imagery is one way to achieve this.

In therapeutic settings, guided imagery is used alone or with other techniques to bring the unconscious into a conscious realm (Mellenthin, in press). Many play therapists incorporate guided imagery into their work including Violet Oaklander, who often incorporated art, storytelling, problem solving, and creativity to assist the client with their connection to self (Oaklander, 1978; Mellenthin, in press). In psychotherapy, guided imagery has been suggested to be taught to and used with children and adolescents so they may reap the benefits which have been shown to help adults. These benefits include relief from physical and emotional difficulties (Hanish, 2013).

Phone and tablet apps, wearables (fitness trackers, smart watches, etc.), and virtual reality systems have led the way in technology's contribution to current mindfulness and guided imagery trends. The top five apps for portable devices in 2018 included:

1)   End Your Day Perfectly
2)   Guided Imagery
3)   Creative Space
4)   Relax with Andrew Johnson
5)   Simply Being

(Bailey, 2018)

There are a number of programs geared toward relaxation in virtual reality. These include programs with visually and auditorily pleasing experiences. Some provide guided pre-set experiences and others allow for customization.

Some are completely passive where the user can simply sit or lie down and experience the program while focusing on being mindful, and others are more active with the creation of a custom world and a more self-guided experience. It is fantastic to have so many options for people to get their needs met in session, at home, at work, and "on the go".

Music and Movement play

Music and movement are integral portions of a human's existence. Throughout time people have created, listened to, enjoyed, and moved to music. "If it is a language, music is a language of feeling. Musical rhythms are life rhythms, and music with tensions, resolutions, crescendos and diminuendos, major and minor keys, delays and silent interludes, with a temporal unfolding of events" (Trimble & Hesdorffer, 2017, p. 30). "When listening to our favorite songs, our body betrays all the symptoms of emotional arousal. The pupils in our eyes dilate, our pulse and blood pressure rise, the electrical conductance of our skin is lowered, and the cerebellum, a brain region associated with bodily movement, becomes strangely active. Blood is even re-directed to the muscles in our legs. (Some speculate that this is why we begin tapping our feet.) In other words, sound stirs us at our biological roots" (Lehrer, 2011, para. 1). Music affects our beings profoundly.

Taylor (in press), also includes movement and dance, along with awareness of breathing, rhythm, and singing along with music play, which culminates into an importance of attunement, safety, and attachment. The therapist is to be aware of overt and subtle communications of one's own rhythm and movement as a communication to and with the client. "Our embodied selves enter the playroom, bringing the tones and rhythm of our sounds and the postures, gestures, and inner sensations of our bodies. Intentional use of music and movement allows clients to access body-based self-discovery and self-regulation through sensation, imagery, and symbolic play" (Taylor, in press, core techniques section).

The modality of music and movement play can be realized through digital tool means. Numerous apps and programs are available for all hardware platforms and allow for the creation and enjoyment of music. The play can be game-based with notes for the user to match as the speed gets progressively faster, or cubes to slash as the music plays on, both of which require body movement as well as active listening. Meditative or creation-based programs allow the user to concentrate on being mindful of their breathing, body, emotions, thoughts, and the like while the music sets the rhythm of their being. Most relaxation apps and programs incorporate music as a key portion of the experience.

The music in video games contribute to the gameplay experience. Margounakas and Lappa (2016), described three types of sounds in video games: interactive, adaptive, and dynamic. The sounds that one hears when the player takes some type of action in the game. It is a resulting sound of the player pressing a key or button to have an action take place in the gameplay and the sound illustrates and confirms the action. Adaptive sounds change depending on the gameplay. An example would be some type of timed mini-game which is accompanied by music. When the end of the mini-game is near, the music's rhythm or speed would change to indicate a change happening. Dynamic sounds in gameplay would include both the interactive and dynamic sounds, those which are in response to the player's actions and the flow of the game itself. Players often attend to the effects and music sounds apart from the image and process their meaning(s) (Margounakas & Lappa, 2016).

Whether a key aspect of the experience or a peripheral inclusion, the vast majority of apps and programs include some form of music. The brain-body experience of the music, and the task (or lack of active task, i.e., meditation, etc.) involved culminates into a powerful experience for the client and therapist. The client can be involved in gameplay, dancing and movement, or creating, and simultaneously be experiencing the body's neurological responses to the stimuli, as they can and do with more traditional forms of play. In virtual reality, an additional sense of freedom is felt by some as the headset can give one the sense that they can "dance like nobody is watching" or they may feel they are already moving about to interact with the program; why not move one's body to the music?

Drawings

Whether led by a clinician in a therapeutic setting or self-motivated, drawing has been part of our history, expression, and storytelling for all time. Cave drawings depict experiences and stories which were probably recorded to be shared for a number of purposes. Drawing can be a complex or simple endeavor and does not require any special talent or age limitations. Anne Quito explains that drawing and art have been intertwined and confused; that drawing is about the process and not the performance (2018). Quito refers to drawing as a problem solving and learning tool which "fosters close observation, analytical thinking, patience, even humility" (para. 8).

Art therapy has a long and important history in the mental health world. In art therapy, "drawings become helpful in communicating what the unconscious is trying to bring into consciousness and gain insight into the underlying issues" (Jiggetts, in press, Therapeutic Benefits section). Quite often children particularly love to draw and explore and depict their process, experiences, and stories. Some stories are left with aspects missing when told purely in a verbal way. Utilizing art allows for different mediums, omissions, additions, colors, and more to illustrate the story more completely.

As discussed in the Hardware chapter, Malchiodi discussed the interplay between the art creation and the digital medium in a powerful way in her book *Art Therapy & Computer Technology: A Virtual Studio of Possibilities* (2000). The process is different than the traditional creation of drawings and artwork, but it is not less than. The ability to manipulate the art to change, expand upon, or manipulate the expression can be very powerful.

In addition to the wide variety of options available in the apps and programs, the benefit of being able to save, print, and share the artwork further expands the experience. Clients can return to previous work to revisit, revise, or complete what they worked on during a different time. Keeping this work safe and holding it until another time is a wonderful metaphor for the work. Literally being able to keep it allows the therapist the ability to witness and monitor any growth, new understandings, and/or backsliding of the treatment process.

There are hundreds of different apps and programs to use to create drawings and artwork. It is certainly best to explore each and determine which will meet your client's needs. The following table (5.2) shows a few to start your therapeutic digital art creation journey.

Table 5.2 2018/2019 Drawing and Art Apps and Programs

Free Drawing	*iPad Sketch*	*Android Drawing*	*Sketch*	*3D*
Adobe Illustrator Draw	Procreate	Infinite Painter	ArtRage	ZBrush
MediBang Paint	iPastels		Autodesk SketchBook	Blender
GIMP	Zen Brush 2		Marmoset Hexels 3	Sculptris
	Pixelmator Pro		Adobe Photoshop	Hexagon
	Assembly		Concepts	
	Graphic		Comic Draw	
	Art Set		Photoshop Sketch	
	Inkist		Clip Studio Paint EX	
	ArtStudio		Tayasui Sketches	
	Brushes Redux		Paper by Fiftythree	
	Pixaki		Sketch Club	
			Ibis Paint X	
			Adobe Illustrator	
			Aseprite	
			Krita	

Adapted from Format Team (2018)

Virtual reality has some amazing drawing and art programs. With VR the user can create work, move it around, become immersed in it, and interact with it. The process and results are enough to give one goosebumps. Google Tilt Brush, Gravity Sketch, Substance Painter, Unbound Alpha, Facebook's Quill, Oculus Medium, and Mozilla A-Painter are all excellent programs to explore (Harris, 2018).

Board Game Play

Board game play is amazingly rich with ample opportunities to engage with the client, learn about a number of patterns and tendencies, and intervene where appropriate (Stone, 2016; Stone & Schaefer, 2019). A rich 5,000-plus-year history of board game play indicates the fundamental and innate level of interest of human beings in engaging in these activities. Often latency-aged children have an increased interest in board games because of their developmental phase; however, people of all ages can and do enjoy this type of play.

Typically, board games have six fundamental characteristics: 1) they are fun; 2) they provide a separation from real life to allow for fantasy experiences; 3) organization and structure for the game is provided through rules; 4) competition occurs within a player or among players; 5) complex games require more intellect, emotional control, and social interaction skills; and 6) two or more players typically are involved in the game play (Schaefer & Reid, 1986). Additionally, games are frequently separated into three major categories – cooperative, strategy, and chance – and offer the following therapeutic benefits: therapeutic alliance, self-control, moral development, self-expression, executive functioning skills, mood elevation, self-esteem, stress release, attachment formation, and social skills (Stone & Schaefer, 2019). Board games are full of therapeutic uses and benefits.

Many different board games are available in electronic board game form. A company called Tabletopia (https://tabletopia.com/) offers more than 700 board games in digital form. These games include classics like Parcheesi, chess, and backgammon and also venture above and beyond into games like Terra Mystica, Tuscony, Noir, and Eight Minute Empire: Legends (Tabletopia, 2020). Ticket to Ride is digital version of a board game that appears on two separate top-ten lists, so I will certainly be checking it out as soon as possible. Other games on the two top-ten lists include: Splendor, Carcassone, Forbidden Island, Lords of Waterdeep, Galaxy Trucker, Neuroshima Hex, Onirim, Colt Express, Exploding Kittens, Pandemic, Scythe, Risk Factions, Game of Life, Twilight Struggle, and Tabletop Simulator (Oliveri, 2019; Sonechkina, 2020). Some of these games are described as better than the traditional versions because of certain features.

Virtual reality has many offerings in the board game arena as well. Multiple people in the same room can interact in the game or people can join remotely. As play therapists we often think of the room as the container, but it is also important to expand that where it is clinically appropriate. For example, if I have a client whose father is stationed in another country and he has a virtual reality head-mounted display (HMD), we can pre-arrange a time to "meet" and the father and daughter can play a game together. If I have two headsets in my office, one for the client and one for me, and we join him from afar, we are all experiencing the game play together. This can also be accomplished with some tablet games. These are pretty exciting developments with far-reaching effects.

Oculus has teamed up with Hasbro to offer classic games such as Monopoly, Boggle, and Trivial Pursuit to VR (ovr news, 2018). Oculus Rooms serves as a space where people can meet privately with others via an invitation, with the caveat that confidentiality cannot be assured. The room will not be invaded by other players, but that does not mean it is HIPAA-compliant. Other games are also available, such as: Tabletop Simulator, Quiz Night Tonight!, Masters of

Chess, Chess Ultra, Ascension VR, Lost Cities, Hack the Gibson, Majong VR, Dungeon Chess, and Kismet (Wear VR, n.d.).

Conclusion

Kaduson and Schaefer (in press) identified 15 play therapy modalities. With the addition of the DPT modality, ten play therapy modalities can be translated into digital techniques quite easily. With an emphasis on the inclusion of the client's culture, it is logical to incorporate such options within play therapy. Accessibility also plays a factor, as inclusion of digital tools in these play therapy modalities increases the accessibility both in ability and distance.

References

Altvater, R. A., Singer, R. R., & Gil, E. (2017). Part 1: Modern trends in the playroom-preferences and interactions with tradition and innovation. *International Journal of Play Therapy*, *26*(4), 239–249.

Annema, J. H., Verstraete, M., Abeele, V. V., Desmet, S., & Geerts, D. (2010). *Video games in therapy: A therapist's perspective*. Academia. www.academia.edu/510695/Videogames_in_therapy_a_therapists_perspective

Bailey, E. (2018, September 10). 5 guided imagery apps. *Health Central*. www.health-central.com/article/8-guided-imagery-apps

Barasch, A. (2019). Clinical psychologists see positive potential in video games as therapy. *Variety*. https://variety.com/2019/gaming/features/clinical-psychologists-see-positive-potential-in-video-games-as-therapy-1203175911/?fbclid=IwAR1__6N cybvkoMPGxE4G6IlqB7LOou94tyDaDu4tuJY96bvimK8XnZT8W5A

Brahnam, S., & Brooks, A. L. (2014). Two innovative healthcare technologies at the intersection of serious games, alternative realities, and play therapy. *Innovation in Medicine and Healthcare*. https://pdfs.semanticscholar.org/1ccc/0ad228fbb5e2eee20 1611c2d213577853f03.pdf

Brooks, A. L., Brahnam, S., & Jain, L. C. (Eds.) (2014). *Technologies of inclusive well-being: Serious games, alternative realities, and play therapy*. Springer.

Carris, M. (2019). Introducing technology-delivered mindfulness interventions into the therapeutic process. In J. Stone (Ed.), *Integrating technology into modern therapies*. Abingdon, UK: Routledge.

Ceranoglu, T. A. (2010). Video games in psychotherapy. *American Psychological Association*, *14*(2), 141–146.

Clarke, B., & Schoech, D. (1994). A computer-assisted game for adolescents: Initial development and comments. *Computers in Human Services*, *11*(1–2), 121–140.

Clement, J. (2019, June 26). *Number of daily Apple App Store app releases worldwide 2016–2018*. www.statista.com/statistics/276705/ios-app-releases-worldwide/

Farrell, A. D. (1989). Impact of computers on professional practice: A survey of current practices and attitudes. *Professional Psychology: Research and Practices*, *20*(3), 172–178.

Fernández-Aranda, F., Jiménez-Murcia, S., Santamaría, J. J., Gunnard, K., Soto, A., Kalapanidas, E., . . . Penels, E. (2012). Video games as a complementary therapy tool in mental disorders: PlayMancer, a European multicenter study. *Journal of Mental Health*, *21*(4), 364–374.

Folkins, J. W., Brackenbury, T., Krause, M., & Hailand, A. (2014). *Enhancing the therapy experience using principles of video game design.* Bowling Green State University. www.bgsu.edu/content/dam/BGSU/health-and-human-services/document/cdis/Folkins-Brackenbury-Krause-Haviland-2016.pdf

Format Team (2018, December 14). *The 34 best drawing apps and art apps for 2018/2019.* www.format.com/magazine/resources/illustration/drawing-apps

Gardner, J. E. (1991). Can the Mario Bros. help? Nintendo games as an adjunct in psychotherapy with children. *Psychotherapy: Theory, Research, Practice, and Training, 28*(4), 667–670.

Guided Imagery (2013, June 16). *History of guided imagery.* www.guidedimagery-downloads.com/history-of-guided-imagery/

Hanish, J. B. (2013). *Guided imagery as treatment and prevention for anxiety, chronic stress, and illness.* https://alfredadler.edu/sites/default/files/Hanish%20MP%202012.pdf

Harris, M. (2018, September 7). 7 best tools for painting, 3D modeling and sculpting in VR. *Digital Arts Online.* www.digitalartsonline.co.uk/features/hacking-maker/7-best-tools-for-painting-3d-modelling-sculpting-in-vr/

Hawkes-Robinson, W. (2008). Role-playing games used as educational and therapeutic tools for youth and adults. *Academia.* www.academia.edu/3668971/Role-playing_Games_Used_as_Educational_and_Therapeutic_Tool_for_Youth_and_Adults

Health Journeys (n.d.). Health journeys guided imagery and mediation. *Google Play.* https://play.google.com/store/apps/details?id=com.release.healthjourneyaudio&hl=en_US

Homeyer, L., & Sweeney, D. (2017). *Sandtray therapy: A practical manual* (3rd ed.). New York: Routledge.

Hull, K. (2016). Technology in the playroom. In K. J. O'Connor, C. E. Schaefer, & L. D. Braverman (Eds.), *Handbook of play therapy* (2nd ed., pp. 613–627). Wiley.

Jiggetts, N. (in press). The use of children's drawing in play therapy. In H. G. Kaduson & C. E. Schaefer (Eds.), *Nuts and bolts of play therapy with children.* American Psychological Association.

Jonas, W. (n.d.). *Guided imagery pocket guide.* https://drwaynejonas.com/wp-content/uploads/2018/05/Guided-Imagery-Pocket-Guide.pdf

Kaduson, H., & Schaefer, C. (in press). Introduction. In H. G. Kaduson & C. E. Schaefer (Eds.), *Nuts and bolts of play therapy with children.* American Psychological Association.

Kottman, T. (2011). *Play therapy basics and beyond* (2nd ed.). American Counseling Association.

Lamb, R., & Etopio, E. (in press). Therapeutic extended reality. In H. G. Kaduson & C. E. Schaefer (Eds.), *Nuts and bolts of play therapy with children.* American Psychological Association.

Lehrer, J. (2011, January 19). The neuroscience of music. *Wired.* www.wired.com/2011/01/the-neuroscience-of-music/

Lexico (2019a). *Modality.* www.lexico.com/en/definition/modality

Lexico (2019b). *Mode.* www.lexico.com/en/definition/mode

Li, J., Theng, Y. L., & Foo, S. (2014). Game-based digital interventions for depression therapy: A systematic review and meta-analysis. *Cyberpsychology, Behavior, and Social Networking, 17*(8), 519–527.

Lowenfeld, M. (1997). *Understanding children's sandplay: Lowenfeld's world technique.* Sussex Academic Press.

Malchiodi, C. A. (2000). *Art therapy & computer technology: A virtual studio of possibilities*. Jessica Kingsley.

Maples-Keller, J. L., Bunnell, B. E., Kim, S.-J., & Rothbaum, B. O. (2017). The use of virtual reality technology in the treatment of anxiety and other psychiatric disorders. *Harvard Review of Psychiatry*, 103–113. www.e-mence.org/sites/default/files/domain-39/Maples-Keller%20Use%20VR%20in%20disorders%202017.pdf

Margounakas, D., & Lappa, I. (2016). Music in video games. *Researchgate*. www.researchgate.net/publication/315959927_Music_in_Video_Games

Mayo Clinic (2020). *Meditation: A simple, fast way to reduce stress*. www.mayoclinic.org/tests-procedures/meditation/in-depth/meditation/art-20045858

Mazuryk, T., & Gervautz, M. (n.d.). Virtual reality history, applications, technology and future. *Institute of Computer Graphics*. www.cg.tuwien.ac.at/research/publications/1996/mazuryk-1996-VRH/TR-186-2-96-06Paper.pdf

Mellenthin, C. (in press). Guided imagery. In H. G. Kaduson & C. E. Schaefer (Eds.), *Nuts and bolts of play therapy with children*. American Psychological Association.

Mendoza, M. (2015, May 1). *The evolution of storytelling*. https://reporter.rit.edu/tech/evolution-storytelling

Merriam Webster (2019). *Technique*. www.merriam-webster.com/dictionary/technique

Murray, S. (in press). Use of stories in play therapy. In H. G. Kaduson & C. E. Schaefer (Eds.), *Nuts and bolts of play therapy with children*. American Psychological Association.

Musser, G. (2018, October 24). How virtual reality is transforming autism studies. *Spectrum News*. www.spectrumnews.org/.../virtual-reality-transforming-autism-studies/?format=pdf

Oaklander, V. (1978). *Windows to our children*. Gestalt Journal Press.

Oliveri, J. (2019, May 20). 10 best digital adaptations of board games. *The Gamer*. www.thegamer.com/best-digital-adaptations-of-board-games/

Orben, A., & Przybylski, A. K. (2019). Screens, teens, and psychological well-being: Evidence from three time-use-diary studies. *Association for Psychological Science*, *30*, 682–696.

Ortíz-Catalan, M., Nijenhuis, S., Ambrosch, K., Bovend'Eerdt, T., Koenig, S., & Lange, B. (2014). Virtual reality. In J. L. Pons & D. Torricelli (Eds.), *Emerging therapies in neurorehabilitation, biosystems, & biorobotics* (pp. 249–265). Springer.

ovr news (2018, May 22). *Oculus rooms gets Boggle, more Hasbro classic games coming soon*. www.ovrnews.com/oculus-rooms-gets-boggle-more-hasbro-games-coming-soon/

Pernicano, P. (2016). Metaphors and stories in play therapy. In K. J. O'Connor, C. E. Schaefer, & L. D. Braverman (Eds.), *Handbook of play therapy* (2nd ed., pp. 259–275). Wiley.

Prensky, M. (2002). *What kids learn that's positive from playing video games*. www.marcprensky.com/writing/Prensky%20-%20What%20Kids%20Learn%20Thats%20POSITIVE%20From%20Playing%20Video%20Games.pdf

Przybylski, A. K., Weinstein, N., Murayama, K., Kynch, M. F., & Ryan, R. M. (2012). The ideal self at play: The appeal of video games that let you be all you can be. *Association for Psychological Science*, *23*(1), 69–76.

Quito, A. (2018, September 18). Drawing is the best way to learn, even if you are no Leonardo di Vinci. *Quartz*. https://qz.com/quartzy/1381916/drawing-is-the-best-way-to-learn-even-if-youre-no-leonardo-da-vinci/?fbclid=IwAR1XZuTLNhxThXeEB_sH2BEEEmSYOaN_Ukvfi7teQaDK3VGnoG7FeP3EMgk

Resnick, H., & Sherer, M. (1995). Computer games in the human services: A review. *Computers in Human Services*, *11*(1–2), 17–29.

Schaefer, C. E., & Reid, S. E. (1986). *Game play: Therapeutic use of childhood games*. Wiley.

Snow, M. S., Winburn, A., Crumrine, L., & Jackson, E. (2012). *The iPad playroom a therapeutic technique*. www.mlppubsonline.com/display_article.php?id=1141251

Sonechkina, A. (2020). The 10 best digital board games for your mobile. *Game Analytics*. https://gameanalytics.com/blog/10-best-digital-board-games.html

Steadman, J. (2014). Using popular commercial video games in therapy with children and adolescents. *Journal of Technology in Human Sciences*, *32*, 201–219.

Stone, J. (2016). Board games in play therapy. In K. J. O'Connor, C. E. Schaefer, & L. D. Braverman (Eds.), *Handbook of play therapy* (2nd ed., pp. 309–323). Hoboken, NJ: John Wiley & Sons.

Stone, J. (in press). Extended reality therapy: The use of virtual, augmented, and mixed reality in mental health treatment. In R. Kowert & T. Quandt (Eds.), *Video game debate* (2nd ed.). Abingdon, UK: Routledge.

Stone, J., & Schaefer, C. E. (2019). Game play therapy: Theory and practice. In J. Stone & C. E. Schaefer (Eds.), *Game play* (3rd ed., pp. 3–8). Wiley.

Strickland, D. (1998). Virtual reality for the treatment of autism. In *Virtual reality in neuro-psycho-physiology*. Ios Press. https://pdfs.semanticscholar.org/358e/28df2cb7 720b7100811f4aee7af731164b08.pdf

Sweeney, D. (in press). Sandtray therapy. In H. G. Kaduson & C. E. Schaefer (Eds.), *Nuts and bolts of play therapy with children*. American Psychological Association.

Tabletopia (2020). *Online sandbox arena for playing board games just like in real life*. https://tabletopia.com/

Taylor, S. A. (in press). The use of music and movement in therapy. In H. G. Kaduson & C. E. Schaefer (Eds.), *Nuts and bolts of play therapy with children*. American Psychological Association.

Trimble, M., & Hesdorffer, D. (2017). Music and the brain: The neuroscience of music and musical appreciation. *BJPsych International*, *14*(2), 28–30.

Wear VR (n.d.). *VR board games and tabletop*. www.wearvr.com/collections/vr-boardgames

Wilkinson, N., Ang, R. P., & Goh, D. H. (2008). Online video game therapy for mental health concerns: A review. *International Journal of Social Psychiatry*, *54*(4), 370–382.

6   Understanding Research

I chatted with one of our esteemed play therapy colleagues about this chapter. As I shared my nervousness about writing it in a way that would entice people to read it, she said, "don't worry, no one will read it". The thing is, *I really, really want you to read it*. I think this type of information and knowledge makes us better clinicians, professionals, and colleagues. Understanding the importance of critically reviewing research articles elevates each of us and our play therapy profession. So, please, let us prove her wrong. Read this chapter and tell others what you now know, post about it, pursue even more knowledge. Let everyone know you will no longer be spoon-fed information. You are an educated, professional consumer!

Why Is This Chapter Important?

As play therapists we want to know that what we are doing with our clients in session is appropriate. We want information from a collection of sources (trusted mentors, supervisors, theorists, experience, and experimental research) that will help to ensure the quality of services we provide. We are quite adept at seeking out mentors, supervision, academic learning, and gaining experience, however, many play therapists do not have formal training in the evaluation of research methodologies or statistics. Most people do not want to learn about experimental research, which can be dry and complicated. There are certainly things we can learn that are more fun and applicable for in-session use, such as techniques. It is completely understandable.

The good news is that you do not have to understand the full scope of statistics and experimental research methodology to begin to read research critically. It is better to understand some basics so you can read additional portions of research articles rather than just the abstract and the discussion. Reading and comprehending research will be very different for the consumer who is armed with skills to analyze these important components.

Research Articles

Research articles typically include the following components (Hall, 2017):

- Abstract
- Introduction

- Methodology
- Results
- Discussion

A key portion of research is the methodology: the setup/structure of the research, the variable identification, and variable definitions, statistics to be used, and so on. If the methodology is poor, the whole study will be poor. Think of it this way: imagine you are building a castle out of wooden blocks with a client. If the floor or is unstable or uneven, it does not matter how wonderful your walls are. They will most likely fall or have other structural issues. A solid foundation is the best way to have your castle solidly stand and it is the best start for research that will yield solid, applicable results.

The methodology is likened to a recipe, which is outlined and described in a way that allows another person to come and replicate the study. The statistical analysis method should be identified within the article; however, evaluating this choice can be difficult. For our purposes, understanding the method of analysis is *less* critical. It is important information; however, most clinicians are not going to attend to that level of research study analysis. The results section includes the results of the statistical analysis; it is the presentation of the data. The discussion section serves to bring together concepts introduced within the article. This is where the author extrapolates and assigns meaning to the data and findings. Additional sections, such as literature review, conclusion, implications, limitations, needs for further research, and a conflict of interest statement can also be included. Recent research frequently includes the statement of conflict of interest, which can inform the reader of any connections the researcher has to the topic. These connections will not always lead to bias, but could, and it is important for the reader to be aware. Pre-registration, another more recent concept, is powerful way to reduce complications in research.

People frequently read research articles, or something that references research, with a focus on the conclusions that the author(s) provide. Often a host of numbers and values are displayed without much explanation in the results and discussion sections, and the reader has minimal understanding of what the provided information means. It can be overwhelming. Blair (2017), has a great recommendation: "Read the article that you have selected or been assigned at least three times. At first you may just skim the article and read the abstract, introduction and discussion sections to get a general overview of the study. Read the paper again in its entirety, paying attention to the methods and results sections. Finally, read the paper a third time with an eye for asking questions about what the researchers have or have not done. Consider alternative explanations for the results from those provided by the authors of the article" (para. 3).

Questions one should ask include:

- What is the research question?
   - Is the question narrow? Broad?

- How was the research set up?
  - ○ Does it seem complete? Well-executed?
  - ○ Does the research structure appear well-poised to address the question?
- What was included and/or excluded?
  - ○ This will be more easily evaluated in pre-registered research.
- What came into the discussion based on data and what was extrapolated?
  - ○ Were the conclusions a direct result of the data?
  - ○ Did the author stretch the findings? Focus on only one aspect?
- What information do you wish you had regarding the topic, research, or researchers?
  - ○ Were there any missing components?
  - ○ Are there any incongruencies?
  - ○ Are there any stated conflicts of interest?

Section Breakdown

Abstract

The abstract of a study is a short summary intended to inform the reader of the key elements and entice them into further reading. The reason and rationale for the study, brief comments about the population studied and the data found, and the conclusions drawn are typically provided. Reading an abstract alone is not sufficient and can be misleading at times. The abstract sets the stage but by no means serves as a substitute for the full production.

Introduction

The introduction section of a research article provides the rationale and support for the study. This section includes the research question, which is best stated clearly and simply to minimize any confusion, and a literature review of the existing research. The literature, or "lit", review supports the need for the current research and explains how it will further or expand the field's current body of knowledge. If the topic does not have an expansive amount of previous research to review, key concepts should be bridged together through research in different areas to explain to the reader why this research question is important. This section should be full of in-text citations and references so the reader can follow up on any questions they have or further research they would like to conduct. The author(s) should walk the reader through the key components they have identified and provide a foundation for the rest of the current study. Additionally, the introduction should describe what the current study will offer or provide to expand the field's body of knowledge.

Methodology

Methodology refers to a systematic plan for conducting the research. It is a recipe to follow. The methodology should be described in a way that would allow another researcher to replicate the work and so the reader can understand how the research was conducted. This is a good area to take notes and create a list of questions. For instance, why did the researchers choose the population, how did they gain access to the population, why was their sample size chosen, why did they use a certain questionnaire, and so on?

Variables

Variables are the items, concepts, and/or categories one is trying to measure. They are called variables because their value varies from person to person or situation to situation. It varies, so it is called a variable. Variables include numbers, measurements, groups, categories, and the like. The information found or collected on the variables are called data.

There are two main types of variables: independent (x) and dependent (y). Independent variables are called the explanatory variables because when x changes, the regression line (the numbers are plotted as a slope on a graph to tell us more about the meaning) explains to us how much y is expected to change (Rumsey, 2011; Helmenstine, 2018, para. 1).

If we think about the slime we make and use in our play therapy sessions, we could use an example about the slime's viscosity (thickness and stickiness) to help illustrate this concept. Independent variables (x) could include things like amount of each ingredient used to make slime, the temperature in the room, or the humidity levels. The measurement of how much the viscosity changes would be our y variable, or the dependent variable, because the viscosity is dependent upon the changes we make in x (amount of ingredients, temperature, humidity, etc.). These definitions matter in the structure of the research. If they are not identified properly the statistics will not run properly and the conclusions would be incorrect. In other words, if we change the glue to mayonnaise and keep everything else in the recipe the same, the mayonnaise becomes the independent variable (x). When we measure the viscosity of the slime, or the dependent variable (y), we will see

Table 6.1 Independent and Dependent Variables

Type of variable	Short definition
Independent (x)	The explanatory variable, the variable you use to make the prediction. If x changes, a regression line can tell you how much y would be expected to change.
Dependent (y)	The response variable, it changes in response to x. This is the variable you want to predict.

what the effect of the mayonnaise was on the slime. We would be testing how much the mayonnaise changed the viscosity of the slime or looking at the effect x (mayonnaise) has on y (slime viscosity). If these were not assigned, defined, or measured properly, the statistics would be based on improper information and the conclusions would most likely offer misinformation. If the researchers did not tell us that the glue was substituted with mayonnaise, yet the results were provided, we would be basing recipe decisions on untrue information.

The independent variable assignments and definitions also let us know what the researchers were looking for. A reader could question why certain variables were or were not included. Alternatively, extraneous and/or distracting variables might be included and could bring the methodology into question. The slime example is simplistic, but the importance stands: the variables and their assigned jobs tell us what the researchers are looking at and how they will be using the variables and evaluating them.

What are the researchers looking at (research question(s), variables)? Why are they looking at them (research questions and literature review)? How are they looking at them/how are they changing components/what are the effects (independent and dependent variables)? What information did the experiments yield (results)? How are they interpreting the results (discussion)? Each section of the research article is important.

Power

Statistical results are interpreted in terms of power. Statistical power refers to the likelihood that the study results will detect an effect. The higher the power, the fewer results will be considered significant. Think of it as a cut-off bar. The higher the power, the higher the cut-off bar is, and the fewer results will be considered significant because they will not reach the bar. If the researcher sets the bar high, fewer results will be considered significant but those that are included can be accepted with a higher level of confidence. If the bar is set low, more significance will be reported and included, but confidence in the results should be lower. It should be noted that the statistical power is only referring to the variables addressed in the study and extrapolation should be done with great caution. There could be other variables which would be most important to you or your work that were not included.

The determination and interpretation of statistical power can result in errors, Type I and Type II. A Type I error is also called a false positive. This is where the results were accepted as positive when they were not. Medical tests provide a perfect example, for instance, a person is told their testing showed they were pregnant when in fact they were not. A Type II error is called a false negative, where the results were rejected when they should not have been. An example would be that a person was told they were not pregnant when in fact they were. (Glen, 2015).

Replication

Replication is important as it allows a variety of researchers to conduct the same study to strengthen or disprove claims. Study replication allows for the conclusions drawn from research (discussion section) to provide the audience with more solid, trustworthy results as they have been found by different groups following the same protocol (methodology recipe). At times this process will lead to an expansion of the topic with new questions, components, or variables. Other times this process will highlight parts of the study that were done improperly, whether intentionally or not.

The more a conclusion is supported by replications of studies, the more we can trust the information, and therefore, the better the programs, interventions, and treatment we can provide our clients. As Hue Green stated, "Experiments should be considered in the aggregate, with conclusions most safely drawn from multiple demonstrations of any given finding" (2015, para. 8). To illustrate the importance of replication, an open-source replication review was led by Brian Nosek of the University of Virginia. The purpose was to look at existing studies, follow the methodologies, and compare the findings to the originals. This project was an enormous undertaking and included 270 researchers from around the world (Open Science Collaboration, 2015). The findings were alarming. A total of 100 study replications were completed. Of these 100 replications, only *36%* had significant results. All one hundred of the original studies reported significant results. This means that *64%* of the studies they replicated were found to be "unstable" (Green, 2015). Unstable here means that subsequent researchers could not replicate the results reported initially and therefore we cannot rely on them. Although it is not clear what this replication percentage should be (Yong, 2015), this is an enormous issue and it brings everything into question. Even if the original studies were well-executed and the initial findings were sound, perhaps the environment, variables which were unaccounted for, or a variety of human factors effected the results and therefore the generalizability could be compromised or over- or under- estimated.

Results

Data are the star of the results section. This is the section which will include numbers, symbols, and formulae which can be confusing. There are a lot of important concepts to understand and this chapter will not address many of them. If you would like to understand these concepts and more in depth, I strongly recommend you take a research design and statistics course. However, here are some fundamental basics. In a few moments those funny little symbols will mean a lot more to you.

Slimy Hypotheses

Hypotheses are really important concepts in research design and identify what is being tested in the research. There are two main hypotheses we will focus on in this chapter. The first hypothesis is the null hypothesis and is shown as H_0. The null hypothesis is the status quo. For instance, if one were to make slime and the container claims it will make a gallon, the gallon amount would be the H_0. The alternative hypothesis, or H_a (also can be shown as H_1), is the claim that the researcher believes is true. Perhaps the play therapist has made the recipe numerous times and each time it yields much more than a gallon Ziploc bag will hold. Therefore, the H_a is that the recipe actually yields more than a gallon of slime. We need to include one more symbol here, the parameter of interest or the population average: μ. The H_0, or the claim that the slime recipe makes one gallon of slime would be written in the results section like this: $H_0: \mu = 1$ (one gallon). The alternative hypothesis, that it actually yields more than a gallon, would be denoted as: $H_a: \mu > 1$. Now you know what a good portion of that confusing stuff in the results section means!

Researchers like to show that their H_a is true and therefore that their basis for the study yielded support for their claim. In our case, we would want to show the world that the recipe makes more than one gallon of slime. In order for the H_a to be true, the H_0 has to be rejected. This is where the p-value comes into the conversation. The p-value tells us what the data is showing about the μ (parameter of interest/population average) and the cutoff value (the number that tells us which decisions to make) $= 0.05$. p-values define whether or not something is statistically significant, or "has a very small probability of happening just by chance" (Rumsey, 2011, p. 62). The p-value indicates that probability. The rules are as follows, according to Rumsey (2011):

1) A p-value of ≤ 0.05 is considered small and indicates strong evidence against the H_0, so you reject the null hypothesis. For our slime study we would then say we could reject the claim that it makes only one gallon. We would feel successful.
2) A p-value of > 0.05 shows weak evidence against the H_0, therefore we would "fail to reject it" (p. 61). In other words, we would *not* be able to reject the claim that the slime made one gallon. We might then wonder what on earth we were doing to create more slime than the company claimed, and the study showed when we are in our office or what might have gone wrong in our research.
3) A p-value which is very close to the cutoff value of 0.05 would not be definitive. It could indicate support for the H_0 or the H_a.

p-values should always be provided so the reader can evaluate them for themselves and decide how close the values were to being able to reject or accept the H_0.

Considered the costliest statistical error, a false positive occurs when the null hypothesis is rejected incorrectly (Simmons et al., 2011). This is costly because money, time, and resources could be wasted trying to replicate the study, programs and policy changes could be formed based on false information, and overall topic or field credibility could be lost. Once false positives are published, it can be very difficult to remove them. A powerful example of this is the widespread phenomena of Andrew Wakefield's study linking vaccinations and autism. Although Wakefield's results have been *discredited multiple times*, the debate still lingers and the spread of misinformation continues (Zane, 2018). Even though these findings are false, many people still link vaccinations and autism, which can hinder the quest for legitimate findings.

Discussion

Most therapists are familiar with the discussion section. This is where we go to find out what the researcher discovered and to determine how these findings fit (or not) with our previous understandings. It is important to remember that researchers are human, and we all have biases. Some biases are recognized and acknowledged, and others are not. I would like to believe that the majority of researchers work hard to acknowledge and control for their biases, so the research is minimally impacted. This is a fundamental reason why understanding all portions of the research paper is important.

Perhaps the conscientious researcher missed something or interpreted data in accordance with their preconceived belief systems. A critical review of the work, which includes an evaluation of the information provided and an attention to questions that arise as a consumer of the information, will likely highlight some of these issues. Additionally, while we would like to believe that researchers have pure intentions which would result in unbiased results, this is not always the case. Some people have agendas for political, professional, academic, or financial reasons and their research can serve as support for their cause. Reading research articles critically and understanding some of the basics will allow you, as the consumer, to evaluate the work, the process, the findings, and the conclusions.

Questionable Research Practices (QRPs)

Questionable research practices, or QRPs, are behaviors which might be known or unknown to the researcher(s) (Chambers et al., 2014; Etchells, 2019). Some researchers may engage in QRPs because of the way they were taught. The QRPs are unintentional. Others might use QRPs to manipulate their findings. It is important to be aware that these practices can and do happen and they effect the research we consume.

Simmons et al. (2011) provided an example of how QRPs can affect research. They described a study involving 34 University of Pennsylvania students who listened to one of three songs, including a song by the Beatles. After intentionally employing a number of QRPs, the properly executed statistical analysis (ANCOVA) yielded that people were one and a half years younger after listening to the song "When I'm Sixty-Four". Certainly, it is impossible for a person to be younger after listening to any song; however, when research components are manipulated in certain ways, the data can still "show" certain results. This example is benign and obvious; however, many are not.

Chambers et al. (2014) proposed that awareness of these QRP practices had been increased, however, despite the increased awareness, the "incentive structure of academia has not changed to address them" (2014, p. 1). It is important for people who read research to be aware of QRPs so they can look for signs that the findings might not be acceptable. Scholars have sought a process which would decrease these concerns, and pre-registration appears to be the next big step. Pre-registration is a way to minimize QRPs.

Pre-registration/Registered Reports

Pre-registration of research requires the authors to register their hypotheses and analyses *before* any data are collected. This model of publishing is called registered reports (RR). Registered reports require authors to submit their work in two stages. stage one includes the submission of the introduction, methods, and results of any pilot experiments. If the stage one submission is accepted, it is given an "in principle acceptance" and is virtually assured publication of the research as long as they follow their proposed stage one protocol. This process frees the researchers from the pressures of having to conform to traditional expectations and allows the work to unfold more organically. Stage two includes the Introduction and Methods from the stage one submission, along with the Results and Discussion sections. The Results section would include the pre-registered outcome and any additional outcomes would be provided in another section entitled "Exploratory Analyses" (Chambers et al., 2014). Data must also be shared on a free, public forum which would allow the reader to more accurately analyze the research study, conclusions, and implications.

This RR process has been adopted by many journals, but certainly not enough. If you find an article that refers to participation in the pre-registration or RR process, you can read with a much greater assurance to the quality of the research. Not only was the work subject to the RR process, but the researchers entered the process with the expressed intention of transparency and minimized QRPs. Look for this type of article and let your favorite journals know you prefer this process.

As with any topic, some people support this move toward pre-registration and some do not (Gonzales, 2015). Some researchers have concerns about the constraints the pre-registration process would require and suppress exploratory research (Chambers et al., 2014). Publishers may have concerns about committing to publish before seeing the completed manuscript (Gonzales, 2015). Although there may be concerns to address and even some changes to the process, the focus on transparency and replicability is critical for research findings to have meaning. The loopholes and concerns identified over many years have cast a shadow on research that must be addressed.

The Center for Open Science has implemented a badge initiative to recognize adherence to the transparent practices of the RR process. There are 66 journals currently using the badge system (Center for Open Science, 2019, para. 2). All research that participates in the RR process will automatically receive the

Pre-registration and Open Data badges. You can find more information about these badges here: https://cos.io/our-services/open-science-badges/. These badges encourage reduced QRPs and increased data sharing. Once you know the badges, you can quickly recognize whether or not what you are reading participated in the RR pre-registration process. Transparency empowers the reader to know the work has been held to a higher standard and, armed with some knowledge about research and statistics, the reader is not left to accept the author's interpretations and can analyze the data and meanings for themselves. Let us look at a few of the QRPs that RRs aim to reduce or remove.

Publication Bias

Researchers who do not participate in the RR process submit their completed work for publication and wait for the acceptance or rejection notification. Publishing companies tend to want to publish new, exciting research that will draw the attention of the academic consumer and/or focus on statistical significance. This practice is referred to as publication bias or "the file drawer effect" (Etchells, 2019, p. 98). This tends to highlight research which fits into certain parameters. Therefore, researchers often focus on studies which have a higher probability of being published (Kerr, 1998). Insignificant results and replication studies are frequently left in the in the file drawer (also known as the file-drawer effect). It is logical human nature to steer efforts toward the mechanism that will yield the desired result, so it makes sense that researchers will primarily embark on certain experimental quests and focus on statistical significance.

However, a byproduct of this approach is that studies that might rule something out because of "insignificant" findings and/or replication studies often are not published. When learning about research and conducting a number of studies in graduate school, I remember being told that not finding significance was still yielding information. The lack of significance told us that either something in the research question, methodology, or statistics choices needed to be changed, the variables we chose needed to be different or could be ruled out, and the like. This kind of information could be helpful to those doing similar work in the future and help them focus their efforts elsewhere. Even having heard this and understanding the value of results that did not show significance, the push to find significance was deeply felt. Anything less than significance felt like failure. Perhaps this is another reason well-conducted studies that do not find significance should be published, to demonstrate the value and help inform future research.

Overall, the research publication industry is antiquated, and reform is warranted. The shift to online databases has had a fantastic effect on the way information is shared. In this author's opinion, research should be pre-registered, to avoid many pitfalls and increase transparency; well-structured and conducted studies should be published, whether the results are significant or not; and all articles should available to everyone. The focus should be on the dissemination of information, the ensuing conversations, and informing future research for the good of all people.

Confirmation Bias

With all these replication issues, cherry-picking of research to be published, and conflicting findings, many of us can be left confused regarding what to believe or not to believe. A common human response to this overwhelm is to revert to a concept known as confirmation bias. Confirmation bias "refers to the unwitting selectivity in the acquisition and use of evidence" (Nickerson, 1998, p. 175) or "the tendency for people to search for or interpret information in a manner that favors their current beliefs" (Nelson & McKenzie, 2009, p. 1). With regard to concerns about confirmation bias of those who conduct research, John P. Ioannidis believed that "claimed research findings may often be simply accurate measures of the prevailing bias" (2005). Basically, we tend to go with what we know, what we think we know, what feels most safe, or what "fits".

Confirmation bias can seem like a safe(r) option when faced with difficult, counter-intuitive, confusing or conflicting information. It is an age-old phenomenon for humans, and it has continued because it serves a purpose: it feels safe and congruent because it fits into our pre-existing paradigm. However, it can be dangerous.

In an attempt to understand confirmation bias further, Nickerson delineates the concept into two main categories: motivated and unmotivated. If people have a motivation to defend beliefs they wish to maintain, then the confirmation bias is considered motivated. For instance, they have a preconceived notion they want to defend, have a monetary stake in the results, or need certain results for other personal gain. If people do not have any known personal interest or material stake, then the confirmation bias is considered to be unmotivated (Nickerson, 1998). Unmotivated confirmation bias could be as simple as something that is congruent with the person's belief system. Often either type of confirmation bias can be balanced by two key concepts: 1) self-exploration, along with awareness of one's beliefs and biases, and 2) a continued openness to information, ideas, evidence, and discussion, which may or may not be congruent with one's beliefs and biases.

Interestingly, as I write this chapter, my daughter is completing a National History Day project about the Salem Witch Trials. As I read Nickerson's article, I came across an example he provided of historical confirmation bias in terms of the Salem trials. The people of Salem held onto their belief systems even under the most horrific circumstances, predominantly out of fear. My daughter's position in her project is that Giles Cory was pivotal in changing the approach Salem took regarding witches and accusations. You may or may not know that Giles Cory *testified against his wife* when she was accused. However, once he was later accused, he began to say that the trials and accusations were a sham and he refused to relent. He was ultimately crushed to death by stones and never entered a plea regarding his charges.

Initially, when he testified against his wife, he could have had a variety of motivations (which is important to include to combat our own confirmation bias in reading this); however, elements of confirmation bias were likely in effect. Perhaps his wife was acting in a way that made him question her and witchcraft was a feasible explanation of the time. It may have felt safer to support the accusations against her and not have a witch in his home. These could be predominantly *unmotivated* confirmation bias. He may also have feared guilt by association or merely did not want to be married to her any longer. This could have been *motivated* confirmation bias. His position changed when he was accused of being a witch. His need for self-preservation superseded any confirmation bias he was previously employing.

p-Hacking

Simply put, *p*-hacking occurs when the researcher only picks out the data they want to include and leaves the rest behind. This assures significance in most situations and therefore an increased probability of the article being published. The name refers to the *p* value having been hacked to give the appearance of statistical significance. Some of the ways *p*-hacking occurs include collecting additional data, leaving out data, excluding less-promising measures, and altering the data analysis *after seeing the results*. This type of manipulation in response to collected data frequently results in false positives (Cummings, 2016).

For example, it is similar to the process of finding the average of a list of numbers and wanting the result to be a large number. A way to reach that goal would be to only include the large numbers in the equation, thereby guaranteeing a large average of the list of numbers. The preconceived "desired" result is realized, but it is incomplete and inaccurate as the left-out numbers existed but were not included. The resulting average is inflated; however, the reader is unaware of the process used to achieve the results.

HARKing

HARK, an acronym for "Hypothesizing After Results are Known", was presented by Norbert Kerr in 1998. This concept specifically refers to the practice of presenting a hypothesis which was formed *after* (post hoc) data collection as though it had been formed *before* (a priori) data collection. He further delineated five types, two of which I will describe here. The others are more complicated and can be found in the original article. For our purposes we will discuss: 1) pure HARKing and 2) suppressing loser hypotheses.

Pure HARKing is deliberate and manipulative. After data collection, the researcher recognizes that the hypotheses are insufficient in some way and they are then changed to be most consistent with the collected results. An example of this could be "the hypothesis does not match the results, so I am changing the hypothesis to make a better match". Suppressing the loser hypotheses is a process of dropping any hypotheses that were contraindicated by the data and keeping those that were not (Kerr, 1998). For instance, "this hypothesis is a winner and I will keep it, the others are not, so I will pretend they never existed".

When a researcher HARKs, the chance of incorrectly rejecting the null hypothesis increases and the effect sizes will be distorted (Bout, 2013). What this means is the wrong conclusions about the data will be made and the entire research project will be suspect. In addition, the research would not be able to be replicated as the rules of the game were changed mid-play and they were not recorded for the next player.

Orben and Przybylski

Amy Orben and Andrew Przybylski published a fantastic paper entitled the *Association Between Adolescent Well-Being and Digital Technology Use* (2019). Not only is this paper a fantastic review of the most prominent research on adolescent well-being and digital technology use, it also provides a remarkable breakdown and education regarding the pitfalls of research, data collection, and data analysis. In reading this paper, you will find many of the concerns raised in this chapter highlighted and explained further. Their analysis is phenomenally well done.

Conclusion

It is my sincere hope that you have gained valuable knowledge about research after reading this chapter. The critical consumption of splashy headlines, polished data, and conclusions made by others stands to improve our day to day work with clients, our standing in the professional communities, and the play therapy field in general. There is certainly a lot more information to learn about these topics, and I encourage you to seek further education when you are able.

References

Blair, K. L. (2017, July 19). How to summarize a psychology article. *Pen & the Pad*. https://penandthepad.com/summarize-psychology-article-7199463.html
Bout, J. (2013, September 18). Why HARKing is bad for science. *Good Science Bad Science*. http://goodsciencebadscience.nl/?p=347
Center for Open Science (2019, December 12). *What are open science badges?* https://cos.io/our-services/open-science-badges/
Chambers, C. D., Feredos, E., Muthukumaraswamy, S. D., & Etchells, P. (2014). Instead of "playing the game" it is time to change the rules: Registered reports at AIMS Neuroscience and beyond. *AIMS Neuroscience, 1*, 4–17.
Cummings, G. (2016). A primer on p-hacking. *Method Space*. www.methodspace.com/primer-p-hacking/
Etchells, P. (2019). *Lost in a good game*. Icon.
Glen, S. (2015, April 2). False positives and false negatives: Definitions and examples. *Statistics How To*. www.statisticshowto.datasciencecentral.com/false-positive-definition-and-examples/
Gonzales, J. E. (2015, August). The promise of preregistration. *American Psychological Association*. www.apa.org/science/about/psa/2015/08/pre-registration

Green, H. (2015, September 14). It's not the lack of replication, it's the lack of trying to replicate! *Social Science Space*. www.socialsciencespace.com/2015/09/its-not-the-lack-of-replication-its-the-lack-of-trying-to-replicate/

Hall, S. (2017, March 23). Definition of a research article. *Pen & the Pad*. https://penandthepad.com/definition-research-article-2711.html

Helmenstine, T. (2018, October 7). What's the difference between independent and dependent variables? *Thoughtco*. www.thoughtco.com/independent-and-dependent-variables-differences-606115

Ioannidis, J. P. (2005). Why most published research findings are false. *PLOS Medicine*, *2*(8), e124. https://journals.plos.org/plosmedicine/article?id=10.1371/journal.pmed.0020124

Kerr, N. L. (1998). HARKing: Hypothesizing after the results are known. *Personality and Social Psychology Review*, *2*(3), 196–217.

Nelson & McKenzie (2009). Confirmation bias. In M. Katten (Ed.), *The encyclopedia of medical decision making* (pp. 167–171). Thousand Oaks, CA: Sage Publications. www.jonathandnelson.com/papers/2009confirmationBias.pdf

Nickerson, R. S. (1998). Confirmation bias: A ubiquitous phenomenon in many guises. *Review of General Psychology*, *2*(2), 175–220.

Open Science Collaboration (2015). Estimating the reproducibility of psychological science. *Science*, *349*(6251). https://science.sciencemag.org/content/349/6251/aac4716.full?ijkey=1xgFoCnpLswpk&keytype=ref&siteid=sci

Orben, A., & Przybylski, A. (2019). The association between adolescent well-being and digital technology use. *Nature Human Behavior*. www.gwern.net/docs/psychology/2019-orben.pdf

Rumsey, D. (2011). *Statistics for dummies* (pp. 43–63). Wiley.

Simmons, J. P., Nelson, L. D., & Simonsohn, U. (2011). False-positive psychology: Undisclosed flexibility in data collection and analysis allows presenting anything as significant. *Association for Psychological Science*, *22*(11), 1359–1366.

Yong, E. (2015, August 27). How reliable are psychological studies? *The Atlantic*. www.theatlantic.com/science/archive/2015/08/psychology-studies-reliability-reproducability-nosek/402466/

Zane, T. (2018, April 18). The vaccine and autism connection: The Wakefield study once again discredited. *Cambridge Center for Behavioral Studies*. https://behavior.org/sfaba-vaccine/

7 Technopanic

"Fear is an extremely powerful motivational force" (Thierer, 2013, p. 311). To state the obvious yet again, play therapists from all foundations have a desire to do no harm. To really understand this, we need to examine what potential harm is, where it comes from, and what might be done about it. These explorations and definitions will shape our field as it moves forward in this technocentric world.

You might be wondering why we are exploring concepts like technopanic, moral panic, folk devils, and more in a book about DPT. These very concepts are prominent in our field when it comes to the integration of technological tools into play therapy, even if we do not use these terms. As a society and a field, we cannot responsibly focus solely on the sensationalism of the world's headlines. The danger is that we will miss any actual underlying concerns regarding society's shift toward a digital world. Our spotlight is not currently on the true, underlying issues at hand. "Tech is bad". What about it is bad? For whom? What kind? In what situations? We are not looking at the important questions or at the most critical components (refer back to the Understanding Research chapter), in so many ways.

Folk Devils and Moral Panic, à la Cohen and Thierer

The terms "folk devils" and "moral panic" were written about extensively in three editions of sociologist Stanley Cohen's book, *Folk Devils and Moral Panics* (1972, 1987, 2002). Originating from a clash between two groups of young people and various political happenings in Great Britain, Cohen's work set forth on an intense sociological and philosophical journey to explore human tendencies to act and react based on fear. Some of his work is outdated and some applies specifically to Great Britain, but much of it applies to human nature and tendencies overall. These concepts are commonly applied to media studies as Cohen focused much of his work on the participation and responsibility of the media in such issues. The clash he refers to sparked fear and outrage as a link between groups of young people and the decay of Britain as British society knew it, among other things, was made.

For some, a difficulty with Cohen's concepts lies in the term "moral panic". This can denote a narrow, irrational, derogatory connotation (Critcher, 2008). Therefore, it is important to have some clarification about the meaning and implications. A good portion of Cohen's (2002) edition is dedicated to addressing critics from the previous 30 years. According to Cohen (2002) "Calling something a 'moral panic' does not imply that this something does not exist or happen at all . . . the attribution of the moral panic label means that the 'thing's' extent and significance has been exaggerated a) in itself (compared with other more reliable, valid and objective sources) and/or b) compared with other, more serious problems" (p. vii). In other words, it may or may not exist, and if it does, it has been exaggerated. Not only exaggerated to the point of sensationalism and the like, but to the point that the real, underlying issues and concerns are not being explored or attended to. A "folk devil" is a scapegoat. The folk devil is whatever topic, group, or person is receiving the brunt of the attention and focus in a negative light, without exploration of other components. Folk devils are the subjects in the moral panic.

Deviance

Deviance is one of the mechanisms for deciding who or what the folk devils are. The concept of deviance brings about a number of questions, such as, what is a deviant and who defines the parameters? In this situation, deviance refers to a person or group or topic that exhibits behavior outside of cultural norms or expectations. The social context is important when evaluating the behavior, such as the group process, judgements, and definitions. Different groups have different norms and expectations, so it is important to evaluate behavior, and thereby define deviance, accordingly (Crossman, 2018).

Regarding deviance, Cohen had great interest in the theory of symbolic interactionism and discovering the motivation of people who opted to engage in groups and behavior which would be considered deviant. Cohen believed that sociological labeling theory, derived from symbolic interactionism, explained a portion of why deviant groups or people engaged in such behaviors (such as the way they dressed, conducted themselves, and any crimes they were involved in). Labeling theory refers to the concept that a "person will generally behave in a manner that is consistent with the way in which that person believes others view him or her" (Criminal Justice, n.d., para. 2; Heslin, 2007). Basically, if you create a situation in which a person or group is an "other" and make assumptions about them, they will "live up to" (or down to) the labels placed on them. They will often play the part defined for them. Cohen expanded upon this with the theory of deviance, or subculture theory, which refers to groups of people (often young) who break off from the mainstream norms and create their own subculture (Cohen, 1972; Critcher, 2008). The young people "become symbols of larger social contradictions" and the contradictions are predominately depicting power struggles (Drotner, 1999, p. 597). If these are the components, who decides if a behavior or anything else is deviant? Where are the lines drawn? When does the subculture become the dominant culture?

In terms of technology within the last 60 years, history shows that a subculture of people were working on advancements and in a way broke away from social norms. They were not committing any crimes; however, they were working on advancements that the average person neither understood nor desired. The first attempts of many types of digital technology in the 1990's to become mainstream were not successful. Often the people who did incorporate such technologies into their lives became part of subcultures: geeks, nerds, gamers, and so on. There has been a lingering demonization of people who are in these subcultures. They could certainly fit into Cohen's theory of deviance. For a period of time all of this could be marginalized, until the use of digital tools became a focus of the mainstream culture.

In the year 2020, these subculture groups are becoming the norm and changing the landscape. As discussed in other portions of the book, digital natives have never known life without technology so, as they age, the norm will include many types of digital tool involvement. Norms shift over time. "For every time a new mass medium has entered the social scene, it has spurred public debates on social and cultural norms, debates that serve to reflect, negotiate, and possibly revise these very norms" (Drotner, 1999, p. 596).

Perpetuating

If the trend is toward a new social norm of inclusion of various digital tools, why does there seem to be such conflict? It is confusing to me to hear and read about adults complaining about youth and the use of such tools; yet when I go anywhere in the public realm, I see adults on their phones, laptops, and tablets. Does it become a conversation of perceived value? Is the belief that the adult is doing something of value on the device, but the adolescent is not? Who determines the value? Perhaps the adolescent is navigating a relationship through Snapchat and learning how to advocate for themselves. This interaction could hold great value for their current and future interpersonal skills. Perhaps the game they are playing is teaching frustration tolerance. The myths and realities of danger must be delineated (Boyd, 2008). How do any of us know what is happening as we are pointing fingers outward as a society?

Technopanic

What Is Technopanic?

In 2008 Alice Marwick was addressing the moral panic she recognized regarding modern technologies. She termed this type of panic *technopanic*. She focused on two major cases where legislation regarding internet content was directly linked to moral panics fueled by the media in which technology was harmful to children: the "cyberporn panic of 1996" and "the contemporary panic over online predators and MySpace" (para. 22). In both situations Marwick argues that "while both panics have their roots in legitimate concerns, I am not primarily concerned with the extent of the purported harms. However, my research demonstrates that the legislation proposed (or passed) to curb these problems is an extraordinary response, it is misguided and, in many cases, masks the underlying problem" (para. 22). Her concern was the extent to which the headlines and claims in the media were influencing policies and masking the important underlying issues. We continue to have similar issues to this day.

A few people have weighed in on the definition of a technopanic. For Marwick, "Technopanics have the following characteristics. First, they focus on new media forms, which currently take the form of computer – mediated technologies. Second, technopanics generally pathologize young people's use of this media, like hacking, file-sharing, or playing violent video games. Third, this cultural anxiety manifests itself in an attempt to modify or regulate young people's behavior, either by controlling young people or the creators or producers of media products" (2008, para. 26). For Thierer (2013), technopanics are "intense, public, political, and academic responses to the emergence or use of media or technologies, especially by the young" (p. 311) and "a moral panic that centers around societal fears about a specific contemporary technology (or technological activity) instead of merely the content flowing over that technology or medium" (Thierer, n.d., para. 1).

The term technopanic is used to describe the media sensationalism regarding the rise of digital tools in our lives. Just like Cohen's moral panic, the term does not negate the concerns about potential issues with the topic; rather, it focuses on the frenzy created regarding certain aspects while others are left to fester. Decisions about legislation, funding, programs, treatment, interventions, and diagnoses are made frequently based on incomplete, and often erroneous, information. O'Byrne offers: "The challenge is that the paranoia and panic that accompanies a technopanic is often overblown and stifles the discussion, examination, and critique that is necessary as we explore these new digital spaces" (2019, para. 4).

Thierer (2013), offers six factors that contribute to the rise of technopanics. Each of these is intended to build on the next one and together create a compounded set of issues. They are as follows:

1) Generational differences: George Orwell offered in his book *In Front of Your Nose*, "Each generation imagines itself to be more intelligent than the one that went before it, and wiser than the one that comes after it" (2000, p. 51). Generation differences are also highlighted by David Finkelhor, who coined the term "'Juvenoia' – an exaggerated fear about the influence of social change on children and youth" (Finkelhor, 2011, p. 13; Thierer, 2013).

2) Hyper-nostalgia, pessimistic bias, and soft Ludditism: Hyper-nostalgia can certainly fan the flames of rejection for anything new, including the use of technology. Humans are generally more comfortable with that which is

known. It can be expected that there would be fear regarding something that challenges the traditional values and norms. History has repeatedly shown that the fear of what is new has caused a fear-driven stir and claims of the next generation's demise. There can also be a positive exaggeration regarding both the positives of the past and the negatives of the present/future.

3) Bad news sells: The role of the media, advocates and the listener – fear-based headlines cause people to pay attention out of the fear that they might miss something, make poor decisions, and ultimately cause harm. Most people operate with some level of negativity bias, or the tendency to attend more to negative events, beliefs, and/or information.

4) The role of special interests and industry infighting: S groups can benefit from certain information becoming big news. Companies that offer services to combat or cure certain "ailments" have an incentive to emphasize the dangers of that which they aim to treat.

5) Elitist attitudes among academics and intellectuals: Those who feel they have a higher position and education will often attempt to guide and dictate the path of those who do not.

6) The role of "third-person-effect hypothesis" – this is very similar to confirmation bias. It is the phenomena of people hearing and seeing that which is congruent with existing beliefs.

(Thierer, 2013, pp. 333–345)

Fear Appeal Arguments

Thierer (2013), introduced the evaluative process of *fear appeal arguments* which he based on Cohen's previous works (Cohen, 1972, 1987, 2002) and Walton's argumentation schemes (2012). He asserted that the process of bypassing a person's critical evaluation of a situation lies in a three-part fear-based process:

1) This situation is fearful to/for you: *Fearful situation premise*
2) If you do x, the result of the fearful situation will happen to you: *Conditional premise*
3) Therefore, you should not do x: *Conclusion*

Thierer applied this fear appeal argument scheme to the common concern regarding children viewing or playing anything that involves violent media and the generalization of violence in their day-to-day lives. He proposed the following fear appeal argument:

1) "Fearful situation premise: letting children watch violent television or movies, or play violent video games, will make them violent in real life.
2) Conditional premise: If we allow children to play games that contain violent content, then those children will behave aggressively or commit acts of violence later

3) Conclusion: We should not let children see violent television or movies, or play violent games"

(Thierer, 2013, p. 313).

Thierer offered a number of issues with this specific violence-begets-violence fear appeal argument: 1) the fearful situation and conditional premise might not be based in solid empirical evidence. The connection between viewing depictions of violence and acting out violently has not been found to be conclusive. A "logical fallacy could also be at work here, just because A preceded B does not mean that A caused B. Correlation does not necessarily equal causation" (2013, p. 314), 2) other potential causes must be explored, 3) children are different and therefore will have different understandings and responses to visual stimuli (2013).

Another example offered by Thierer (2013), is one regarding the fear of online predators. Despite information which narrows the typical online predator situation, the generalized fear spread like wildfire.

1) Fearful Situation Premise: Predators are out to get your kids and they are lurking everywhere online.
2) Conditional Premise: If you allow kids to use social networking sites, predators could get to your kids and abuse them.
3) Conclusion: You should not allow your kids on social networking sites (and perhaps policymakers should consider restricting access to those sites by children).

(p. 323)

Janet Wolak, J.D. has researched this topic extensively and offers that "reality about Internet-initiated sex crimes – those in which sex offenders meet juvenile victims online – is different, complex, and serious, but less archetypically frightening than the publicity about these crimes suggests" (Wolak et al., 2012, p. 28). They found that "victims are most often at-risk youth who have previously been abused or already have problems in school or at home" (p. 34). This illustrates the most important distinction: delineating the fear appeal argument or challenging the technopanics is *not* to suggest or state that there is no reason for concern. In this last example of online predators, the focus could stay on the general child user and widespread panic can ensue without looking further into a variety of factors, or the factors can be investigated, and the findings can be targeted for a more effective approach. In this case, Wolak, et al., presented information to government officials after analyzing data regarding arrests, risk factors, internet sex crimes, and more. Their findings assisted in the ability of the government to target specific populations for specialized interventions, education, outreach, and law enforcement policies.

Potatoes

The headline reads: "Screens might be as bad for mental health as potatoes" (Gonzalez, 2019). Say what? Gonzalez is referencing a paper published by Amy

Orben and Andrew Przybylski from the Oxford Internet Institute in 2019. *The association between adolescent well-being and digital technology* use was a review and analysis of three "large-scale exemplar datasets" (p. 2) to "rigorously examine correlational evidence for the effects of digital technology on adolescents" (p. 1). As stated in the earlier chapter regarding understanding research, this is a phenomenal paper.

The premise for the paper and the underlying analyses was to explore the disagreements in the literature regarding the impact of screen time on children's psychological well-being. They analyzed and evaluated the Monitoring the Future (MTF), Youth Risk and Behaviour Survey (YRBS), and Millennium Cohort Study (MCT), the first two from the United States and the third from the United Kingdom (Orben & Przybylski, 2019). They identified the main analytical decisions for each of these large-scale studies. Astonishingly, they discovered that the YRBS had 372 "justifiable specifications", the MTF had 40,966 "plausible specifications", and the MCS had a 603,979,752 "defensible specifications". What this means is that each of these studies had x number of possible specific data definitions within the studies. When you look at independent and dependent variables, the MCS study's specification possibilities would rise to 2.5 trillion specifications. Traditional statistical analyses cannot possibly explore this many pathways, therefore researchers choose particular variable pathways and utilized those.

Orben and Przybylski chose to use the SCA, or specification curve analysis, method which maps "the sum of the theory-driven analytical decisions that could justifiably been taken when analysing quantitative data. Researchers demarcate every possible analytical pathway and then calculate the results of each. Rather than reporting a handful of analyses in their paper, they report all results of all theoretically defensible analyses" (2019, p. 2).

In an effort to compare the findings with other variable associations regarding adolescent mental health, the researchers compared specification curves for the following items along with those found for the MTF, YBRS, and MCS studies: getting into fights, binge-drinking, smoking cigarettes, smoking, marijuana, being bullied, being arrested, eating potatoes, perceived weight, drinking milk, having asthma, doing homework, religion, listening to music, going to the movies, height, handedness, wearing glasses, cycling, eating vegetables, eating fruit, eating breakfast, and getting enough sleep. Interestingly, "in all three data-sets the effects of both smoking marijuana and bullying have much larger negative associations with adolescent well-being ($\times$ 2.7 and $\times$ 4.3, respectively for the YRBS) than does technology use. Positive antecedents of well-being are equally illustrative; simple actions such as getting enough sleep and regularly eating breakfast have much more positive associations with well-being than the average impact of technology use (ranging from $\times$ 1.7 to $\times$ 44.2 more positive in all datasets). Neutral factors provide perhaps the most useful context in which to judge technology engagement effects: the association of well-being with regularly eating potatoes was nearly as negative as the association with technology use ($\times$ 0.9, YRBS), and wearing glasses was more negatively associated with well-being ($\times$ 1.5, MCS)" (p. 5–6). In other words, technology use was approximately the same negative association as regularly eating potatoes for a teen's mental health. *Regularly eating potatoes had about the same effect on a teen's mental health as tech use.* Wearing glasses affected an adolescent's mental health more negatively than the use of technology.

These findings are not claiming that there are no negative aspects of the use of technology, but they are telling us that there are significant issues with 1) the way research is conducted, 2) the way research is reported, 3) the way research findings are interpreted, and 4) that the flashlight is directed in only certain areas, most of which feed into the technopanic realm. How on earth can we truly dissect technology use and the effects of such use with such a plethora of confusing information? This is exactly why I did not dedicate a chapter of this book to a literature review. It would have been a mishmosh of conflicting information that we would not have been able to decipher or depend upon.

Ultimately, Orben and Przybylski concluded: "We know very little about whether increased technology use might cause lower well-being, whether lower well-being might result in increased technology use or whether a third con-founding factor underlies both. Because we are examining something inher-ently complex, the likelihood of unaccounted factors affecting both technology use and well-being is high. It is therefore possible that the associations we document, and those that previous authors have documented, are spurious" (2019, p. 7). The Gonzalez write-up referenced earlier offers this quote but does not provide a reference. It appears to be a response to the Orben and Przybylski analysis. "The level of association documented in this study is incongruent with the level of panic we see around things like screen time", says University of California Irvine psychologist Candice Odgers, who researches how technol-ogy affects kids' development and was unaffiliated with the study. "It really highlights the disconnect between conversations in the public sphere and what the bulk of the data are showing us" (Gonzalez, 2019, para. 11).

Orben likens the global questions regarding the use of technology to whether or not food is good or bad for you. How can one even answer that question? There are so many caveats, other questions to be asked and answered, information to be gathered. The more important questions regarding the use of technology are: what kind is being used, who is using them, and how they are being used (Gon-zalez, 2019). O'Bryne also offered: "Rather than assuming all technology use is equal (and equally bad), perhaps we should take a more nuanced approach as we discuss these issues. We might, for example, consider different types of screen-time, and the affordances of each of these texts, tools, and spaces". "Perhaps if children and adults spent time coconsuming this content, and had dialogue about the experience, we might have a better understanding of screentime" (2019, p. 7).

What Is the Play Therapist's Role and Conclusion

The play therapist's role regarding technology use and technopanic is to be informed and to apply digital tools within play therapy as they speak the cli-ent's language, honor the client's culture, and activate the therapeutic powers of play. Find the original research referenced in headlined articles, read research critically, and understand that only a handful of statistical pathways were most likely followed when analyzing data and that they were most likely ones that supported their hypotheses because of such issues as publication bias. The play therapist is in an amazingly powerful position: you can offer powerful therapeutic digital tools, understand the tenets and underpinnings to such use, educate families, and help shape the future of proper research regarding such usage, both within and outside of the therapeutic session.

References

Boyd, D. M. (2008). *Taken out of context: American teen sociality*. www.microsoft.com/en-us/research/wp-content/uploads/2016/02/TakenOutOfContext.pdf

Cohen, S. (1972). *Folk devils and moral panics* (1st ed.). MacGibbon and Kee.

Cohen, S. (1987). *Folk devils and moral panics* (2nd ed.). Basil Blackwood.

Cohen, S. (2002). *Folk devils and moral panics* (3rd ed.). Abingdon, UK: Routledge.

Criminal Justice (n.d.). Labeling theory and symbolic interaction theory. *iResearch*. http://criminal-justice.iresearchnet.com/criminology/theories/labeling-theory-and-symbolic-interaction-theory/2/

Critcher, C. (2008). Moral panic analysis: Past, present, and future. *Sociology Compass*, 2(4), 1127–1144. www.penelopeironstone.com/Critcher.pdf

Crossman, A. (2018, April 23). Sociology of deviance and crime. *Thoughtco*. www.thoughtco.com/sociology-of-crime-and-deviance-3026279

Drotner, K. (1999). Dangerous media? Panic discourses and dilemmas of modernity. *Paedagogica Historica*, 35(3), 593–619.

Finkelhor, D. (2011, January). *The internet, youth safety, and the problem of juvenoia*. www.unh.edu/ccrc/pdf/Juvenoia%20paper.pdf

Gonzalez, R. (2019). Screens might be as bad for mental health as . . . potatoes. *Wired*. www.wired.com/story/screens-might-be-as-bad-for-mental-health-as-potatoes/

Heslin, J. (2007). *Sociology: A down to earth approach* (8th ed.). Pearson.

Marwick, A. E. (2008, June 2). To catch a predator: The MySpace moral panic. *First Monday*. https://firstmonday.org/article/view/2152/1966

O'Byrne, I. (2019, June 14). Addressing technopanic in the age of screentime. *Literacy Worldwide*. www.literacyworldwide.org/blog%2fliteracy-daily%2f2019%2f06%2f14%2faddressing-technopanic-in-the-age-of-screentime

Orben, A., & Przybylski (2019). The association between adolescent well-being and digital technology use. *Nature Human Behavior*. www.gwern.net/docs/psychology/2019-orben.pdf

Orwell, G. (2000). *In front of your nose*. Godine.

Thierer, A. (n.d.). Ongoing series: Moral panics/techno-panics. *Tech Liberation*. https://techliberation.com/ongoing-series/ongoing-series-moral-panics-techno-panics/

Thierer, A. (2013). Technopanics, threat inflation, and the danger of an information technology precautionary principle. *Mercatus*. www.mercatus.org/system/files/Technopanics-by-Adam-Thierer_MN-Journal-Law-Science-Tech-Issue-14-1.pdf#page=71

Walton, D. (2012). Using argumentation schemes for argument extraction: A bottom up method. *Semantic Scholar*. https://pdfs.semanticscholar.org/da5a/fc5074b71463cda7cc35805781cbbd333a5e.pdf

Wolak, J., Evans, L., Nguyen, S., & Hines, D. A. (2012). Online predators: Myth versus reality. *Purdue*. www.purdue.edu/hhs/hdfs/fii/wp-content/uploads/2015/06/s_mafis03c03.pdf

8 Hardware

Consider this a place to start for those who are beginning this DPT journey. Fully recognizing that even by the time the ink is dry on these printed pages things will have changed regarding computers, tablets, and the like, let this serve as a general guide. You can certainly take this information to your trusted computer person and ask what the current version of these items are.

A key recommendation I offer is to have equipment designated for your office. To save money, many people purchase a tablet or laptop with the intention of it serving both professional and personal needs. This is a short-term gain but a long-term problem. It is important to keep your personal and professional equipment and data separate. I have found that to be true even with board games and other toys. The moment I take them home, something gets broken or crushed or lost, either in transit or otherwise. It is better to have a version of Candy Land at home and one at the office. It is better to have a tablet designated for the office. The division between personal and professional will be much easier to establish and maintain. What if the photographs you took of a client's sandtray should have been transferred to their file, but you were running late and did not get to it? That evening, your eight-year-old is playing a game on the tablet and runs across your work sandtray photos. It should not happen, but it does. Life can get hectic and it is best to set up a clean, separate system. Work items for work. Home items for home.

This leads to a conversation about professional investment. I was on a presentation panel with several esteemed colleagues in 2019, and one of them said something that struck me in a really profound manner. A psychologist himself, he was talking about mental health providers in general and how we go to school, we do our hours, we get licensed, we rent a space or work for an agency, we might spend some money to furnish our space with chairs, and so on, and then we are done. The expectation for many is that there will not be many more major expenses during our careers and, really, the initial ones for a therapist are not that enormous. If we think about an optometrist, for instance – the cost of the practice, the office, the equipment, the furnishings, the staff, and the like – are all amazingly high. They typically have to take out business loans to get started. I had never thought of it that way. I was really struck by these statements. It is true, therapists do not typically need any major materials to do the work. As play therapists, we have ourselves, our office, and our toys. I am certain that some people are thinking about the expense of the toys. I am not downplaying that at all. However, I am thinking more about the hundreds of thousands of dollars an optometrist spends on the eye exam equipment. Spending even $1,000 on toys and sandtray items is a lot, but not compared to the set-up costs of many other professions. I think it is more about mindset. If our mindset is one of expecting to not have a lot of start-up cost, then it is alarming when we have to spend larger amounts on our business.

As I digress for a moment or two, I would also like to say that I think a lot of play therapists do not charge enough money for their services. I know I went through my own difficulties in private practice regarding what to charge. What is the going rate? What does the market bear? What do I believe my services are worth? I think it is not only the insurance companies who question the worth of what play therapists do, but play therapists question it as well, overall. I do not mean in the moment when we have an amazing session and feel on top of the world, but in general. I think of my massage therapist, who is amazing, by the way. We are in a rural area and the going rate is probably lower than many other areas, but she charges $80. Her services are certainly worth more and my stress muscles are no picnic for her to deal with. However – not to disparage her in any way, or even the massage therapy field – why is there such a discrepancy?

This is not about the value of others' work; it is about play therapists and what we accept as being appropriate for the service we provide. If we compare the process of becoming a master's- or doctorate-level therapist, and a registered play therapist on top of that, to many other fields, how on earth is it acceptable to pay play therapists $20 or so per hour? I was recruited to work as a program director for a major mental health company a few years ago. It was to include clinical and supervisorial work. They offered me – a person with a doctorate and 20-plus years of experience at the time – $26 per hour. I did not accept the job. Eighty dollars for a massage and less than $30 for a mental health session? Even if we think about any other service industry: plumbing, electrical, or construction, the financial comparisons are confusing. Again, not disparaging anyone as I am grateful for their services, but what are we saying as an industry that we accept so little. What are we saying as a society? How does all of this contribute to the mental health crisis we are facing today? Do not even get me started on the Medicaid rate of reimbursement or other payor sources like low-income programs here in Colorado, which reimburse $31 per session for a doctorate level and even less for master's level. Thirty years ago, my post-doctoral fellowship charged clients $150 per session for my services and I was paid $8.24. That was *30 years* ago. I had graduated. I had more than 2,000 hours of experience by that time, but I was unlicensed, so: $8.24. The systems in place are not okay.

There are many aspects which are systemic and political in this equation and we are not going to solve them in these few paragraphs, but I also think it is time for play therapists to begin the process of realizing that what we do has great value. The changes we guide and facilitate, the heart and soul we offer, and the time, energy, and money we invest have great value. If we change the conversation from "I'm a play therapist" to "I. AM. A. PLAY. THERAPIST", perhaps some of the current systems will begin to shift.

Along these same lines of thought is the idea of investing in our businesses. Being self-employed helps quite a bit, or at least as a contracted person, so purchased items can be considered deducted expenses when tax time comes around. If you can find a way to accomplish this, it will help quite a bit. Consult your accountant and see what is possible. It is important to ask ourselves: what contributes to our overarching professional goals? For me, I want to offer my clients quality services (which means I strive for the 4 Cs from earlier in the book), prescriptive interventions which focus on speaking the client's language, and honoring their culture and continuously working toward accessibility for people with whatever different needs they might have. I have increased my yearly budget for investing in my business so that I can purchase for these items which support my business and professional goals.

I purchased an enormous, oversized lawn Connect Four game this year because I wanted my clients to have the option of experiencing a more active, outdoor play, and it was very pricey. However, I felt the experience was important for my clients and therefore I purchased it. Having increased my yearly budget, it was important to be smart about the purchase, search for the best price, and so on, and then make it happen. The equipment for DPT is a little overwhelming for some and pricey for most, but this is an investment in providing culture specific, accessible tools for your clientele. Sales can be found and with a little savvy and knowledge you can save some money here and there. One of the benefits of ever-changing technology is that people who are really technophiles upgrade their equipment often and frequently sell their "older" things for decent prices. I am not talking about therapists; I am talking about technophiles. We therapists keep things forever. I still have Playmobil from the 1990's in my office.

Hardware

The following sections of the chapter will present the hardware and software available as of this manuscript being written (late 2019). It is important to:

1) Do your homework and research the hardware you are interested in (cost, space, portability, uses, quantity, etc.).
2) Examine how it relates to the interventions and accessibility you want to provide.
3) What the long-term goal is for your business (i.e., invest in something more initially to have longer, run more complicated programs, etc., or get something "starter" knowing you will most likely replace it at some point in the not-too-distant future).
4) Evaluate what kind of programs (software) you want to use, which will inform the kind of hardware you will need.

5) Have long and short-term goals. Perhaps this year you invest in certain things and others the next. The goal could be that you want to have x, y, z in your office, along with training and supervision, by the year 20XX and each year you work toward that goal in a purposeful way.

Digital Cameras

Digital cameras have been replaced by our smartphones in most instances. I am still including them here because this advancement was pretty amazing for play therapists. Gone were the days of having to sketch out a scene of the sandtray or elsewhere. A quick, portable, downloadable, printable method of preserving the client's work was absolutely freeing and important. Diagrams and descriptions have always been less-than when it comes to explaining the client's work; whether it be to one's self, in one's notes, to a caregiver, or a supervisor, a picture can literally tell a thousand words in our work. The important shift was figuring out how to protect such information.

Most people have either taken the plunge into electronic health records or have at least looked into it knowing that it has to be done. External powers are forcing us in that direction, no matter how satisfying it might be for some to hand-write everything out. (I am speaking for myself here. I still use a paper and pencil yearly planner for my schedule. I also have one included in my HIPPA compliant electronic health records service, but I like the book infinitely more.) Remember, I am a technonecessist (Chapter 2) and I see the importance and necessity of technology in our lives and our work. As stated in Chapter 1, I resisted getting a cellphone, stating to numerous people that I "don't need to be that connected", and that makes me giggle now because I do; I do need and want to be that connected. I do not personally need the newest or latest or greatest or best. I need functional, with functional meaning it serves the intended purpose and needs.

Digital cameras still meet many of those needs, and the newer ones with Bluetooth or wireless capabilities for ease of information transfer are fantastic. If you do not want a separate phone for your office, a newer digital camera might meet your needs. You could also repurpose an old phone which no longer has service. If you connect the phone via Wi-Fi and/or use a cable (to download photos, etc.), this designated work phone could serve your purposes and be an at-work-only tool. Be sure to think through and set up as simple a process as possible for your data transfer and retention. If your process is complicated, chances are it will not work for the long term. I am a big fan of figuring out ways to work smarter and not harder, especially when it pertains to the things we are required to do for our client care and while we are trying to manage many other things simultaneously.

Smartphones

Nikola Tesla participated in an interview for Collier's magazine on January 30, 1926 (Kennedy, n.d.; Nguyen, 2019). I was not able to find the original source, that is, a copy of the 1926 magazine, but John B. Kennedy has posted a transcript of the interview and it was corroborated by the other author I have referenced for you. Amazingly, it appears that Tesla predicted the smartphone during this interview: "When wireless is perfectly applied the whole earth will be converted into a huge brain, which in fact it is, all things being particles of a real and rhythmic whole. We shall be able to communicate with one another instantly, irrespective of distance. Not only this, but through television and telephony we shall see and hear one another as perfectly as though we were face to face, despite intervening distances of thousands of miles; and the instruments through which we shall be able to do his will be amazingly simple compared with our present telephone. A man will be able to carry one in his vest pocket" (Kennedy, n.d., para. 9; Nguyen, 2019, para. 2). What an amazing forward thinker.

The smartphone has many capabilities that I certainly did not think were possible. I remember the first answering machines, two- and three-way calling, call waiting, pagers, and more. As mentioned earlier, I resisted getting a cellphone decades ago and did not have internet service until I felt I needed it to complete my dissertation more easily. After writing all that, you probably expect me to yell "get off my lawn" because I sound ancient, but I am not (yet). Technology has merely had a few decades long burst in ingenuity and growth and we are all working to figure it out. I just did not jump on the bandwagon quickly.

Within play therapy we can use our phones in place of cameras, as mentioned earlier; communicate; look up information through internet searches; run thousands of different applications; watch videos; and more. As long as your ethical responsibilities are taken care of regarding personal health information, confidentiality in general, and informed consent is in place, HIPAA-compliant use of a cellphone in session can be very powerful. The digital camera section mentioned the possibility of using an older cellphone, perhaps one you retained after an upgrade or purchased used, for a work phone. The benefit of this is not only keeping work and personal use separate, but that the apps, contacts, photos, and more can be specifically tailored to mental health and play therapy foci. Turning the phone's Wi-Fi on and off will allow the therapist to further control how the phone is used in session.

RxTxT

Parson et al. (2019), detailed the use of smartphones in therapy via therapeutic texting with clients (RxTxT), especially with adolescents, in the book *Integrating Technology into Modern Therapies*. They posit: "Human beings navigate the digital world concurrently with the physical world and therefore it is important for practitioners to consider if (and if so, when) it may be appropriate to integrate a range of digital communication aids" (Parson et al., 2019, p. 67). RxTxT can benefit the therapeutic relationship and alliance in general and also serve those in rural communities.

I have noticed that adolescent clients have a particularly difficult time retaining experiences, emotions, and introspections over the time between sessions.

The ability to text between sessions in order to share something, even a something as "simple" as a meme, can be very powerful in building and maintaining
the therapeutic relationship. It is important to set boundaries around it, however.
In my practice these boundaries and uses include:

1) The client can text any time and I may or may not be able to respond
    quickly, but if I am able to I will, even if to simply acknowledge receipt
    of their text. I do not have my phone set to indicate when my messages
    are "read" for this reason. They are not aware of when I have read the
    message based on phone notifications.
2) The purposes of texting between sessions include a) updating, b) sharing
    thoughts or experiences for discussion during the next session so they
    are not lost in between, c) enquiring about appointment days, time, and
    more. This is not a "therapy by text" situation and we will not be process-
    ing anything in ways we might in an in-person session.
3) The client should be aware that the texts are protected via my own phone
    privacy and password protection and professional software on my end,
    but that they have their own rules in their family about cellphone privacy.
    They also have friends, etc. who could be on their phone. It is important
    for them to be aware that text messages can be read and shared, and they
    must take that into consideration when texting in general and to the
    therapist. Some software programs require the client to log in to text the
    therapist, which is ideal. Even in that situation, parents may have the login
    information and read what they write. In other words, therapists can
    protect the personal health information and communications through
    professional service programs, but the client must be aware that the
    information on their end may or may not be secure. Parents should also
    be made aware of the process and potential pitfalls during the informed
    consent discussion and paperwork. The possibilities should improve as
    the software improves; however, the results have been very positive thus
    far and have even led to some much-needed safety checks on occasion.

The needs of our clients have changed, and mental health is struggling to figure
out what those needs are and how to appropriately meet them.

Tablets

In 1987, an early version of the tablet was born. The "Linus Write-Top" had a
green screen and a stylus. One could write on the screen with the stylus and the
computer would recognize the handwriting. Two years later came a product by
the Palm company called the GridPad. In 1993 Apple released the Newton Mes-
sagePad, which was a personal digital assistant, or PDA. Shortly thereafter quite
a few PDAs were launched, including the once famous PalmPilot (Bort, 2013).
    Fast forward a bit to the year 2000, when Bill Gates released a prototype
for the type of tablet we know and love today. A few more were released

in-between, and in 2010 Apple offered the first iPad (Bort, 2013). Since then numerous companies have released their versions and there have been many upgrades with different features, sizes, and easy to use functions. The process from clunky, bulky, difficult to use, and very limited units to the tablets of today has been a long journey.

The tablet has been a welcome tool in many different arenas and professions. Tablets can be used as portable way to collect information, payments, run programs, share data, and so much more. Environments include hospitals, retail, research, education, and more. Touch screens allow for a different way of interacting with the hardware and software. There is no longer an "triangle", as in the person, mouse, computer, now it is a dyad: the person and the tablet. Phones have this benefit as well, but the tablet has a much larger screen with a wider range of uses.

Cathy Malchiodi published a fantastic book in 2000 entitled *Art Therapy & Computer Technology: A Virtual Studio of Possibilities*. This book is certainly dated, but it demonstrates her amazing ability to use and envision how digital tools can offer new possibilities within art therapy. She stated, "If we view computer technology as an ally, art therapists have the potential to expand their work into a new world of possibilities" (p. 30). The reason I have placed mention of Malchiodi's work here in the tablet section is because she described the "interplay" between the client, therapist and the art image being created in a beautiful way. She was speaking about the use of computers in art therapy at the time since tablets as we know them were not in use then, but I think the concepts still apply here. She described the following: "The spatial separation between the mouse and the image being shaped offers new qualities to the three-way interplay between client, therapist, and image. The picture on the screen is equally accessible and visible to both therapist and client and there is far greater perceptual fluidity among the three participants" (p. 95). This applies to so many programs one can use with the tablet in session. The triad has been reduced with the advancement of technology to a dyad and the interplay and benefits of the special separation have been preserved.

iPads have been in my office for many years and have been used with great success. At this point my favorite is the iPad Pro, 12.9". I prefer iPads because of the predominate consistency in the use and functions from version to version. At times there are new things to learn – for example, how to turn it on or swipe away screens – but overall the consistency and standardization is a plus, so I do not have relearn everything each time I upgrade my tablet. The iPad Pro 12.9" is my favorite because of the screen size. The general public seemed to believe it was too big, as the recent focus has been more on the 10"- and 11"-sized versions. The 12.9" version allows for a larger workspace for art or sandtray work or to play a game together. If a therapist uses the iPad Mini, which is 7.9", the client can easily curl their body around the iPad and obscure the therapist's view. This is certainly informative, but it hinders the process and the connection.

A lot of people ask about the need for memory in their iPad. This is a tough thing to answer for people. I liken it to someone asking me how big of a piece of chocolate cake they should have. I am not sure how to answer that question either. Not too much, but not too little so that you run out too quickly. You need what is enough. That answer works for both questions but still does not tell us much. However, the more helpful answer is that there are a number of options. iPads come in 32 GB (gigabytes), 64 GB, 128 GB, 256 GB, 512 GB, and 1 TB (terabyte). The amount you will need depends on the programs you want to run and what you want to do with the iPad. If you want to record every session and not transfer the videos daily, you will need to go for the 1 TB option. If you want the iPad purely to look things up on the internet and run very simple programs, the 32 GB will most likely be sufficient. The questions are: 1) what kinds of programs do you want to run on the iPad (game apps, serious apps, or creating and projecting presentations from your iPad?), and 2) how often will you realistically transfer information from your iPad to your client files (electronic health records)? iPads cannot be upgraded after purchase, which means you cannot add memory later. If you do not have enough at some point, you will have to buy a new one or remove items from the iPad.

Another issue is that Apple launches new versions of the iPad periodically. This can be great with new features and capabilities, but it also means that the older versions will become obsolete at some point. The applications (apps) available in the AppStore (iTunes) have minimum requirements dictated by Apple. This means that if the app initially ran on a Generation 2 iPad, by the time the Air 2 model is out the app on the Generation 2 will most likely be unable to update. If the user wants to update the app, a new iPad will need to be purchased. So the dilemma is, how much memory (capacity) is enough to run what I want knowing that at some point I will have to upgrade my iPad anyway? Now this is not an every-year issue. I have been using my 64 GB iPad Pro for approximately 5-plus years at this point and it has not been deemed obsolete yet. This is just food for thought and it is important to be aware.

Many other companies produce tablets as well and some of them are amazing. The reason I focus on the iPad is because the processors (CPU, or core processing unit) in the iPads are consistent and made by the same company. Android-based tablets are made by so many different companies that the processors are not standard. Why does this matter, you might ask? The processor is the brains of the unit. It performs calculations and runs programs. The processor affects the experience you have using the tablet and the ease/smoothness of the program running. It is my belief that any digital tool used in a therapeutic setting should be as smooth as humanly possible. Glitches, or funky things that happen when using programs, will always be part of the process. They happen with every hardware and software platform. However, if there are things we can do to minimize these issues, I believe we should do them, as the effects can alter the therapeutic process. We desire a fun, engaging, immersive, highly motivating experience and subpar equipment can make that much more difficult.

Whether the tablet is an iPad or Android based tablet, choose based on the needs of your clientele, the therapeutic goals you have for the use of the tool, and what is compatible with your other systems. Look through the AppStore and GooglePlay and see what is available within both. Make informed decisions and you will feel better about moving forward with DPT.

I leave my tablet leaning against my bookshelf in my playroom. As with any other item in the room, I typically allow clients to choose the activity they would like to do during our session. At times I will take a more directive approach, particularly with clients who are stagnant, shut down, or do not "know how" to play (parentified, etc.). For these clients, I might suggest we play something on the tablet or other DPT item to see if they can be engaged with the gameplay. I have even engaged in some parallel play or even solo play and narrated my struggles in hopes they will come help me and therefore become engaged. These tactics have worked quite well.

One might imagine that the inclusion of digital items would result in clients never wanting to use anything else in the playroom, but that has overwhelmingly not been my experience. There are weeks in which the items do not get touched at all, just like any other item in the room. Things seem to be used in some cycle or schedule in which an item will not be touched for a long time and then every client pulls it out throughout the day, even though no one was aware that anyone had used it. Digital tools fall into the same patterns. When you introduce it as something new, almost everyone is enamored and then it wears off and it falls into the unspoken schedule along with everything else.

Gaming Consoles

Gaming consoles are units that hook up to a television screen or monitor and typically have controllers used for gameplay. The controllers can be wired (connected to the console by a cord) or wireless (powered by rechargeable batteries). The controllers can be the classic controllers with "X", "Y", "A", and "B" buttons to make a character move around, jump, battle, and so on, or they can be specialized into specific shapes including joysticks (i.e., for controlling an airplane) and steering wheels.

The first gaming console, the Magnavox Odyssey, was released in 1972. The games were very basic, and it had no CPU (see the tablet section). The year 1979 and the 1980's experienced a boost with the first Atari systems. There were some lulls in the console market, but the 1980's saw Sony and Sega continuing the development. In 1994 the PlayStation was born, and the in-home gaming console became a household staple for millions. In 2019, Xbox, PlayStation, and Nintendo continue to develop their hardware and available software and dominate the market (Njiri, 2016).

As discussed in the Video Game Genre chapter, a number of video game genres have great value in the mental health setting and particularly in DPT. The gaming console set up, however, takes up more space than many play therapists are willing to devote. Unless you already have a large screen monitor or television, the traditional gaming console might not be the best option for the playroom. If you do have the large screen or have decided to have a dedicated DPT room as some people do, then consoles have an enormous library of games available. The controllers can be customized with "skins", wraps, or decals for a fun look.

Handheld Consoles

This is a category I had not really considered for DPT until the release of the Nintendo Switch. This little game changer, pun intended, has been a fantastic addition to my playroom. With the joy con controllers on each side of a handheld screen, the console can be held by one person and played OR the joy cons can be removed, the screen propped up on a surface, and each person can have a controller. This is my preferred method of use for the Switch. If you have a large monitor or television in your office, the Switch can also be viewed through the larger screen.

The late 1970s were a time of great industry for many computer-driven companies. The first handheld console was released in 1979 by Microvision. Technical problems and a very limed supply of games led to the demise of the groundbreaking device. A few other consoles were released but it was not until 1989 with the birth of the first Game Boy that the industry experienced a resurge in popularity. Game Boy released many new advances over the years, such as Color and Advanced. Nintendo entered the race with the DS (Dual Screen) as well as PlayStation with the PSP (PlayStation Portable) units (Codex Gamicus, 2019).

These units may sound great for DPT initially, but until the Nintendo Switch was released with the removable joy con controllers, the same issue that was discussed earlier with the iPad Mini could easily occur. The unit is small and could easily be played in a way that excludes the therapist. Having the screen visible to both the client and the therapist, as Malchioldi described, allows for both people to be engaged and involved in the play. The removable joy cons of the Switch allow the screen to be seen by both and a controller is available for each player. Another fantastic byproduct of this design is that each controller provides different functions. If I have the controller that makes Link in the Legend of Zelda game look around, the other person has the ability to make him walk. If we do not communicate, Link will most likely fall off a cliff or walk into something dangerous. I have had to selectively mute clients who, because of their own high motivation to play the Legend of Zelda, talk to me for the first time during this type of play. Their desire to communicate a move or a direction was greater than their fear of speaking to me and therefore they spoke.

The Nintendo Switch is also by the bookshelf in my office and it experiences the same unspoken cycles of use. There are many titles to choose from and the same rules of vetting games prior to clinical use applies. One tip is that you might want to purchase your games through the Nintendo store. If you connect your Switch to Wi-Fi, you can access the store through the unit. When you purchase the game through this store you can load the game from the store to your Switch. If you buy the cartridges in a brick and mortar store you run the risk of losing them, or worse, having them be stolen. The cartridges are really small. Once the cartridges are lost, the game is unusable, as in, you need the cartridge to play the game. If you purchased it from the Nintendo store, there is nothing to lose and you an reload it onto any Switch once you have signed into your account. I discovered this the hard way.

Computers

The computer was born out of the need for efficiency. Punch cards, which were used in early computers, were designed by Joseph Marie Jaquard in 1801 to weave fabric designs automatically in a loom. In 1880 that punch card design was put to great use when the government needed a way to complete the census more quickly than was traditionally accomplished. A process which had previously taken seven years to complete was reduced to three using this punch card "computer" for the calculations. Beyond the construction of computers and the necessary parts, languages also needed to be invented and the size and cost had to be reduced dramatically. With enormous of advancements between 1880 and the computers we know now, computers are a marvel of science, math, and determination to meet the ever-growing needs and desires of human beings. I was surprised to discover that the first computer chip was created in 1958 and the first mouse in 1964. From computers that filled rooms 20x40 feet and included 18,000 vacuum tubes, to the smartphones that fit in our pockets, the advancements have been remarkable (Zimmerman, 2017).

Desktop computers may or may not have a place in DPT. By desktop I mean the traditional large unit where the processor and all the inner workings of the computer are housed and the monitor on a desk. The games available for the personal desktop computer are limited and the mouse use, at this point, is not optimal. When tablets and Nintendo Switches were not available, computers had more of a place. I never wanted a bulky computer and desk with the logistics of two chairs as a focal point in my office, so I steered away from the use. Perhaps you have had good results in this arena; I did not embark on this venture because of logistics and the new tools available at this point supersede my desire to test it out. The subtle tablet leaning up against my bookshelf is a very different visual experience than the desk with all the components in the playroom. I want the tools to be a part of the whole, not an "other" or a predominate focal point. These items are just another tool and should blend in as best they can with the other tools in the room.

Laptops certainly afford a different experience and logistical arrangement than desktops. Laptops (and tablets) are commonly used for psychometric testing at this time. A touchscreen laptop increases the involvement of the therapist and client as both can reach over and touch the screen to manipulate what they would like. A laptop is easily stored and presented as a part of the room. I do not have a desktop or laptop computer available to my clients. I feel the tablet, either of our phones, and/or the Nintendo Switch meet our needs at this time. Unless we are speaking about VR.

Virtual Reality, Augmented Reality, and Mixed Reality = Extended Reality

Extended reality includes the DPT tools that have me the most excited. I believe the immersion and expansion qualities of virtual reality will fill in many swiss-cheese type gaps that have existed in mental health treatment for well over one hundred years. The days of "try to imagine" and "let's paint a picture in your mind", while the therapist is unable to witness what is being created, and the unknowns about whether or not client grasps the process, are gone. With VR the scene can be entered, created, shared, experienced, and engaged while both the client and therapist can bear visual and emotional witness. The scope of possibilities with extended reality use within many fields, but particularly mental health, are in their infancy but growing quickly.

Stanley G. Weinbaum wrote *Pygmalion's Spectacles* in 1935. This was a science fiction story about man who used a pair of goggles to experience "a fictional world through holographics, smell, taste, and touch" (p. 5). Little did Weinbaum know that less than a century later these imaginings would be a reality. The equipment to date can provide each of these experiences except for taste. I am not sure taste will ever be an important feature, but the holographics, smell, and touch are all possibilities for inclusion. The smell feature is being used in such research labs as the University of Southern California with Dr. Skip Rizzo and his team, but not yet for the consumer.

Virtual Reality

Jaron Lanier coined the phrase "Virtual Reality", or VR, around 1985, with inspirational credit given the Susanne K. Langer (Virtual Reality Society, n.d.; Langer, 1955). The VR experience is immersive with a 360-degree view of video with computer generated content, real-world content, or a combination of both (Irvine, 2017). The use of virtual reality synthesizes many of the elements desired in mental health and reduces the separation between the machine and the user. This is a more direct, intuitive interaction with the technology than we have ever had before (Bricken & Byrne, 1993). Sensors are used to track hand, head, and body movements in natural ways which contributes to a sense of congruency and immersion (Maples-Keller et al., 2017).

The VR head-mounted display allows the user to engage multiple senses. When a user is in a world and high on a cliff, the autonomic system is activated and the heart rate will increase, the sinking-stomach feeling will happen, and other fear and arousal responses will happen. These responses happen instinctually when a person senses a dangerous environment and they happen in VR because the mind believes the scenario is real due to the immersive features of the programs.

Augmented Reality

Augmented reality (AR) is computer-generated content shown as an overlay of the physical world environment. The computer-generated content does not interact with the environment; rather, it appears as though it is a layer over the real-world material, thus it is referred to as an overlay. For instance, in AR, if the computer-generated content was a rabbit, the screen would appear to look exactly as though one was using a camera feature, but a rabbit would appear in the screen. In another use, AR programs can be used to translate information from one language to another (Irvine, 2017). In this scenario, the camera of a smartphone or tablet is held over the text and the program translates the text and displays the translation as an overlay on top of the image in the camera.

Mixed Reality (MR)

Mixed reality utilizes occlusion, or the ability for the computer-generated objects to interact with the environment (Irvine, 2017). Returning to the example of the computer-generated rabbit: in MR the rabbit could hop behind a chair or under a table, whereas in AR the rabbit would be superimposed upon the table which exists in the real world. Occlusion allows for a higher level of interactivity between the computer-generated object and the physical real-world environment. When thinking about MR and AR, Irvine offers the following: "The general distinction is: all MR is AR, but not all AR is MR. AR is a composite. MR is interactive" (Irvine, 2017, p. 12). According to Dudley (2018), some predict that AR and MR are possibly more useful as the user does not need to be "sealed off in self-contained artificial environments" (p. 6); however, one can also argue that it is exactly the sealed off environment of VR which allows for the immersion and flow necessary to elicit a therapeutic process.

The VR headset is called a "head-mounted display", or HMD unit. Historically these units have been bulky, uncomfortable, and expensive (Virtual Reality Society, n.d.; Brooks, 1999; Mandal, 2013). A burst of activity regarding VR began in the 1960's and fizzled out by the late 1990's. The fizzle has been attributed to many factors with expensive, cumbersome, uncomfortable gear; a lack of available software; and a lack of true immersion leading the list (Dudley, 2018). Luckily, an 18-year-old named Palmer Luckey essentially dusted off these somewhat forgotten ideas and created a new type of HMD in his garage (Dudley, 2018; Rubin, 2014). Whereas VR was previously limited to academic, research, and industry laboratories with enormous machines, Luckey created a system for commercial use using a personal computer. Luckey launched a Kickstarter campaign to fund his development and production and soon Mark Zuckerberg purchased his start-up company for over $2 billion (Dudley, 2018). VR creation and sales quickly became an explosive market with many companies rushing to create HMDs for everyday use.

Rather than present a few of the current VR HMD units in historical order, these will be presented in terms of quality and experience. It is important to remember that some features of each, especially in a clinical setting, will matter greatly and price should not be the only factor. Overall, mental health clinicians will want to attend to factors such as depicted in Table 8.1.

Table 8.1 Virtual Reality Hardware Selection Factors

Hardware Factor	Description
System set-up logistics	What is the required space needed for the chosen system? How will the system affect the visual aesthetics in the office? Will this be permanently mounted, or will it need to be mobile?
Complexity of available software	Currently the tethered units can run more complicated programs; does the HMD support the level of software desired?
Computer-dependent or self-contained unit	Do the HMD and controllers need a computer? A computer-dependent or tethered HMD can be expanded upon and will run more complex programs. A self-contained unit cannot be expanded.
Wireless or wired headset	Is the HMD tethered to the computer or not? The answer to this is not as simple as it may seem. A wireless headset has a freer range of motion; however, it needs to be plugged in and charged frequently. A wired headset allows a more complex and detailed experience and does not need to be charged. Wireless adaptors for tethered headsets are also available.
Sensors or no sensors mounted in the room	Do sensor boxes need to be mounted in the room? Is that possible in the setting? Sensor boxes track the movements of the HMD and controller handsets. Sensors contribute to field of vision and range of motion, which will affect the experience of the user.
Level of haptics	Does the set have one controller or two? Level of haptics available will vary depending on the unit. Haptics contribute to immersion.
Dexterity needed to use the controller	What is the learning curve for the use of the controller? For the most part, the learning curve is very short even with more complex controllers. The movements are reinforced through use. A more complex controller allows for more interaction with the virtual world. A less complex controller requires less dexterity and limits the interaction within the world.

Basically, a clinician will want to attend to the following: what do you want it to do, what purpose will the use of VR serve clinically, and does the chosen unit meet those needs or not? Clinical use of VR will need to be as problem-free an experience as possible to achieve the desired therapeutic goals. As a general rule, at this time in development, the higher end, computer-run, tethered VR setups have more power for graphics, memory, and speed, which equate to a more rich, smooth running, complex experience. The self-contained/all-in-one units, despite having made significant leaps in development, are limited in these ways. This is demonstrated by even a relatively simple relaxation program such as *NatureTreks* offering a truncated version of their program in the self-contained units.

The clinical purpose of the VR use will and should drive the chosen device(s). If the HMD is chosen, for instance, for use as a mobile unit to run specific programs for home visits or within a hospital setting, then a wireless self-contained system would be worth the lessened ability to run more complex programs. However, if the unit is to be mounted and stable in one location and the programs desired are more complex, and therefore often more immersive with more options within the play, then a higher end, computer dependent HMD would be warranted.

The HTC Vive and Oculus Rift S are computer-dependent, tethered-headset, two-controller, sensor-dependent VR units. The primary benefit of this type of unit is the ability to run more complex programs and experience an increased level of interactivity and immersion. For both, the HMD itself has a higher level of adjustability, particularly for people who wear glasses, and for many this increased customization and comfort leads to a more integrated experience. The headset feels like less of an "other" and more an extension of the head. Cleanable face shields are available for hygienic purposes.

The Vive and Rift S HMDs will both run the most complex software programs. An exploration of the online stores "Steam", "Viveport", or "Oculus" will reveal that many programs are designed specifically for use on certain HMD systems. Some developers have programmed software for multiple systems, and some have not for a multitude of reasons. Each system has their own development parameters and requirements and some programs work best on specific systems.

The Vive and Rift S both have the capacity for the clinician to either enter into the VR program with the client through another HMD (software permitting) or to watch the view on the computer screen. Once the items are downloaded onto the computer, internet connection is not needed unless a program specifically has an online component, such as team play with others outside of the session room. Since the client view can be watched by the therapist, the interactivity is established verbally by the narration of the process by the client, therapist, or both.

Quite recently (June 2019), Oculus has released the Oculus Quest in the United States. This HMD is an advancement on the Oculus Go, which included one controller and very limited abilities, both in function and available software. The newer Quest includes some much-needed improvements and is worth the increased cost as compared to the Go.

The Quest includes two controllers which run on AA batteries, a headset with a greater ability for adjustment than the Go (however, not as solid a fit as the Vive or Rift S), and a processor equivalent to some older Android-based smartphones. Truncated versions of some more complex software are available for the Quest and the experience is positive overall. A recent Oculus beta update released a hand tracking feature, so the user does not have to have controllers. This is amazing, but right now it needs some work before it is session ready.

A clinician can pair two Quest headsets for use in family sessions or to include the therapist (software dependent feature and additional purchases might be necessary) or the images can be "cast" to a device such as a smartphone or monitor and the view of the user can be seen (requires internet connection). The casting feature can be unreliable at this time, which leaves the clinician without a view of what the client is doing, seeing, or experiencing.

When evaluated for clinical use, this untethered VR system has a lot going for it in portability and ease of setup but lacks in the ability to run more complex programs, which can be important in a mental health setting. Additionally, if the client is not able to initiate programs or navigate the library of options on their own, the use of the Quest becomes more difficult. When the HMD is used by one person and passed to another, the system closes. There is a sensor you can cover so this does not happen, but it is a flaw in the system. Having attended Oculus 6, their annual meeting to launch and showcase products, this problem was discussed and hopefully they will have a solution soon.

A consideration for clinicians is whether or not the purchased system has staying power. Does the system have the capacity to run the desired types of software? Will the system last over a significant portion of time or will it need to be upgraded frequently to keep up with the demands and abilities of the technology?

This author prefers the Vive as the clinical mainstay in the office at this point in hardware development. Once the computer is in place, the sensors are simple to mount, the controller handsets are easy to use, the HMD is simple to adjust, and it can run the most complex programs of the day. The computer does not require a desk and can be tucked away. Having used this same unit for three years, it has not needed any hardware updates or equipment changes. However, having purchased the Oculus Odessey, Go, and Quest for clinical-use evaluation, the Odessey and Go were quickly replaced by the Quest, equaling substantially more money spent on HMDs and controllers than the initial Vive purchase. The untethered, all-in-one headset is quite attractive, and more advancements will certainly happen, however, at this point, clients have routinely started sessions using the Quest and then requested the use of the Vive as their perception of the limitations is expressed. As more clinically specific programs become available, such as social skills training programs or those for PTSD, a more complex system will be required to allow the clinical aspects to be explored. To clarify earlier statements regarding a computer in the office, my VR set up is not in my playroom.

VR Computer

The computer needed for a virtual reality system is equivalent to a high-end gaming computer whether it is a desktop-type tower unit or a laptop. There is a need for a quality processor (CPU), video card, and memory (RAM). Once you have decided which type of tethered headset you would like to purchase it would be best to refer to the user's manual or minimum computer specifications listed on their website to begin the process of buying a computer. This is certainly a significant investment; however, the return is the increased power. The increased power equals a more immersive experience and the more immersive experience equals a mind which is fully engaged in the task at hand.

This parts list is for your reference regarding building the VR computer. If possible, it is best to *not* buy a pre-made computer. You can buy the parts separately and have a specialist put it together for you. The pre-made computers will rarely have the combination of features you will need.

Please consult your trusted computer specialist as these items might be outdated tomorrow. An SSD drive that is top of the line as of this list creation might be replaced by another more powerful drive tomorrow. You do not have to know what the SSD drive is, rather understand that the advancements happen quickly, and you might be able to get something more powerful than what is listed here but going below these requirements is not advised.

Parts List

- Processor
  - Intel I7–9700
  - AMD Ryzen 7 2700X
- Motherboard
  - Reliable brand such as ASUS
  - 2x NVME slots
  - 4x RAM slots
  - ATX form factor
  - Enough USB (3+) slots for VR hardware
- Case
  - ATX
  - Mid-tower or larger
- SSD
  - Using multiple SSDs is best if you will be recording the VR use
  - Operating system and programs, 500+ GB NVME with >3000 MB/sec read and >2000 MB/sec
  - Recording drive, mid speed 1 TB NVME
- Storage and archiving
  - 2+ TB, 7200 rpm drive
- RAM
  - 4 x 8 GB for 32 GB total
  - 2 x 8 GB for 16 GB to save money up front and expand later
  - Speed to utilize full potential of processor

- Video card
  - ○ Nvidia GTX2080 from a reputable brand
- Cooling
  - ○ Corsair liquid cooler for CPU
- Operating system
  - ○ Windows 10

Conclusion

The hardware provides the power and mechanism to run your chosen software. Making sure you have some basic knowledge in this area will enhance your DPT experiences. The software will only be as good as your hardware allows. Different devices provide different interactive experience for the user, the therapist, and the dyad of both. Continuing the learn about the devices to come in the future will allow for adaptation and further inclusion as the digital play therapist deems therapeutic and appropriate.

References

Bort, J. (2013, June 2). The history of the tablet, an idea Steve Jobs stole and turned into a game-changer. *Business Insider*. www.businessinsider.com/history-of-the-tablet-2013-5

Bricken, M., & Byrne, C. M. (1993). Summer students in virtual reality: A pilot study on educational applications of virtual reality technology. In A. Wexelblat (Ed.), *Virtual reality applications and explorations*. Cambridge, MA: Academic Press Professional.

Brooks, F. P., Jr. (1999, November/December). What's real about virtual reality? *Computer Graphics and Applications Special Report*. www.cs.unc.edu/%7Ebrooks/WhatsReal.pdf

Codex Gamicus (2019, November 4). The history of handheld game consoles. *Fandom*. https://gamicus.gamepedia.com/History_of_handheld_game_consoles

Dudley, D. (2018, December). Virtual reality used to combat isolation and improve health. *AARP Magazine*. www.aarp.org/home-family/personal-technology/info-2018/vr-explained.html

Irvine, K. (2017). *XR: VR, AR, MR: What's the difference?* www.viget.com/articles/xr-vr-ar-mr-whats-the-difference/

Kennedy, J. B. (n.d.). When woman is boss. *Twenty-First Century Books*. www.tfcbooks.com/tesla/1926-01-30.htm

Langer, S.K. (1955). *Feeling and form: A theory of art*. Scribner.

Malchiodi, C. A. (2000). *Art therapy & computer technology: A virtual studio of possibilities*. Jessica Kingsley.

Mandal, S. (2013). Brief introduction of virtual reality & its challenges. *International Journal of Scientific & Engineering Research, 4*(4), 304–309. www.ijser.org/researchpaper/Brief-Introduction-of-Virtual-Reality-its-Challenges.pdf

Maples-Keller, J. L., Bunnell, B. E., Kim, S. J., & Rothbaum, B. O. (2017). The use of virtual reality technology in the treatment of anxiety and other psychiatric disorders. *Harvard Review of Psychiatry, 25*(3), 103–113.

Nguyen, T. (2019, June 25). A brief history of smartphones. *Thoughtco.* www.thoughtco.com/history-of-smartphones-4096585

Njiri, M. (2016, February 15). The history of gaming consoles. *Techinfographics.* https://techinfographics.com/the-history-of-gaming-consoles/

Parson, J., Renshaw, K., & Hurt, A. (2019). RxTxT: Therapeutic texting. In J. Stone (Ed.), *Integrating technology into modern therapies* (pp. 64–79). Abingdon, UK: Routledge.

Rubin, P. (2014). *The inside story of Oculus Rift and how virtual reality became reality.* www.wired.com/2014/05/oculus-rift-4/

Virtual Reality Society (n.d.). *The history of virtual reality.* www.vrs.org.uk/virtual-reality/history.html

Weinbaum, S. G. (1935). *Pygmalion's spectacles.* S.l.: Project Gutenberg.

Zimmerman, K. A. (2017, September 7). History of computers: A brief timeline. *Livescience.* www.livescience.com/20718-computer-history.html

9 Software

Having reviewed a number of the types of hardware available, our focus turns to the software. Software includes many types of computer programs which "allow a computer to do a multitude of things" (typesof, n.d., para. 1). Think of the hardware as the limbic system of the brain and the software as the frontal lobe. Without the software, the hardware would not be able to execute complex functions.

There are many different types of software including operational and application. A quick description of these two are provided. There are many other types, but further research into the others reveal that they do not directly apply to our purposes. Most of this is over my head and honestly it does not really matter for our focus. We want to use a program and have it work properly. Events such as "glitches" affect us more than anything to do with the types of software.

The latter part of the chapter offers lists of programs and apps which have been used and recommended by several play therapists. An overview of a few programs is provided and organized into different levels of sophistication. This will be an ever-changing list depending on what is available and released, what hardware you acquire, your knowledge of DPT, and the needs of your clients.

Operational Software

The operational software includes drivers (like instruction manuals for the hardware but "spoken" to the hardware internally) and utility programs. This type of software "controls and manages the hardware and other software" on your device (Fisher, 2019, para. 1) and "manages and allocates memory space" (Amuno, 2019, para. 9). Windows, Linux, Android, and Mac OS (operating system) programs fit into this category. Operational software is typically device specific and application software will frequently specify which operating system in necessary for use.

Application Software

Application software primarily includes spreadsheets, databases, and word processing. These programs are often sold in a bundle called an application suite to meet a variety of needs, such as the Microsoft Office 365 bundle. These programs have features which complement and interact with each other. Enterprise and enterprise infrastructure software supports and assists companies with data flow and distribution. These are primarily used with really big businesses. Educational software is created specifically for students in academic settings or individually (Techopedia, n.d.).

Issues That Can Happen

Any hardware and software can have unintended issues. Sometimes these can be relatively easily identified, such as a low battery or lack of memory available in the device. Other times it has to do with "bugs" or updates or other malfunctions. We are actually venturing back into the hardware category a bit, but they play off each other and are not mutually exclusive. The possible issues one can have can relate to the hardware, software, and/or the interplay between them. These items listed can affect your experience of the software chosen. The best remedy is to look at the minimum requirements listed either on the software cartridge's box, the website, or even within the AppStore or GooglePlay Store for more information.

Battery Life

Keeping your device's battery charged is very important in a therapeutic setting. Not only will the client who wants to use the tablet or Nintendo Switch be disappointed when they find that it will not turn on, but the session is then full of lost opportunities. The best-case scenario is to have a system for plugging these items in, but not for 24 hours per day. The more devices that offer wireless charging, the easier this will be for the mental health setting, as you can just place the unit on the charge pad and move on with your day.

Lack of Memory

Nerds on Call can help us understand memory a bit more. They state "The memory is known as RAM. It is a part of your computer that it uses while it's powered on. Your computer stores everything that it's thinking about in RAM. If you're running a program, it's in RAM. If you're looking at a webpage, it's in RAM. RAM contains everything that's currently going on with your computer. And when RAM is in a computer that isn't powered, the RAM is empty. It's just waiting for something to think about. The more memory your computer has, the more it's able to think about at the same time. More RAM allows you to use more complex programs and more of them" (Callnerds, 2019, para. 2). For therapists it can be helpful to think of a device's memory in terms of working memory, as discussed in psychometrics and the like.

The memory is often a fixed amount for devices other than computers. In most cases the RAM is not upgradeable and if you have an older unit that is a bit tired and sluggish, it might be the lack of RAM. For instance, if you purchased a first-generation iPad you received a unit with 256 MB of ram. The newest models of iPad come with 2 GB or more, depending on the model.

Lack of Available Memory

When your device becomes sluggish it is important to shut down any programs you are not currently using. This can make more of your unit's memory available to the task at hand. You can also remove programs you are not using; however, this often becomes a "fun" game of delete-install-delete again. This brings us back to the how much is too much and how much is enough conversation from the hardware chapter. The more complex and visually stimulating programs become, the more memory the programs will use.

Storage

Storage is the device's equivalent of a closet. It can hold what it can hold and no more. Nerds on Call helps us out again with an explanation: "Storage refers to long-term storage. Everything that your computer knows, but isn't thinking about, is in storage, written on the Hard Disk Drive (HDD). This is a permanent type of storage: hard drives can be unplugged and contain the same information as when they're plugged in or turned on. Nothing actually gets changed on the hard drive: it gets pulled off the hard drive, into RAM/Memory. While it's in memory, you as the user can change it. When you save the information, it gets sent back to the hard drive storage in a different version. More hard drive storage allows you to store more things on your computer. However, it rarely affects your computer's performance. A computer with 1 gigabyte of RAM will work at the same speed whether it has 2 gigabytes of storage or 2000 gigabytes" (Callnerds, 2019, para. 4).

Processor

The processor was discussed a bit in the hardware section. It is the brain of the computer, the CPU, otherwise known as the "chip". The CPU "takes instructions from a program or application and performs a calculation. This process can be broken down into three key stages: Fetch, decode, and execute. A CPU fetches the instruction from a system's RAM, then it decodes what the instruction actually is, before it is executed by the relevant parts of the CPU" (Martindale, 2020, para 6). Older, less-powerful processors have difficulties running newer programs.

Graphics

Graphics cards (also called video cards) can be something to think about in computer units. Most other devices have these decisions premade and decided by the manufacturer. The graphics card renders the visuals seen; the more realistic, complex, and often visually pleasing a scene, the more work the graphics card is doing. Think of a lower-level card as similar to creating artwork with crayons and a higher-level card as more similar to oil paints. Both of them are fine enough, but the visual experience is different. A software program might not run, or might not run properly, if the graphics card is not powerful enough.

Programming/Development Bugs and Glitches

This section is a lot more complex and intricate than our needs dictate; however, there are a few important concepts you might benefit from knowing. Program and app software are developed in some type of platform system. Additionally, the company who distributes the software has some type of platform system. On top of that, the hardware has some mechanism for updates to their own system. Sometimes these different systems are compatible, and they work well together. Other times they do not. "Bugs" can happen when changes happen anywhere along the road with the multiple systems or when there is a problem in the source code (the writing of the software).

Glitches happen when information is not being processed properly by the CPU, the brain of the computer. Sometimes these glitches are transient, and it can be hard to discover what happened. The common recommendation to "reboot" (turn off the device and turn it back on or close the program and restart it) often works well as it resets the unit. If the problem persists, look for an update in the software. The company may be aware of it and has already fixed the issue or is working on it. If you do not find an update you can contact the company and let them know of your concern. Some larger companies have forums (people who use the same program post tips and concerns there) where information can be found and shared. At times a quick search of the issue can also yield helpful information.

Spontaneous, undesired quitting can happen when any of these systems have a problem. The best thing to do in the moment is to not panic. Moderate your response to what is appropriate for the client and the situation. Be sure to save periodically while using a program so if it quits, all is not lost. Digital natives understand the possibility of a program quitting unexpectedly; however, the hope is to avoid it or the negative impacts as much as possible, particularly in the therapeutic setting.

Be Prepared

Overall, the digital play therapist will be well prepared in having their devices charged and ready to use, and understanding the need for sufficient memory, storage, processors, and graphics. If a program is not running properly, start with the basics and close down unnecessary programs which drain that working memory. Reboot your device from time to time to give it a reset. Once you have your setup you will not need to focus on any of these things as you will have systems in place. When anything does happen, have fail-safes thought through to save work as much as possible and moderate your own response to pair with the dynamic.

Apps and Programs

The list of apps and programs in Table 9.1 is a mere introduction to the options available for your review. The items listed are ones that play therapists have used successfully in session. A few of these are further described later in the chapter to give you some ideas regarding what is available. They are separated into three sections: simple, medium, and more. Simple refers a very minimal amount of technological skill needed to use the software. The medium designation indicates a higher but not advanced level of skill, knowledge, and comfort with the use of apps and programs. These items are still relatively simple. The

Table 9.1 Sample Beginner Apps (Stone et al., 2019)

Apps:	Agar.io
Best Behavior	Breathe 2 Relax
Bubbles	Calm
Castle Story (Farm Story, all this genre)	Chicken Scream
Clash Royale	Crack and Break It
Dumb Ways to Die	Finger Fights
Fingle	Felt Board
Fluid	Fluidity
Hidden Folks	Instant Heart Rate
June's Journey	Memorise
Moving Child	My PlayHome
Plants v Zombies 1	Pictorial
Puppet Pals	Red Hands
Sand Draw	Sesame Street Breathe
Snap's Stories	Storybird
Thumb War	Touch and Learn Emotions
Virtual Sandtray (Including the AutPlay expansion pack)	Zones of Regulation
Virtual Reality:	TheBlu
NatureTreks	Beat Saber
Virtual Sandtray	Tilt Brush
Bogo	Job Simulator
Vacation Simulator	Minecraft
Wander	Google Earth
Bait	First Steps
Oculus First Contact	Richie's Plank Experience (intense, but useful in certain cases, determine carefully)

more category is yet one step above medium but is by no means highly complicated. It is important to remember that these all have either tutorials, videos, or
classes available regarding their use.[1] You are not alone in process of learning
how to integrate these tools into your play therapy work.

Simple

Bubbles

Bubbles, by Hog Bay Software, is a very simple and satisfying app. Everywhere
you touch on the screen a bubble will appear and when you touch the bubble it
will pop. There are sound effects of a popping noise when you touch them. If
you rotate your phone or tablet you can make the bubble movements speed up
or slow down. You can draw letters, fling the bubbles about, or just create them
and pop them as you please.

Fluid

This app by Nebulus Design is another simple yet satisfying app. As you touch
the screen a colorful fluid moves across it. The colors and level of light change
every time you touch the screen. The effect reminds me a bit of the aurora
borealis, or northern lights.

Sand Draw

There are numerous sand draw apps and it might be best to look at them and
decide which one you want. Some of them are beach-themed and have waves that
remove your sand drawings when you shake your device. Other versions have
different sands to choose from and preset backgrounds to accent the drawing.

Breathe2Relax

Breathe2Relax guides the user through breathing exercises and provides information about the effect of stress on the body. New updates allow the app to be
connected to an Apple Watch. This app was created by the National Institute of
Telehealth and Technology.

Calm

Calm, by Calm.com, is a visual and auditory experience. There are settings to
assist with breathing, sleeping, meditating, and music. They have specific programs such as: Calm Kids, Calm Masterclass, Calm Body, breathing exercises,
and a variety of sounds and scenes to choose from. This app has a free version
and a premium version. The good news for therapists is that they will give you
the premium version for free if you apply.

Instant Heart Rate

This app by Azumio provides heart rate information in ten seconds. This is a simple way to provide limited biofeedback information. Graphs and charts of heartrates are available. This might be best to have a client download onto their own device, so the information is only theirs. You cannot make an infinite number of accounts within the app and even if you do not enter any identifying information, it could become difficult to navigate.

theBlu

theBlu is a VR program created by Wevr. I like to start people with this program because there is no need to use the controllers. I can start the program for the client from my computer and help them put on the HMD and the controllers into their hands. I start people sitting down and they can choose to stand up after they have acclimated to the process. The controllers are not necessary; however, the haptic (vibration feeling in the controllers tricks your mind into thinking you have touched something) response in the controllers is activated when you touch a fish or sea anemone and it is a fun experience for most. There are three scenes: underwater with turtles, fish, manta rays, and jellyfish; a sunken ship where a whale comes close, looks at you and swims off; and a deep underwater scene with lighted fish and more. This program is peaceful and visually gorgeous.

Wander/Google Earth

Wander (Oculus) and Google Earth (Google) are similar programs that are available on different systems. The basic premise is that you can type in any address or famous location and the program will "take" you there. You can go up and down streets, over some formations, and explore familiar or unfamiliar territory. You cannot venture into private property or into someone's house, and so on. There are so many possibilities for this program in mental health settings. Initially it is just fun to see a house one used to live in or a school one attended, but if you think about people who have moved from locations they miss (i.e., children in foster care, people who have moved frequently, seniors, etc.), who have never been able to travel to places they had hoped (especially seniors), or who would even like to show the therapist the house they currently live in or a landmark nearby, this program could have infinite uses. Since it is in VR, it feels like you are really there, heading down the street or up the hill or looking at the Eiffel Tower.

Medium

Storybird

This fun app provides scenes, environments, and characters for the user to create a variety of stories. It was created by the developer Magikid. The author can write a graphic novel or an illustrated poem, it is up to them. This is a valuable tool as an in-session activity, singularly created, co-created, or as a take-home exercise. Stories can be saved, printed, shared, and even published if so desired.

June's Journey

Produced by Wooga, this hidden-objects-type game has some great aspects and a potential drawback. This game is great for the part-to-whole attention to detail needs that some clients have. The scenes are full of items to distract one from finding the hidden objects which are revealed as the play progresses. Multiple levels and peripheral components keep the play enticing. The energy provided to play the levels is limited so the time taken to play the game will be limited as well. The potential drawback is the storyline. For some clients I tap the screen and skip through the storyline, as it focuses on a family's 1920-era family secret and intrigue. The scenes are cartoon and are predominantly benign, but at times there are such items as a handkerchief with a blood stain or a cartoon drawing of a person on the floor. With the strong recommendation to play all games yourself in advance of the use in therapy, you can better determine which clients would be best to use this game in session. If you desire a part-to-whole, attention to detail game experience, there are others to choose from.

Nature Treks VR

Nature Treks by the developer GreenerGames is fantastic. This virtual reality experience is a mix of simplicity with interaction. Depending on the virtual reality system used, the program will have more or less to offer. The basic premise is that the person in the HMD is presented with a number of environment panels to choose from. Once chosen, the environment loads in a 360-degree view. The user can move around in the world, move close to the trees, rocks, flowers, animals, buildings, and water features. The headset provides corresponding sounds to deepen the immersion. The interactive features include orbs which can be activated to customize the area, that is, rock, tree, flower placement, lighting changes, butterflies in flight, and more.

Virtual Sandtray App and VR Programs

The Virtual Sandtray tablet and virtual reality programs are designed for in-session use. The purpose is fundamentally to provide access to the tried-and-true process of sandtray therapy for people with whom and in place where the traditional process is not possible. Additionally, this professional program allows clients to create trays that are not possible in the traditional process. Each client has their own secure login within the therapist's tablet/account only (meaning they cannot log into their account elsewhere) and trays can be saved for future use. Supervision and trainings can be held in person or by distance with an increased ability to have others explore the created tray. Privacy and confidentiality measures have been painstakingly included.

The VR program allows the client to have an even further expanded experience of the sandtray process. In addition to the creation of worlds with trees, houses, people, animals, fences, dragons, fire, special effects, and more (there are currently more than 9,000 3D models available), the client can now enter and interact with their world if they choose. The VR user can be in what is called "God mode" (not my term) where the person is looking down on the world or can be down on the sand moving around in the world. This immersive experience allows the client to create scenarios that will benefit greatly from the additional feature of being able to feel you are personally interacting with the people, animals, or structures in place.

Zones of Regulation

Created by Selosoft, this app is sold separately or part of a bundle with another program called Exploring Emotions. Based on the Zones of Regulation by Leah Kuypers, the Zones of Regulation app helps the user to categorize feelings and use tools to develop awareness and coping skills. This app may be best utilized if loaded onto the client's own device, if possible.

Bogo VR

Bogo is a pet simulator program created by Oculus. This virtual pet alien has big eyes and a cute little body that changes colors as he advances. This program is quite engaging and fun for all ages. The entire program can be completed within a session if desired. There are minigames within the program that complement the pet care given and keep the user engaged and active. The user progressively figures out what Bogo's needs are and works to meet them for in game reinforcements, including Bogo rolling over onto his back for belly rubs.

Chicken Scream

By Perfect Tap Games, Chicken Scream is a simple game where the main character, a chicken, is controlled by your voice. The more noise made, the more the chicken runs or jumps. The less noise is made, the more slowly the chicken moves. The chicken navigates different levels and tries to avoid water and other obstacles. With a focus on learning how to self-regulate and about cause and effect, this game is easy, interactive, and fun.

Puppet Pals 2

This app by Polished Play, LLC, allows the user to create their own puppet show with a number of characters and scenes to choose from. A video of the puppet show can be created, saved, and shared if desired. You can make custom puppets with your own photos or backgrounds using your own space. This app is simple yet fantastic for telling your own story.

More

Plants vs. Zombies

This game has long been a go-to game in my sessions. Offered by Electronic Arts, this game provides many metaphors. The original version of the game is my preferred version for in session use, but you can certainly explore the subsequent versions. I like the first version because it is simple. The premise is that you are working to protect your house from the invading zombies by choosing particular tools to ward them off. The zombies are cartoonish and cute, not gory. Each has a particular skill set as do the plants you place to fight them off. To play together, I often have one person collect the suns (the in-game currency) and the other plant the plants for protection. What does one need to keep themselves safe? With 50 levels and a whole host of minigames, including a garden to nurture, this game is engaging and fun. I even taught a class to a room full of play therapists in Denmark once and everyone was loving this game.

Job and Vacation Simulator VR

These two games are quite similar in premise. Both by Owlchemy developers, these games feature bots who speak to the player and guide them through the gameplay. Job simulator allows the player to become a worker in four possible vocations: cook, auto mechanic, store clerk, and office worker. The player can complete tasks as they are given or explore the scene on their own. Bottles can be opened and poured out, food can be "eaten", copies can be made, cars can be painted, and so much more. Vacation Simulator has the same gameplay mechanics and graphics. The bots guide the player through the three vacation locations: mountain, beach, forest, and ultimately the resort. The player customizes an avatar with skin, hair, and eye color, clothing, and accessories. These are super fun games and I recommend getting them both.

Beat Saber

Beat Saber sounded so strange to me when my children first told me about it. Created by Beat Games, this movement, action, and focus driven coordination game is quite engaging. Initially the game starts out simple with blue and red cubes which move toward the player while coordinated with music. The player has a corresponding colored light saber in each hand and moves the light sabers to slice the cubes. The gameplay can be customized in ways that work well in therapy, such as selecting the speed of the cubes and music, choosing the no-fail option, or removing some of the more advanced obstacles like bombs (which are to be avoided and not sliced but there is no explosion). This game is great for in session and your own personal workout.

Legend of Zelda, Breath of the Wild (BOW)

This game is available for a number of Nintendo devices and my favorite is to use the Nintendo Switch within session. An installment in a long-standing franchise, this game focuses on the main hero character, Link, and his adventures to save the land of Hyrule. His mission is to find resources, protect himself in battles, and complete quests. With each player holding a joy con as described in the Hardware chapter, Zelda BOW activates many in-session skills, tendencies, and techniques that a therapist would want and need to work with. A fun tip my clients and I have discovered is that you can hold a chicken in the game and jump off a cliff or roof and the chicken will act as a parachute. This provides an enormous amount of giggles.

Vader Immortal Series

This is a three-part series available through Oculus. The exciting features of these games, beyond the allure of the Star Wars franchise, is the ability for earned mastery and power. Learning the force, the player can enter Darth Vader's fortress and work with allies and against enemies. Using the lightsaber and the force, the player works through levels to accomplish the ultimate feat in the Star Wars realm . . .

Conclusion

Carefully choosing software and understanding potential pitfalls will allow the play therapist to be well-prepared for the therapeutic inclusion of DPT materials. The mantra of play it first, play it often, and play it more applies to any and all of the software choices made. The new and exciting programs available will keep the client's motivation to engage high, and the multi-dimensional aspects will provide a tremendous amount of clinically relevant material.

Note

1. All app information has been collected through the iTunes Apple AppStore, the Android-based GooglePlay Store, the Oculus Store, the VR gaming platform Steam, and www.sandtrayplay.com.

References

Amuno, A. (2019, February 8). Five types of system software. *Turbofuture*. https://turbofuture.com/computers/The-Five-Types-of-System-Software

Callnerds (2019). *What is the difference between memory and storage?* https://callnerds.com/whats-difference-memory-storage/

Fisher, T. (2019, November 8). Types of software. *Lifewire*. www.lifewire.com/operating-systems-2625912

Martindale, J. (2020, March 14). *What is a CPU?* https://sports.yahoo.com/cpu-210041849.html

Stone, J., Gran, R. J., Goodyear-Brown, P., & Hull, K. (2019, October 5). Play it forward: Incorporating therapeutic digital tool benefits and client driven interests in play therapy [Conference session]. Association for Play Therapy Conference, Dallas, TX, United States.

Techopedia (n.d.). *Application software.* www.techopedia.com/definition/4224/application-software typesof (n.d.). *Types of software.* www.typesof.com/types-of-software/

10 Video Games and Genres

Stating that someone plays video games, or is a "gamer", conjures up a few thoughts, beliefs, and visuals for most people. However, the term *video game* is really amorphous and not very specific. The type of software and hardware involved is not delineated whatsoever, nor is the type, frequency, or length of play, and so on. Play therapists who understand more about the many types of video games, characters, story lines, goals, and gameplay will benefit both in conversation and play with their clients.

Understanding some of the different genres of video games will help the play therapist connect with their client(s) and further highlight any therapeutic properties within the gameplay. The empowered and knowledgeable digital play therapist will be capable of entering the client's world and be able to have conversations about the characters and gameplay that the client is interested in. Additionally, the digital play therapist will be able to identify the therapeutic value in the character development, story line, or in-game play included in the experience.

Video games are defined as "an electronic game in which players control images on a video screen" (Merriam-Webster, 2019). This book is full of widely used terms that have many different colloquial meanings. In my mind, when someone uses the term "video game", an image of a person playing a game on a computer comes into view. Really, though, if we think of the components of the video game definition, we are talking about 1) an electronic game, 2) players controlling images, and 3) the controlled images are on a video screen. By this definition, playing Tetris or Candy Crush on my phone counts as video game play as well as those played on a computer, handheld consoles, traditional consoles, tablets, and even VR headsets. Video games are everywhere, and based on the definition, most of us are playing them in some form.

Since the term *video game* seems to be a very large umbrella term with numerous important components to explore, I will list many different types here. The field is ever-changing; new programs are released, updated, and discovered daily. Furthering our knowledge of the different genres and meanings under this umbrella will serve us well when we are speaking with our clients, using digital tools in play therapy sessions, and/or researching different games for potential therapeutic inclusion. Meanings matter. I even had to research the difference between "game play" and "gameplay" and I will have to go through this document a hundred times to see if I caught the nuances and worded them correctly. Game play is the act of playing the game or describing the act of playing the game, and the like. Gameplay is "the specific way in which players interact with a game, and in particular with video games. Gameplay is the pattern defined through the game rules, connection between player and the game, challenges and overcoming them, plot and player's connection with it" (Wikipedia, 2019).

Genres

It is important for play therapists to understand that there are many different types of video games, game play, and gameplay. This is particularly important from a prescriptive viewpoint as the better one can pair the intervention with the client, the more successful the intervention and therapeutic process. As an example of the importance of some basic knowledge: if a client comes into session and speaks about the MMORPG they love to play, a knowledgeable digital play therapist would have a general idea of what type of game is being played. Even if one is not an expert, breaking down some of the acronym can give a hint: MMORPG ends with RPG, which stands for "role-playing game". MMO refers to "massive(ly) multiplayer online", which means this is a very large, online, multiplayer game in which thousands of people are joining in to play from all over the world 24 hours a day. Therefore, the initially scary looking MMORPG, which could make one feel inadequate, is not really scary at all. MMORPG is a game where a lot of people join online and play a role-playing game. The genre of the game begins to tell us something about what the client is talking about, and, in turn, some things about the client.

Video games are commonly categorized by their genre, despite some inherent difficulties and even some controversy. The controversy is born predominantly of two groups who believe their foci regarding game play are superior. One group focuses on the mechanics and rules of the play, which is a field of study known as ludology or the study of games. Ludologists feel strongly that what the player is doing in the game play (the choices made, the moves, etc.) includes the most important components. Narratologists, however, feel that the storyline, emotions, metaphors, and representations are most important. Narratology is the study of the narrative, the storyline. We will discuss ludology and narratology, and their importance in DPT in detail in the Ludology chapter. For now, the importance of these two concepts lies in the identification of what is happening in video game play. By definition there are visual components, but often there are also sounds and haptic movement (vibration in the controllers) included. There can also be a storyline which fuels the quests, battles, and goals of the play. For me, it seems strange to try to separate out the mechanics and rules of the game from the storyline, emotions, and more. They all come together and inform and shape the experience for the player(s).

Thomas Apperley wrote an impressive analysis of game genres, the historical viewpoints of genres before 2006, and offered suggestions for future categorizations of video games (2006). Apperley suggests that it might be best to combine these two viewpoints of ludology and narratology for a more comprehensive approach and introduces the idea of "interactivity", that there is an interactive component to the many facets of video games. The main take-away is that games are complex. They do not fit into neat categories. The idea of organizing video games into genres originally stemmed from the way the film industry organizes film categories. It is true that films can have aspects of more than one category, but generally there is a fundamental theme or approach that will be dominant. Video games, on the other hand, are multifaceted and often branch out into many different arenas. The game play can move in many directions based on the player's choices, character, skill, and development. Additionally, there are often social, role, and team aspects that bring other facets to the game play. The game design and storyline also come into the equation. The result is complex and ever-changing, with millions of possibilities.

The importance of ludology and narratology lies in the identification of key, core factors which begin to explain what the components of the gameplay are. As these factors are defined, play therapists and others can begin to better identify the therapeutic components of the gameplay. Once the therapeutic factors are identified, then research can be more properly designed and defined. Play therapists who strive to be educated in the components of video game play will find an enormous amount of therapeutic material and interactions to choose from. Clinicians will be able to tailor the DPT treatment for the client in a prescriptive way or allow the child to lead with their chosen games while the therapist identifies therapeutic aspects and utilizes them in the treatment.

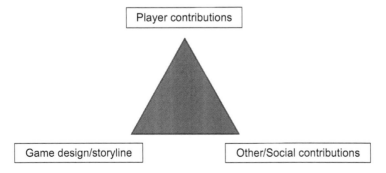

Figure 10.1 Game genre classification complexities.

GAMER Genres

The University of Washington has a program called the "Information School". The Information School runs a group called the Game Metadata Research Group, or the GAMER group. Members of the GAMER group project and the Seattle Interactive Media Museum have been working for years to develop a complex scheme which includes 12 facets and 358 foci toward the description and representation of video game classification (Ha Lee et al., 2014; Ha Lee, 2015a). As stated earlier, if we think of video games in terms of research, the more we can delineate the various components of the games and game play, the more specific we can be in our variable and hypotheses definitions. Some groups are motivated by identifying the components of the games that contribute to popularity and factors regarding game design. Fortunately, these classifications also help play therapists make decisions regarding the therapeutic use.

Most video game descriptions include information such as the title, age range, requirements for the platform (the equipment it runs on), a broad category genre, the player's expected experience of the game world, and the storyline (Ha Lee et al., 2014). For therapeutic evaluation, a therapist would want to know more about the type of play involved. Although categories are helpful to narrow down one's search, the best way to evaluate a game for therapeutic in-session inclusion is to watch videos of the game play (you can search the name of the game or even the category via your web browser and choose "videos") and, ultimately, play the game for yourself. Often there are components that non play therapists would not highlight so it is important to have your own experience.

The following are recommendations regarding the identification of video game genres and which to consider including in your treatment protocol:

1) Research the genres of games your clients talk about or bring into session.

   a. Watch videos of gameplay online. YouTube typically has hundreds to choose from. You can watch with or without sound. Sometimes the constant chatter of the vlogger can be too much.
   b. Search for information about the game: recommended age range, genre, content, focus, platform, and so on.

2) Research the genres of games you hope will have therapeutic value.

   a. Same process as for the first recommendation.

3) Purchase the game, borrow from a friend or colleague, check it out from the library, or another source. Some stores also sell used games. Be sure to ask about the return policy.

4) The best-case scenario is to play the game before in-session use. Play it until you are no longer focused on the mechanics of the play (i.e., how do I walk, how do I jump, etc.). The goal is to focus on the unfolding process, the interactions, and the play styles and not the mechanics.

(Stone, 2016)

5). If the client brings a game in to share (discussion or brings the actual game):

    a. Listen, explore, discuss, and the like, just as you would anything else a client brought in to share.

    b. Allow the client to demonstrate their mastery-to-date of the game. Work to discover what the client:

        i. Enjoys about the game play.

        ii. Wants to share with you about the game play.

        iii. Is challenged by, comforted by, and so on within the game play.

    c. Research the game outside of the session.

Existing Genres

The list of existing video game genres is long, and it took some time to determine what would be the best way to present the information. If I were bookmarking a resource, I would want these in a format that would allow me to easily refer to the information as needed by looking through the alphabetized list and finding the genre I was looking for. Therefore, these genres are listed for you to read over now and refer back to in the future. You could very well need this list for clarification during discussions with clients, while reading a description of a game or program, or when writing case notes. Although this list is long, it is by no means exhaustive in the genres included nor are the genres indicating clear-cut classifications; they are not mutually exclusive. A list which indicated the interactivity qualities of video games would be fantastic; however, it would be very long and an ever-changing project. Therefore, this list is presented with the knowledge that there is much more to be known about each game and your own exploration will be invaluable. Since there are so many games within each (and within multiple) categories, if a client presents with a game that might not be suitable for in-session use, chances are you could find another game with similar gameplay style and more appropriate content for in-session use once you know what to look for.

Video Game Genres[1]

Digital play therapists can explore the following questions and concepts in each of the genres regarding their specific clients:

1) What kinds of gameplay is your client attracted to?

2) Why is the client attracted to this type of gameplay?

3) Is this gameplay reenacting real life experiences? Or not?

4) Is this gameplay allowing for the exploration of other-than-real life experiences? (i.e., exploring different roles, perspectives, approaches, skills, etc.)

5) Do the results of this type of gameplay reinforce positive aspects of activity, interaction, skill building, and the like, or not?

6) Is this the type of gameplay (digital or not) this client seeks elsewhere? What are those experiences like for them? How might this experience be the same or different?

7) If the client plays the game outside of the therapy office, what is/are the social aspects of the game (if any)? Is there an in-game chat feature? What is that experience life? What friends have they made? Where do they live? What kinds of things do they talk about?

8) What kind of character development is in the game? Did the client create the character, choose the characteristics, etc. and if so, why were the particular choices made? What do they mean to the client?

9) Does the client engage in any team play? What is their typical role in a team if they are part of one? What kind of experiences does the client have as part of a team?

10) Is their game play congruent with their regular-life persona or not? Why or why not?

11) What themes emerge during the play or the discussion of the play?

12) What can the therapist do or not do within the gameplay interaction that will elicit critical reactions or enact interventions, (just as one would do within Playmobil play, etc.)?

13) What are the client's frustration tolerance levels?

14) What is the client's level of mastery?

15) What are the client's coping skills?

16) What are the client's strategic skills?

17) What is the client's social interaction abilities?

18) What is the client's level of competitiveness?

19) What is the client's norm-compliance levels?

20) How do the answers to any and all of these questions affect the client's life and where might some skill building be beneficial?

Genres

4X – The four Xs stand for the followin: explore, expand, exterminate, and exploit. Diplomacy and conquest utilize the 4Xs to create an empire. This strategic game genre has merit in helping clients explore how to identify and meet goals, just make sure to choose which games to include in session wisely.

Action – This type of game includes a narrative which focuses on fast-paced experiences where the characters are engaging in intense physical activities, often in a timed manner, with eye-hand coordination and high reaction speeds as central aspects. Many action games include additional puzzles, races, or challenges in addition to the main gameplay.

Adventure – Adventure games are well-suited for DPT as they are firmly rooted in a storyline. The player gathers and collects items to work through barriers and complete quests, all of which further the storyline toward completing the adventure. The play is linear, and plot driven. These games are particularly appropriate for play therapy when they are played on the Nintendo Switch handheld console as each player can have a controller and must communicate to coordinate the character's movement and progression.

Action–adventure – Action–adventure games are also well-suited for DPT, for the client who wants a little more action but not the intensity of pure action games. This is a marriage of the components from action and adventure games. Some people became bored with the pace and lack of quick moving components of the adventure game, so they added in some action. There is a storyline which includes a hero, an enemy, and someone or something which needs to be saved by the hero, typically the person playing the game. Challenges include cognitive skill puzzles and navigation to progress toward the goal.

Arcade – These games have their roots in classic arcade games. Typically, the graphics are simple, and the goal is to achieve a high score.

Art – Another genre well-suited for DPT, art games focus on the creative expression and creation of art using a variety of mediums. Typically, the artwork can be saved and continued another time, printed out, and/or included in the client's file.

Block breaking – Scores are achieved typically through the use of a paddle and a ball which is moved strategically to break blocks.

Board game – Great for DPT, these games have their roots in traditional table-top board games. These are particularly great for play therapy on the go as many games can be stored in one device, such as a tablet, and no pieces will get lost.

Brawler – Brawler games focus on combat, either hand to hand or using weapons.

Breeding – These games focus on the care, breeding, and development of animals or other creatures. This type of game can be valuable in the identification of and meeting the needs of others.

Card game – Similar to the board game genre, these games have their roots in traditional table-top card games and there is no fear of losing any of the cards.

Construction & management simulation – These games are great for the builder and planner, or for one who would benefit from practicing such skills. Resource management and multitasking are the main foci.

Crime – This genre focuses on committing crimes. This is a genre which has been blamed for the violence–gaming connection, although the research does *not* support such a connection. It is more likely that people who act out some type of violence may also play such games (the player has a predisposition, preexisting mental health condition, etc.).

Cyberpunk – Themes and plots of these games use futuristic, computer focused, science fiction driven human–technology interactions. These types of games could really engage your science fiction loving clients.

Dancing – Dancing is fantastic – get up and move! These games focus on dance, whether it be following the lead of the game and mimicking the movements, or free-play dance.

Dark fantasy – This story driven fantasy game world contains scary, dark, gothic themes and elements. Better suited for older clients.

Documentary – Documentary games use a historical or factual perspective to tell a story. This could be great with clients who are really interested in history but should be chosen carefully.

Drama – These simulation games tend to focus on young adult social interaction drama. There are most likely other ways to access and address dramatic situations, however, this type of game would certainly present material for discussion.

Driving/racing – With a goal of winning the race against computer or human driven opponents, these games involve driving a vehicle in a highly skilled manner to cross the finish line first. These games are competitive and strategic. These games can be stand alone or highlighted as mid-game challenges in other games.

Educational – Educational games focus on the introduction, practice, and mastery of provided educational material.

Exercise – These games focus on the goal of exercising. Components of these might be useful in therapy for mind–body movement and connection but would need to be pre-screened carefully.

Fairytale – Pre-screened carefully, these games are based on traditional folklore stories and elements. Often talking animals, creatures, fairies, and magic are included. These games are great for use in DPT.

Fantasy – These fantasy worlds include magic, sorcery, dragons, and other mythical creatures. There are a number of fantasy world sub-genres.

Fighting – Individual characters or teams are controlled by the player and engage in fighting with other character(s). The characters are chosen based on their aesthetics, style, and skills. The fighting aspect might not be everyone's style, but the character choice and strategic approach to this type of game might be useful in *some* therapeutic interactions. This is another carefully selected and paired intervention.

First-person shooter (FPS) – First-person shooter refers to the player operating as though they were the shooter in the game. The view the player has of the character is as though they were looking at their own body, arms, legs, etc.

Flight simulator – Some of these games are more realistic and some are more action oriented, but either way the gameplay simulates flight. These types of games are particularly useful in VR for exposure therapy.

Folklore – Based on traditional cultural stories, legends, and indigenous tales, these games are often fantastic in DPT.

Game show – Game show games are modelled after television game shows and can be a lot of fun!

Gambling – These are based on traditional gambling games.

God game – As an all-powerful entity the player will interact with a world. Chosen carefully, this game concept could be very empowering for some and help with control, organization, and multi-tasking for others.

Hack and slash – Think of the ancient Romans and their displayed combat fighting with one person fighting many enemies at a time. This type of game focuses on multiple levels of fast-paced combat.

High fantasy – These games focus on struggles between good and evil and based in a fantasy world. The virtuous hero will set out to avenge the evil antagonist. Depending on age-appropriate content, this genre could be useful in DPT.

Historical – The gameplay storyline takes place in the past.

Horror – Just like a horror film, this type of game includes stories that intend to scare and use frightening and supernatural material.

Interactive movie – These movies are altered by decisions the player makes along the way. This could be a fantastic future genre for DPT with specific materials created for therapeutic purposes.

Japanese role playing (JRPG) – Often designed in Japan, these games focus on themes of romance and dramatic personal stories. Predominately depicted in anime style with an emphasis on visual representations. Possibly useful with older clients (age-appropriate) who have an interest in anime.

Light gun shooter – This shooting game uses an external gun (not the player holding the gun) to shoot objects or enemies.

Low fantasy – This fantasy world has little to no magic and minimal other fantasy elements.

Mascot fighter – One or more characters from a franchise engage in combat in free-for-all type fights.

Massively multiplayer first-person shooter (MMFPS) – From the first-person perspective, this shooting game is played online with potentially many, many other players at the same time.

Massively multiplayer online role-playing game (MMORPG) – This type of game includes many people from around the world playing online together. It includes character choice and development and often team play involvement. This type of game would be great for discussion within DPT regarding characters, strategy, and social interactions, and even a short demonstration of the game play could be useful, but not for direct in-session use because of the online gameplay and team play involvement.

Maze – These games focus on the completion and navigation of a maze or mazes. This type of game would be potentially helpful for problem-solving skills.

Military – Armed forces engage in armed conflict.

Military science fiction – This type of game includes armed conflict in a science fiction world or setting.

Military simulator – These strategic military games simulate realistic events.

Multiplayer online battle arena (MOBA) – From a third-person perspective, online players control a character on two or more teams who compete against each other to achieve goals or domination. This is another game that has a lot of value in discussion about gameplay but not direct in-session use appropriateness. See MMORPG.

Music – Music, beats, and rhythm are the key components of this gameplay experience.

*Mystery – Finding clues, exploring and investigating help the player solve a mystery or puzzle. These types of games can be useful in DPT, depending on the content.

*Party – These collections of mini games are intended for small group play during a get together. This type of game collection could be a great activity in group or family therapy, depending on content.

Pinball – These games are direct simulations of traditional pinball machines.

*Platform – Players in platform games are moving from one platform to another and navigating obstacles along the way. These games are great for practicing and developing hand-eye coordination.

Programming game – This type of game uses computer code programming as the primary game play and way to achieve various goals.

*Puzzle – Puzzle games focus on organizing puzzle pieces and solving the puzzle. This type of game can be helpful for clients who could benefit from focusing on strategizing, organization, part-to-whole conceptualization and whole-to-part and working memory skills. These could be literal puzzles which contain x number of pieces, or some type of mystery that needs to be solved through manipulation and reconfiguration.

Rail shooter – The rail in this type of game refers to a set course. Players are propelled along this set course after participating in various tasks.

Real time strategy – These strategy games are not driven by turn-based sequences. Players strategize regarding goals in real time without waiting for another player to do something (move, etc.).

*Rhythm – Players complete actions that are synchronized to a rhythm. This type of game could be useful for those who need to connect to their own body or the rhythm of others or work on coordination.

*Role-playing games (RPG) – These extremely popular games are related to table-top role-playing games and focus on characters leveling up while they explore a game world. The information a DPT therapist can gather from the discussion of character development is phenomenal. Role-playing games are perfect for eliciting this type of information.

*Rogue-like – Randomly generated environments allow the player to discover items and treasure. This type of game would be great for discussion within session but might be too much for in-session use.

*Romance – Romance games focus on intimate relationships, dating, and other related interactions. This type of game could be good for the older client (age-appropriate), depending on the content and the needs of the client.

*Sandbox/Open world – This sandbox is not to be confused with sandtray! In this gameplay, players are encouraged to explore the open environment,

create, and act freely. These games can be very valuable in DPT, depending on the content.

Science fiction – The gameplay takes place in a world of science, advanced technology, and space travel, aliens, and futuristic devices.

Shooter – The player shoots at targets and objects to progress through the game.

Simulation – These games simulate real or fictional reality through actions or situations. These games can be valuable in DPT, depending on the content.

Social simulator – This type of game depicts social life, interactions, and situations. Depending on the content (age-appropriate), this type of game-play can inform the therapist about family and social dynamics for the client, similar to how many projective drawing techniques are beneficial.

Sports – This type of game depicts sports play.

Stealth – Stealth games focus on not being detected while accomplishing tasks. This type of game could be good within DPT, depending on content, however, it is also a genre that could benefit from the play therapy specific situation development.

Steampunk – Engineering concepts and aesthetics from Victorian and Edwardian eras are used within this genre of gameplay.

Strategy – Strategic decisions and interventions are used to meet a goal. Strategy is an important skill to learn and practice in DPT and then apply in real life situations.

Survival – Limited resources and difficult situations dominate survival games. Numerous skills, such as organization, management, strategizing, and more can be learned and practiced in this type of game, depending on age-appropriate content.

Tactical shooter – These are shooter games that simulate a tactical or military environment.

Tactics – Small-scale conflicts have the player(s) working to position and control assets with a focus on achieving a goal.

Time travel – Time travel or manipulation are major plots in these stories which include multiple time periods. This type of exploration game can be very useful in DPT, depending on the content.

Tower defense – These games focus on defending a location, such as a tower, from an onslaught. This type of game, depending on age appropriate content, can be very useful in DPT. The concept of recognizing, nurturing, and using skills to protect oneself is very valuable.

Traditional – Traditional games exist in the real world and have been created in digital form.

Trivia – Trivia games are based on answering obscure questions.

Turn-based strategy (TBS) – These games have the players/characters take turns with the task at hand instead of real-time which would not include turns. This can be helpful with clients who have difficulty taking turns, waiting, patience, and the like.

Vehicle combat – This type of game focuses on the combat of vehicles.
*Virtual life – Through the creation of an avatar, the player controls the living in a simulated life. This is often an online gameplay with the avatars of many interacting with each other. This type of gameplay would be great discussion material, particularly the creation of the avatars and how the avatars interact online, but not for in-session use because of the online use, unless appropriate precautions were taken to protect the confidentiality of the client.
Western – Western video games focus on the post–Civil War era Western United States region with cowboys, horses, and the law.
**Western role-playing game (WRPG)* – These role-playing games focus on character development and customization. Realistic visual styles and open worlds allow for creativity and exploration. Depending on the age of the client and the content of the game, this type of gameplay is perfect as a digital projective process.

*denotes a recognition of usefulness in digital play therapy.

Role-Playing Games

Role-playing games are the type of video games in which I tend to find the most therapeutic value. This type of video game also has a rich history in table-top gaming. The transition from table-top to video game has resulted in amazing characters, gameplay, and storylines for all types of players. RPGs grew out of a desire for people to play a game in which they work together as a team rather than battle each other. This is referred to as a "nonzero sum" game or one that has "no single optimal strategy that is preferable to all others, nor is there a predictable outcome" (Stanford.edu, n.d., para. 1).

Sarah Lynne Bowman (2010) defined three basic functions of general role playing:

1). Role playing "enhances a group's sense of communal cohesiveness by providing narrative enactment within a ritual framework";

(p. 1)

2). Role playing "encourages complex problem-solving and provides partici-pants with the opportunity to learn an extensive array of skills through the enactment of scenarios"; and

(p. 1)

3). Role playing "offers participants a safe space to enact alternate personas through a process known as identity alteration".

(p. 1)

The roles one's society and culture offer for people to embody are somewhat limiting. Engaging in fantasy allows these constraints to disappear for a period of time. Throughout time, humans have sought these escape mechanisms, whether it be through art, dance, music, writing, movies, television, hobbies, work, or any other type. Over the past 40 years, role-playing games have grown immensely in popularity. These types of games allow people to be an active participant in the enactment of their own alternate identity expressions, explore parts of themselves that were dormant or suppressed, and escape from the day-to-day expectations of life. Role playing can be part of many types of play: table-top, virtual, and live. Often gamers think of LARP, or live action role play: activities in which people dress up as characters and play out a scenario or event; however, as play therapists we can think of many different forms of live action role playing that happens in our offices (Bowman, 2010).

Role playing allows a person to occupy the headspace of someone or something other than their primary identification, through a process called identity alteration. Participating in role play can allow for people to practice a variety of cognitive, personal, interpersonal, and occupational skills without great risk. Players can explore, learn, and master skills which can be generalized to their day-to-day lives. Role playing, and in turn, RPGs have an important function of providing healthy outlets for exploration, development, skill building, creativity, self-expression, responsibility, and communal connection (Bowman, 2010).

To qualify as a role-playing activity, the player must alter their primary self and develop and assume an alternate one for use in a "co-created story space" and shared storytelling experience (Bowman, 2010, p. 12). The concept of a co-created story space is one with which play therapists are quite familiar. A co-created story is one that may have been created by one participant but develops through a "continual process of involved interaction and creativity on the part of the participants. Thus the 'audience' of a role-playing game invents the narrative as well as experiences it" (p. 13). Historically, we looked to fairy tales, legends, and myths as representations of the human experience. These stories have been passed on through the generations and continue to have meaning. They commonly contain recurring archetypes, messages, ritual, and structures.

Archetypes and symbols are used to represent concepts, ideas, stories, emotions, experiences, and so many other things. Those who use sandtray in their work are very familiar with these concepts. RPGs and many other video game types rely heavily on the use of archetypes and symbols. Some are game specific, but many are those that have survived over centuries. They contribute to the meaning and purpose of the experience, the feasibility of the identity alteration, and the immersive quality of the play. When one can suspend belief of the day-to-day and fully embody the narrative, immersion can be accomplished. The role play can provide a window into the player's life conceptualizations, wishes, experiences, and beliefs.

Bowman (2012), delves deeply into role playing games and Jungian theory in Torner and White's book, *Immersive Gameplay*. It is difficult to pick out a few key points as they are deep, connected, and complex, as studying Jung tends to be. However, the chapter discusses the importance of immersion and how this process is "nearly identical to Jung's concept of active imagination, only distinct in the fact that role-playing takes place in a group setting rather than an individual one" (Bowman, 2012, p. 35). Per Daryl Sharp, a Jungian analyst, active imagination is the "method of assimilating unconscious contents (dreams, fantasies, etc.) through some form of self-expression" (2019) and this process leads to a stripping of one's Ego identity (Bowman, 2012). The archetypes reside in the collective unconscious which is accessed through the personal unconscious after the Ego identity is out of the way. Role playing is a way to put aside the Ego identity and personal unconscious, reach the collective unconscious in a safe space through the embodiment of "other". Through this embodiment, and the emergence from the embodiment, a new inner balance could be achieved (Bowman, 2012).

For me, it is a conceptualization that allowing ourselves the freedom and safety of the exploration and embodiment of something "other" results in the ability to heal psychological wounds, adopt new ways of being, and become a more complete and whole person. This is a fundamental reason I believe role-playing games are so valuable within the mental health setting. As therapists, our job is to assist the client in accessing these processes, guide them through, assist where needed, and deliver them back to their lives with new ways of being. If role-playing video games allow this process to happen for any portion of my clientele, I am going to utilize it. The fact that this particular genre of games mirrors many fundamental human needs and experiences tells me the power I witness clinically of their use is grounded in age-old concepts.

Role-playing games have the potential to fulfill a variety of different needs. Some people enjoy RPGs for the development of character and story. Other people enjoy the problem solving, skill acquisition, and strategizing which can result in a feeling of accomplishment and even mastery. Some use the game components to engage in self-reflection and analysis, especially while engaging in identity alteration. Yet others primarily enjoy the camaraderie and connection with others through working together on teams and chatting during (and outside of) play. Multiple different needs can be fulfilled during RPG gameplay. Role playing video games are fun, entertaining, connecting, challenging, and allow for the embodiment of "other". Utilizing them directly in play therapy sessions, talking with clients about their gameplay, and continuing to learn more about the therapeutic value will greatly benefit the play therapist.

Conclusion

Whether video games are casual (sold for entertainment purposes) or serious (sold for educational or therapeutic purposes), the genre of game, the therapeutic components, and purpose within the therapeutic setting are the most important factors. Clinicians who are aware that these games are multi-faceted and complex, with powers to illustrate the client's perspectives and needs, will benefit greatly from the game play and gameplay interactions. Researching and playing the games will allow the clinician to identify the therapeutic components and recognize the core agents of change within.

Note

1. (Adapted from Ha Lee et al., 2014, 2015a, 2015b; Grace, 2005; Bean, 2018, 2019; Jackson & Games, 2015; Stone, 2016, 2019).

References

Apperley, T. (2006). Genre and game studies: Toward a critical approach to video game genres. *Simulation and Gaming*, 6–23.

Bean, A. M. (2018). *Working with video gamers and games in therapy: A clinician's guide.* Abingdon, UK: Routledge.

Bean, A. M. (2019). I am my avatar and my avatar is me: Utilizing video games as therapeutic tools. In J. Stone. (Ed.), *Integrating technology into modern therapies* (pp. 94–106). Abingdon, UK: Routledge.

Bowman, S. L. (2010). *The functions of role playing games.* McFarland & Co.

Bowman, S. L. (2012). Jungian theory and immersion in role-playing games. In E. Torner & W. J. White (Eds.), *Immersive gameplay* (pp. 31–51). McFarland & Co.

Grace, L. (2005). *Game type and game genre.* http://aii.lgracegames.com/documents/Game_types_and_genres.pdf

Ha Lee, J. (2015a). *Video game metadata schema: Controlled vocabulary for gameplay genre, v. 1.1.* https://gamer.ischool.uw.edu/wp-content/uploads/2018/04/VGMS_CV_Genre_v.1.1_20150622.pdf

Ha Lee, J. (2015b). *Video game metadata schema: Controlled vocabulary for narrative genre, v. 1.2.* https://gamer.ischool.uw.edu/wp-content/uploads/2018/04/VGMS_CV_NarrativeGenre_v.1.2_20150622.pdf

Ha Lee, J., Karlova, N., Clarke, R. I., Thornton, K., & Perti, A. (2014). Facet analysis of video game genres. *Ideals.* www.ideals.illinois.edu/bitstream/handle/2142/47323/057_ready.pdf

Jackson, L. A., & Games, A. I. (2015). Video games and creativity. In G. P. Green & J. C. Kaufman (Eds.), *Video games and creativity.* Academic Press.

Merriam-Webster (2019). *Video game.* www.merriam-webster.com/dictionary/video%20game

Sharp, D. (2019). *What is active imagination?* www.carl-jung.net/active_imagination.html

Stanford.edu (n.d.). *Non-zero-sum games.* https://cs.stanford.edu/people/eroberts/courses/soco/projects/1998-99/game-theory/nonzero.html

Stone, J. (2016). Board games in play therapy. In K. J. O'Connor, C. E. Schaefer, & L. D. Braverman's (Eds.), *Handbook of play therapy* (pp. 309–323). Wiley.

Stone, J. (2019). Digital games. In J. Stone & C. E. Schaefer (Eds.), *Game play* (3rd ed., pp. 99–118). Wiley.

Wikipedia (2019, December 18). *Gameplay.* https://en.wikipedia.org/wiki/Gameplay

11 Digital Citizenship

The play therapist serves as a guide for clients to navigate the steps toward their defined treatment goals within session. Clients and families often seek guidance as they define the components of their digital lives and seek balance. Understanding digital citizenship can help clients, families, and therapists align the needs of the client and the family with the experiences and expectations of the digital world. As stated earlier in the book, it is important to respect the value systems of families while providing unbiased-as-possible information for families to assist them when they are having conflict and/or struggling. The overall development of the youth who play therapists serve is paramount and includes navigating the new world of digital citizenship, the potential impacts of having digital lives, and the importance of parental and intergenerational involvement both within and outside of the therapeutic session.

Digital Citizenship

Digital citizenship is defined differently by numerous people; however, it generally addresses concerns regarding approaches and behaviors within a digital lifestyle. People who adopt the tenets of digital citizenship aspire to achieve a safe, ethical, and responsible existence in their digital worlds. Digital citizenship certainly includes concerns about safety for the user, but the focus is much more on maintaining a thoughtful, conscious existence online. Some people feel as though the "digital" portion of this is unnecessary, that these are tenets of citizenship, however, as the Digital Citizenship Institute asserts, digital life is different enough from day-to-day life that special circumstances arise (Curran et al., n.d.). In the digital realm, people can explore different portions of themselves, interactions, and existence and therefore some situations will warrant a different structure of conduct.

Curran, et al., have identified three core themes and nine elements of digital citizenship. The three core themes include respect, educate, and protect, and the nine elements are depicted with each core theme (n.d.).

1) Respect

    a. Etiquette

        i. Includes social norms and expectations of pre-digital world interactions.

        ii. Includes social norms and expectations specific to post-digital world interactions.

    b. Access

        i. Connection to resources and information.

        ii. Hardware, software, and bandwidth.

    c. Law

        i. Collecting and sharing of personal information.

        ii. Copyrights and other protected material.

        iii. Scams, hacking, stealing online identities.

        iv. Sexting, cyberbullying, and so on.

        v. Any other existing state and federal laws.

2) Educate

    a. Digital literacy

        i. Evaluate and integrate information in multiple formats.

        ii. Evaluate, navigate, and use digital tools.

        iii. Evaluate, navigate, and use online resource.

        iv. Includes media and visual literacy.

    b. Communication

        i. Effective and relevant ways of defining, sharing, and organizing information.

        ii. Communicating as creatively, clearly, and inclusively as possible.

        iii. The message is the core of online activities as it is a majority of the information available to evaluate.

    c. Digital commerce

        i. Use of personal information.

        ii. Digital footprint.

        iii. Understand the risks involved with online financial tools.

        iv. Understand how to protect personal information.

3) Protect

    a. Digital rights and responsibilities

        i. Be aware and watch for problems online.

        ii. Address problems within the tenets of digital literacy.

b. Digital security

 i. Firewalls and virus protection.

 ii. How much personal information should be revealed online.

c. Digital health and wellness

 i. The importance of balance.

 ii. Monitor and improve physical health.

 iii. Monitor and improve mental health.

 iv. Understand the potential physical, social, and interpersonal ramifications of unbalance.

Common Sense Media released a white paper about this new frontier for children in 2009. The acknowledgement of the important integration of digital tools into our lives and our children's future led the authors to include important 21st-century tools such as innovation, communication, creativity, civic participation, and critical thinking along with the traditional reading, writing, math, and science. It was predicted that children would/will need skills and education in these areas to be prepared for the future. Proposed initiatives included: 1) redesigning curriculums in all American schools to include digital citizenship and literacy, and 2) disseminating information to students, teachers, and parents about citizenship, literacy, and ethics. "The nation whose children best harness the educational and creative powers of digital media will write the economic and educational success story of the 21st century. Digital media is bringing significant changes to the ways that kids live and learn – and those changes can create opportunities or pose potential dangers. We need to fund teachers, curricula, and parenting tools that teach kids to understand and manage media's role in their lives. The emerging fields of Digital Literacy and Citizenship are the keys to that preparation" (Common Sense Media, 2009, p. 12). This paper was released eleven years ago at the time of this printing; however, the sentiments remain. Our children's lives will continue to further integrate the use of digital tools. Adhering to and continuing to teach and expect digital citizenship will increase their positive experiences and help shape the environment for all.

Digital Footprints

Most people have heard some version of the warning that, once something is posted online, it will be online forever. This is one's digital footprint (Impero, n.d.). The footprint a person leaves online can typically be found if someone looks hard enough and we can never fully predict who those people might be. A footprint frequently contains items a person did not share, rather, things were shared by family, friends, enemies, and/or strangers. Others can impersonate, take screenshots, take photographs or videos, and so on, and share that information without the knowledge of the person involved. This digital footprint emphasizes the need for and importance of citizenship – digital or otherwise.

How a person behaves, what they say and do, can be online material within seconds whether it was wanted or not. This is an era of information being shared more quickly than ever before. Desired positions for college, sports teams, employment, relationships, and more can all be affected greatly by what is found regarding a person's online presence.

SAFE Framework

The SAFE framework was created as a digital citizenship scale for adolescents. With a focus of the "emotional aspects of adolescents", the researchers combined previously identified components and combined them with specific adolescent features to create this framework. The acronym SAFE is: S – Self-identity, A – Activity online, F – Fluency in digital environment, and E – Ethics for digital environment (Kim & Choi, 2018, p. 162). It is important to note that this study and structure were conducted in Korea and some phrasing, wording, and/or concepts may be specialized to the Korean language and culture. This author made some minor grammatical changes for ease of reading, but not to any content. This article, *Development of Youth Digital Citizenship Scale and Implication for Educational Setting* is not ideal, but the identified components can be useful for our purposes.

Listing the items under each SAFE quadrant in the framework allows the reader to 1) understand what the variables of the study were and 2) recognize a number of aspects of the digital world and online life which affect our clients (and all of us). The following is adapted from Kim and Choi (2018, p. 162).

1) Self-identity – to cultivate and manage digital reputations and identities

   a. Upholding basic and equal digital rights
   b. Achieving digital safety
   c. Protecting personal information
   d. Pursuing digital ownership
   e. Performing individual management
   f. Limiting physical and psychological health risks

2) Activity online – positive and safe behavior

   a. Digital communication
   b. Digital commerce
   c. Appropriate decision making
   d. Political, economic, cultural engagement
   e. Balancing digital use
   f. Healthy and safe relationships

3) Fluency in the digital environment – knowledge of digital literacy

   a. Digital health and wellness
   b. Digital access

    c. Digital literacy

    d. Technical skills

    e. Using technology to learn

    f. Using technology to keep up to date

4) Ethics for the digital environment – understand and respect one's rights and obligations

    a. Digital law responsibilities

    b. Digital awareness

    c. Ethical use of technology

    d. Digital etiquette

    e. Treat others with respect

    f. Do not cyberbully

    g. Do not steal

    h. Do not damage others

    i. Ethical digital use

Digital citizenship aspirations provide a structure for play therapists to guide the use of digital tools in session, for clients to use in their personal lives, and for parents to implement into their family values as they see to be appropriate. It can be helpful for people to understand that this is a focus for many and that their interactions online seem be relatively anonymous, but they do matter. How users/participants treat others online, and how others treat them, contributes to the wellbeing of others, and their own overall well-being.

Identity

One of the interesting byproducts of the digital citizenship conversation is the concept of identity. Not in terms of protecting one's identity, of course that is an important component, rather, for this portion of the exploration, the concept of one's self-identity. What is it, what does it mean, how fluid is the construct, how is it portrayed, how is it accepted, how is it formed? We certainly will not answer all of these questions in this text, but it is an interesting discussion at this time in our professional era. The accessibility for people to share, seek, explore, learn, experiment, experience, and more in our online lives has certainly shifted the development process. It will be fascinating to look back in 10 to 20 years and map the path.

For the developing adolescent, we can look back to Erik Erikson's identified stages. As a little trip down graduate-school memory lane, we are reminded that Erikson identified a stage called Identity vs. Confusion for the approximately 12–18/19-year-old age range (Cherry, 2019). The primary focus of this stage is self-identity. "As they seek to establish a sense of self, teens may experiment with different roles, activities, and behaviors. According to Erikson, this is important to the process of forming a strong identity and developing a sense of direction in life" (para. 5).

Early adolescents (11–14) want to define and identify themselves apart from their family and their role in the family and become an important part of a peer group. They want to assert themselves and their newly forming values. Fourteen- to 18-year-olds begin the journey of assuming different roles and choosing which aspects are most congruent. They begin to understand themselves and their beliefs in context of others within their culture and the world. They may form stances regarding important issues and their identity is becoming more consistent across different environments. Older adolescents (18–24) are moving out of Erikson's Identity vs. Confusion stage and into the Intimacy vs. Isolation stage. Regarding identity, people within this older stage are forming more realistic views of their belief system in context of adult roles, career, intimate relationships, and who they might become. Those in this group often commit to particular cultural and sub-cultural groups (Williams, 2018). "Typically, young people will shift from not giving much thought to identity to actively engaging in the process of exploring identity options. This shift can be prompted by an experience – sometimes positive, sometimes negative – that creates just enough conflict to get them thinking about their place in the world" (para. 6).

The online world affords adolescents today both a luxury and a potential lure regarding the freedom one has to explore different ways of being. The self-identity identification process within the digital age is fantastic for a more experiential process of exploration, whether through gaming and character representations, social media, or other experiences. This process is also a potential lure because the identity is fragile and not formed and this can be difficult to navigate without support. This is another area in which a therapist can be of assistance. By discussions and experiencing how a client is working through the self-identity formation process in any number of digital environments, the therapist can assist through processing the experiences, providing guidance, and emphasizing components of digital citizenship (both for self and others).

The Importance of Co-Play

Co-play refers to playing a game together at the same time or taking turns playing the same game (Wang et al., 2018; Chambers, 2012). As a prefix, the term "co" indicates with, together, or jointly (Merriam-Webster, 2020). The benefits of playing with children are well known to play therapists and directly circle back to the therapeutic powers of play. Our work revolves around co-play. We can borrow a "page" from the pro-family-game-night book and reap the benefits of family co-play and apply them to the play therapy process. Some of the touted benefits to family co-play include: 1) developing strong character by learning to win and lose gracefully; 2) promoting problem-solving skills by strategizing and thinking critically; 3) reducing stress by having fun and laughing together; 4) focusing energy in a positive direction by working toward a common goal; 5) encouraging and modeling positive social skills by taking turns, working toward goals together, and so on; 6) enhancing communication skills by negotiating steps to meet goals, discussing strategies, and the like;

and 7) promoting family bonding, togetherness, and traditions by repeating the play over time (Atkins, 2017). Applying these to DPT and providing co-play recommendations to families will create very powerful interventions.

Wang et al. (2018), set out to discover the effects of video game co-play among family members. Most of the research prior to Wang et al. focused on "traditional media effects issues" such as violent content (p. 4075). As discussed in the Technopanic chapter, a predominant focus on such media effects issues (i.e., splashy headlines based on poorly executed or incomplete research, or even pure opinion) leaves little space for the exploration of other possible factors. Familial and intergenerational co-play is an important focus for play therapy work, both for assisting the families we work with and to highlight the effects of therapist–client co-play.

Family closeness (cohesion) and family satisfaction were defined as distinguished by Wang, et al., for the purpose of their study (2018). These types of definitions are crucial to understanding the research as they are putting it forth. They defined family closeness as it referred to as the "children's feeling(s) about parental warmth and involvement, and the relationship between parents and children" (Wang et al., 2018, p. 4078; Strage, 1998). Family satisfaction is the "degree to which family members feel happy and fulfilled with each other and include cohesion, flexibility, and communication" (Wang et al., 2018, p. 4078; Olson, 2004; Carver & Jones, 1991). Their research focused on whether or not video game co-play facilitates family closeness or cohesion.

Ultimately, Wang et al. concluded that "video games could help improve family relationships, in terms of family closeness and family satisfaction" (2018, p. 4086). Video games appear to contribute positively to the connection between family members "much like any other shared recreational activity, providing and important option for families" and "playing video games together can be a great resource for family members to connect with each other and share thoughts and feelings" (p. 4087). Participants in their study found the video game co-play to be fun, cooperative, and a way to talk to each other. As one parent stated, "it is the chance for us to talk with our children" (p. 4087).

Intergenerational Disconnect?

Intergenerational gameplay has been of some interest to researchers as often the difference in knowledge, experience, and comfort between the groups is cited as being a source of disconnect between youth (digital natives) and digital immigrants. This can also be said about some play therapists and their clients; therefore, we will explore this a little further. Often the client is a digital native and the therapist is a digital immigrant or even a luddite (one who rejects modern technology), technoskeptic (one who is skeptical), or technophobe (one who is afraid). I present these terms for clarity, not for any negative categorization to occur.

Vioda and Greenberg (2012), along with Aarsand (2007), found great value in intergenerational video game co-play. Co-play between different age groups, elderly and youth, yielded a decrease in anxiety, an increased attraction to the other group, and positive attitude changes (Chua et al., 2013). There is much for each participant to learn in intergenerational co-play.

A developmental perspective and concern was presented by Vioda and Greenburg regarding the decline in intergenerational interactions at this point in time. They stated, "interactions with individuals of different generations are critical to human well-being" and "interactions with their elders provide important opportunities for youth to expand the diversity of people with whom they interact" (2012, pp. 1–2). It is important to note that this study focused on intergenerational *co-located* (in the same physical space) interactions, as many intergenerational studies focus on distance interactions (such as video chat, etc.). They also focused on people who were one generation apart (parent–child) and many others focus on a two-generation gap (grandparent–grandchild).

Vioda and Greenburg distinguished five roles the intergenerational participants could be categorized into: 1) decision maker/negotiator, 2) configurer/bystander, 3) instructor/instructed, 4) discouraged gamer/encourager, and 5) performer/audience (2012). These are particularly interesting to digital play therapists as we negotiate what our role is in our therapeutic interactions, what the client's role is, and also, what the roles might be if/when the client and parents or others play when not in session. As you read the role descriptions in Table 11.1, explore which roles you feel would best fit the DPT dynamic.

Table 11.1 Game Play Dynamic Roles

Decision maker/ negotiator	Decisions in these roles included 1) when gaming activities would begin and end, 2) who would get a turn to play, 3) what game would be played, 4) what character or role would be played by whom, and 5) specific actions undertaken within the game. The negotiator would accept or protest the decision maker's decisions. The adults/mature adults decided when game play would begin and end, and most other decisions were made by the younger player.
Instructor/ instructed	The instructor teaches, the instructed attempts to learn what is being taught.
Performer/ audience	The performer dramatically acts out portions of the gameplay, excitedly dances in celebrations, etc. The audience member watches the performance.
Configurer/ bystander	Configurers set up the gaming environment. They were responsible for switching among game consoles, selecting character profiles etc., while the other gamer(s), the bystanders, stood by and waited.
Discouraged gamer/ encourager	Discouraged gamers become discouraged in the game play and the other gamer, typically an adult or mature adult, would take on the role of encourager and strategizer.

Adapted from Vioda, A. & Greenburg, S. (2012). Console gaming across generations: exploring intergenerational interactions in collocated console gaming. Universal Access in the Information Society 11(1), 45–56.

It is my hope that the play therapist and their clients each occupy these roles in a fluid interplay between them during the digital play intervention.

Findings of the Vioda and Greenburg study indicated that intergenerational gaming can provide "some of the developmental benefits crucial to individual well-being" (2012, pp. 24–25), such as:

1) Younger-generation gamers being exposed to older-generation gamers who were:

   a. Models of prosocial behaviors
   b. Shared knowledge
   c. Shared experience

2) Different generation gamers took on different roles with more flexibility than previously observed in traditional play settings.
3) Younger gamers:

   a. Took on more leadership roles
   b. Had opportunities to practice:

      i. Being gracious experts
      ii. Patient teachers
      iii. Being more thoughtful hosts

(2012, pp. 24–25)

Digital Divide and Social Space

Aarsand (2007), found that play between family members of different generations, such as a grandparent and a grandchild, decreased the "digital divide". The digital divide refers to the chasm of knowledge and comfort often found between generations regarding digital information and experience. This was referred to as the "Fourth Cultural Technique" in the information technology world (Scavenius, 1998; Aarsand, 2007). The concern about the fourth cultural technique revolved around the worry that discrepancies in digital knowledge and experience were as concerning as discrepancies in math, writing, and reading. Emphasizing education and experience with digital tools allows students and professionals to have more equal access to opportunities and knowledge. Regarding the fourth cultural technique, the author offers: "It ensures that everybody has access to the most important sources of power in the information society, i.e. information and knowledge, and polarization is therefore avoided" (Scavenius, 1998, para. 5).

Aarsand conducted research which focused on the digital divide and the components which created such a divide (2007). The pure generational distinctions such as grandparent, parent, child, etc., were not sufficient. He wanted to discover what components contributed to/created this divide. One section of the research included a sibling dyad and a mother. It was noted that the older, more experienced sibling "exploited the knowledge asymmetry" and became the instructor in the process (p. 243). There can be a perceived knowledge asymmetry (Aarsand, 2007) where one participant has more knowledge regarding the task at hand than the other(s). This asymmetry can be used to distinguish the hierarchy within the play, that is, one player assumes the teacher role and the other(s) learn from them.

The dynamic is labeled as "unknown" to the mother as the eldest daughter is the one with the most knowledge of the computer game in the scenario. Typically, the adult has more knowledge so this dynamic shift can spark a host of reactions. This is seen as an unknown and uncomfortable situation for the mother due to her lack of knowledge. The mother becomes a bystander in the experiment as she is standing behind the children seated at the computer and not engaging directly in the gameplay for the majority of the interaction. Her attempts to engage include adding an additional component to the interactions; she asks multiple times if the children want food, along with very brief questions regarding the game play. The youngest daughter minimally answers her and the older one does not (Aarsand, 2007). It could easily be interpreted that the older daughter is so entranced by the gameplay that she does not hear the mother or does not want to attend to her, but it can also be possible that the injection of the request for feedback regarding food was incongruent. The request appears, based on the description of the scenario, to be based on the mother's exclusion and discomfort with the situation and the children might be reacting (ignoring) more to the incongruence than anything else. If children are on the playground playing soccer and another child comes into the play and wants to have a chat about dinosaurs, the people playing soccer will most likely not engage, or engage very minimally, about the dinosaur conversation, primarily because it is incongruent to the task already in motion.

The mother, as a bystander, was not directly engaged in the interaction between the children, however, if she had entered into the play the scenario could have been very different. She could have engaged in the play, learned along with the younger sister, entered into the social space and occupied it along with them. (Creating a social space includes the participants acting as competent participants together (Aarsand, 2007).) If her knowledge in her role as mother indicated that a snack was important, the momentary interruption of the task in motion to say, "hey, anyone want a snack while we play?" would most likely have been received very differently. The incongruence would not have been experienced in the same way. It would have been an added component to the task in motion as opposed to a disruption. I believe many play therapists fear that the inclusion of digital tools in therapy would place them in a similar role as this mother assumed; detached and unengaged, searching for a defined role and purpose. This does not need to be the case. Play therapists have a critical role and position when utilizing DPT.

Ultimately, Aarsand concluded, "Children display a competence in playing computer games that parents do not display, and it could therefore be claimed that the traditional knowledge asymmetries between children and adults are bracketed. But it is not that the generation gap exists de facto: it is not a black and white situation where children just display superior know-ledge in the field, while adults display a total lack of knowledge. Rather, the digital divide seems to be a result of joint actions taking place in encounters between children and adults, where the child is placed and ratified as some-one in the know, while the adult is placed and ratified as the less knowledge-able" (2007, p. 251). Rather than the digital divide indicating that the different generations are divided in a way that will not allow them to join, Aarsand finds that the divide helps to define the roles of the participants and thereby the interactions. He asserts, "The digital divide in fact becomes a resource for both children and adults to enter and sustain participation in activities. The digital divide is not seen as a essentialist gap, or a fixed divide between the generations, but it emerges as asymmetrical relations that get co-construed in social action" (2007, p. 251).

In digital play therapy we want the therapist to be as well-versed as possible regarding the hardware and software available, along with the therapeutic powers evoked by the interactions. This will eradicate the role assumed by the mother in this research. In a situation where the therapist is not familiar, the best-case scenario is for the digital divide to become a resource as Aarsand indicated. Additionally, we do not want the therapist to be a bystander or one who disrupts by injecting other "more therapeutic" features such as, "how was recess today?", and the like. The play therapist is to be involved in the co-created social space as a participant fully engaged in the interaction and gameplay. This is the space within which the therapeutic powers of play will be activated and experienced by both the client and the therapist. Additional conversations could certainly be held as they are congruent with the gameplay or even parallels made regarding their day to day experiences, however, they are to be experienced as congruent with the flow and dynamics of the play, not incongruent. It is similar to the concepts of "the real work", that is, the traditional example of playing a board game as an ice breaker or rapport builder in an effort to then get to "the real work". In that scenario, the board game play *is* the real work. Game play does have therapeutic components and value (please refer to the three editions of the book *Game Play* for more direction in this arena if desired) and can be used as the therapeutic interaction toward the treatment goals.

Digital Natives and Digital Immigrants

Mark Prensky (2001), discussed his term for people who are native speakers of the digital language, or "digital natives". In contrast, "digital immigrants" are those who were not born into the digital world but have interest and have integrated aspects of the digital world into their lives (Prensky, 2001). The comingling of digital natives and digital immigrants is very important for current digital co-play. At some point all parties involved in digital co-play will be digital natives and there will probably be other defined distinctions.

Many of the current licensed and registered play therapists today are digital immigrants. We were not born into this digital world, yet we are working to properly integrate and incorporate aspects into our therapeutic work. However, the next generations of play therapists will be predominantly digital natives and, as previously mentioned, they will be asking why digital tools are not utilized more in play therapy. The tides will certainly shift.

Conclusion

The navigation of this relatively new digital world is important for play therapists to explore. Finding therapeutic value in the DPT interactions rests on fundamentals outside of the play therapy world, such as the importance of co-play interactions and ethical and responsible online behavior. Continuing to explore these concepts will contribute to the play therapist's quest for competence and capability.

References

Aarsand, P. A. (2007). Computer and video games in family life: The digital divide as a resource in intergenerational interactions. *Childhood: A Global Journal of Child Research, 14*(2), 235–256.

Atkins, M. (2017). *Benefits of family game night.* Mommy University. https://mommyuniversitynj.com/2017/02/01/benefits-of-family-game-night/

Carver, M. D., & Jones, W. H. (1991). The family satisfaction scale. *Social Behavior and Personality: An International Journal, 20*(2), 71–83.

Chambers, D. (2012). Wii play as a family: The rise in family-centred video gaming. *Leisure Studies, 31*(1), 69–82.

Cherry, K. (2019, December 7). Stage 5. *Very Well Mind.* www.verywellmind.com/identity-versus-confusion-2795735

Chua, P. H., Jung, Y., Lwin, M. O., & Theng, Y. L. (2013). Let's play together: Effects of video-game play on intergenerational perceptions among youth and elderly participants. *Computers in Human Behavior, 29*(6), 2303–2311.

Common Sense Media. (2009). *Digital literacy and citizenship in the 21st century.* http://www.katyisd.org/parents/Documents/Digital%20Library.pdf

Curran, M., Ohler, J., & Ribble, M. (n.d.). White paper: Digital citizenship: A holistic primer. *Impero.* https://kc0eiuhlnmqwdxy1ylzte9ii-wpengine.netdna-ssl.com/us/wp-content/uploads/sites/16/2017/03/Digital-Citizenship-A-Holistic-Primer-v1.9.2.pdf

Impero (n.d.). *Being a good digital citizen and why students should care.* www.imperosoftware.com/us/blog/being-a-good-digital-citizen-and-why-students-should-care/

Kim, M., & Choi, D. (2018). Development of youth digital citizenship scale and implication for educational setting. *Educational Technology & Society, 21*(1), 155–171.

Merriam-Webster (2020). *Co.* www.merriam-webster.com/dictionary/co

Olson, W. H. (2004). *Family Satisfaction Scale (FSS).* Life Innovations.

Prensky, M. (2001). Digital natives digital immigrants. *On the Horizon (MCB University Press), 9*(5), 1–6. www.marcprensky.com/writing/Prensky%20-%20Digital%20Natives,%20Digital%20Immigrants%20-%20Part1.pdf

Scavenius, C. (1998). IT: The fourth cultural technique. *Educational Media International, 35*(4), 289–291.

Strage, A. A. (1998). Family context variables and the developments of self-regulation in college students. *Adolescence, 33*(129), 17–31.

Vioda, A., & Greenburg, S. (2012). Console gaming across generations: Exploring inter-generational interactions in collocated console gaming. *Universal Access in the Information Society*, *11*(1), 45–56. https://amy.voida.com/wp-content/uploads/2013/04/consoleGamingAcrossGenerations-uais.pdf

Wang, B., Taylor, L., & Sun, Q. (2018). Families that play together stay together: Investigating family bonding through video games. *New Media and Society*, *20*(1), 4074–4094.

Williams, J. L. (2018, September 4). Developing adolescent identity. *Center for Parent and Teen Communication*. https://parentandteen.com/developing-adolescent-identity/

12 Digital Play Therapy Interventions

Most play therapists love to learn about specific interventions. With DPT, though, the available hardware and software can evolve rapidly, so providing a few very specific interventions might not be helpful over time. It will not be long before the following interventions are outdated in some way. It is hoped that they represent ways one can think about using the different genres of digital play and allow the clinician to explore current options with more confidence.

A variety of interventions is really useful so the clinician can customize what is offered based on the needs of the client. This customization could be more non-directive in that the therapist offers a suite of options, or more directive by offering one or two options. Different therapists will approach interventions in different ways, and it can be eye-opening to read what others are doing. For this reason, intervention ideas were solicited from people who are actively using technology in mental health sessions. A special thank you to Dr. Robert Jason Grant, Leslie Baker, Kevin Hull, Jennifer Taylor, Dr. Rachel Altvater, Theresa Fraser, Sueann Kenney-Noziska, Tammy Pawlak, Michael Ehrig, John Burr, and Dr. Ryan Kelly for contributing to this chapter.

Privacy and Ethical Considerations

- Confidentiality is of utmost importance and the same rules apply to DPT.
- Be diligent and protect your client's identity.
  - o This includes usernames, passwords, and registration information.
- Follow HIPAA regulations and the ethical guidelines defined by your licensing body.
- Register any new accounts in the therapist's information or anonymously unless the program has compliant mental health specific confidentiality features in place.
- Save, transfer, and/or print any creations as appropriate for inclusion in the client's record.
- Delete any images from your hardware's camera roll and be sure to save, transfer and/or print.

Phone/Tablet/Computer

Social Media Madness

Author: Robert Jason Grant Ed. D, LPC, RPT-S, ACAS
Hardware: Phone or tablet
Software: Facebook, Twitter, Instagram, and similar
Population: Preteen and teen (who use social media); individual or group work
Instructions: Social media sites are very popular among adolescents and many adolescents lack the social skills to navigate social media sites. It is not uncommon to find adolescents' social media use to include a lack of boundary awareness, lack of appropriateness, inability to navigate through challenging situations, and sometimes ethical and legal issues. This intervention teaches adolescents how to identify appropriate and inappropriate ways to use social media sites and how to stay safe with their interactions.

Before implementing this intervention, the practitioner should communicate with the parents about the child's social media use. The practitioner will want to find out what social media the child uses and if the parents have been monitoring the use and what issues have arisen. The practitioner and child can sit anywhere in the practitioner's office and will view the chosen device (phone or tablet) together. The practitioner will begin the intervention by telling the adolescent that they will be discussing appropriate ways to use social media. The practitioner and adolescent will discuss the various social media options that the adolescent currently participants in. This might include Facebook, Twitter, Instagram, Snapchat, Discord, or any number of programs. The practitioner and child will choose one of the child's social media accounts to use for the intervention. If the child does not want to use any of their accounts, the practitioner can use one of the practitioner's accounts. The following acronym is written down on a piece of paper and will be used for the intervention (the acronym guide is used even if the account being viewed is not Facebook):

F=friend
A=angry
C=careful
E=embarrassing
B=bad
O=odd
O=oh no!
K=kind

The practitioner and child look at and discuss different posts on the social media account and label them in one of the acronym categories. For example: a post might be labeled by the child as a friend's post. The practitioner would then ask, "Who is a friend?", "Why is this person a friend?", or the child might find a post and indicate the post is an angry post. The practitioner would ask, "Why is it an angry post?", "Is it appropriate to post angry things?". The practitioner and child will try to find examples for each category in the acronym. Once they have found and discussed an example of each one, the adolescent can show the practitioner one of his or her favorite things online. Some additional example practitioner questions include "What would be an embarrassing post?", "What would be an odd or bad to post?", "What is a post that could get someone in trouble?", and "What is a kind or appropriate post?".

Rationale: This technique helps adolescents work on social skills related to participating in and socializing through social media. This technique requires the child to have a social media account or permission from parents to develop one. The practitioner should discuss with the child appropriateness and inappropriateness in regard to navigating social media. By looking at and talking about real posts, the practitioner and child can apply what they are discussing for better understanding and application. The practitioner may want to talk to the parents about monitoring the child's social media account and practice this intervention periodically at home with their child.[1]

Animating Self Intervention

Animating Self

Author: Leslie Baker, MA, MFT, NBC, RPT-S
Hardware: iPhone or iPad
Software: *Morfo 3D Face Booth* by SunSpark Labs; iOS only
Population: Ages 5 and up

Instructions

Step One: Create rapport with your client to develop trust and safety. The therapeutic alliance is key in introducing any intervention. Discuss the opportunity to create a self-expressive art piece to be animated by your client, leaving room to hear their concerns. Always be open to the pace of your client. It is key to honor their feelings and understand that they may choose to not participate in any art or play intervention until they feel safe and ready. Once a client feels ready, proceed with the Animating Self Intervention, introduce the expressive art part of the Intervention and proceed with the creation of the art piece.

Step Two: Create a self-expressive art piece (this is not digital). Any expressive art media, from crayons, markers, paints, clay, collage, to finger painting, can be utilized to create a self-expressive art piece for this intervention to be effective. The creative art piece simply needs to contain two eyes, one nose, and a mouth. Including details from pens, markers, sparkles, glitter, googly-eye stickers, or other crafting materials can bring a face to life. Complete the expressive creation and place for it to dry.

Step Three: Once the object of self-expression is completed and contains eyes, nose & mouth. Take a photo of the art. Point the camera straight onto the "face" of the creation. Save the photo to your photo roll. Open the Morfo 3D Face Booth and upload the photo into the app.

Step Four: Once the photo is uploaded into the Morfo 3D Face Booth app, adjust the art piece to fit the face form provided in the app. Using your fingertips, adjust the eye forms to fit each eye on the art piece and then use the mouth form to fit the mouth. This allows for the animation to be in best place to create the most accurate facial movements. Press "save".

Step Five: Press the "record" button and have the client record a sentence or two that they would like their art to say. This can be something spontaneous or a script the client developed. A short poem can be written and recited, or words can simply be spoken that express their feelings or thoughts. Press play and their art will repeat the message with the Animating Self creation will come alive. One can change the voice pitch to high or low or leave it as the client's voice. This is another opportunity to explore voice and narrative with your client. Therapists can explore: as you hear what your creation is saying, what feelings arise? Do your feelings change when you hear the different voice tones? Describe the feelings in your body as you listen and watch the animation. The application also allows for other costumes, facial expressions, makeup, dance, and music to change and decorate a client's Animating Self.

Step Six: The image can be saved and shared (with the client only) if it is appropriate. Otherwise the images can be saved as a photo, printed and stored, or uploaded into their file.

Rationale: The Animating Self Intervention was inspired by the Animated Mask intervention by Dr. Jeffery Jamerson, MS (2019). In therapy, creating self-representation masks is often an intervention used in order to explore the development of the self in children, teens, and adults. Moreover, masks have often been a part of therapy not only to express one's inner self, but also to provide an outward form of expression of the self the client presents in the world. *Morfo 3D Face Booth* allows a further dimension of this self-exploration by blending art therapy and narrative therapy to create a mask, animate the mask, and then to explore the clients story through the words the client adds as they voice the mask through this application.

In the exploration of this media application, I began to expand the use of the Morfo 3D Face Booth beyond the use of Animating Masks. The Morfo 3D Face Booth app allows for any self-expressive art piece to be voiced by the app. In the exploration, this opened an opportunity for clients to give voice and story to many art forms. Clients can create a collection of Animating Self creations by exploring their trauma stories, exploring their healing process, exploring their loss and grief stories and unfolding narratives of their self-development in the therapy process, simply by adding a face and a narrative to their Animating Self creations.

In closing, the Animating Self Intervention allows the therapist and client the ability to expand beyond the mask and to move into multiple expressive modalities for creating and voicing their stories. What's more, the Morfo 3D Face Booth app can animate and play back the client's voice in real time, thereby creating one or a series of these stories to process an experience in a powerful journey of healing for the client. Applying this tool provides an opportunity to assist the client in voicing their stories; in having their stories witnessed; and in the ability to process their trauma, loss, grief, discovery and growth of their self.

Minecraft to Help With School Fears

Author: Kevin B. Hull, Ph.D., LMHC
Hardware: Tablet/phone/console/computer
Software: Minecraft
Population: Child/Pre-teen
Instructions: School is a large part of a young person's daily life. For those with emotional issues, sensory problems, and neurodevelopmental delays, attending school can feel like a war zone. As a result, many young people are terrified to attend school and experience fear on a daily basis. Fear results from many sources: bullying, rejection, and failure. Games like Minecraft are fun and inviting to young people and are useful in the therapy room because it is usually familiar and fun, while providing the young person with a sense of being in control. Just like life, Minecraft has themes and metaphors of overcoming challenges, decision-making, relying on others for help, developing attributes and abilities, creating tools for survival, and finding spaces of safety and comfort. Therapists can use these themes and metaphors in Minecraft to help young people broaden perspective taking and increase self-confidence, while developing better decision making and overcoming fears.

Before implementing this intervention, it is helpful to explain the use of Minecraft during the therapeutic process to the parent. Explanations of how themes and metaphors can broaden the child's perspective and coping skills enables parents to be supportive of the tools and techniques, instead of thinking that the therapist and young person are "just playing" and "wasting time". This can also be a teaching tool to help the parent see how they can join in their child's play and not only promote relationship but also help their child feel supported as they face the problems and issues of school.

Mode of Play: The therapist may be an observer while the child plays as a single player, or the therapist may join in the game and play together with the child. It is interesting to note the various "modes" of play in Minecraft:

• Survival Mode: Enemies exist, resources must be gathered, and damage can happen to the player's character.

- Creative Mode: Unlimited resources, flying is possible, and no damage occurs.
- Flat World: A virtual sandbox in which the player may create on a completely flat surface.
- Infinite World: A realistic world complete with mountains, rivers, and biomes.

As play begins, the therapist should look for themes in the child's play. What mode is chosen? How do they create a character? If playing together, how does the child relate to the therapist's character within the game. The therapist can assess decision making, planning, and how the child deals with challenges and obstacles as well as enemies. In creative mode, does the child finish a creation or is there a chaotic nature to the interaction with the game?

Game play opens discussion of metaphors through reflective statements by the therapist.

- Facing that enemy seems like what you face at school each day. I'm wondering what you're feeling now as you tried to get out of that situation.
- You figured it out! Good for you! You didn't give up. I'm wondering if there are some things you can think of to make the situation at school better.
- I noticed to asked me to help you build our house. Is there anyone at school that you feel safe with to help you during times when you feel afraid?
- This shelter we built feels really safe. I'm wondering if there's a way to make a "safe place" at school when you're feeling out of control and afraid.

Rationale: The goal is to help the young person make the connection between the situations in the game and the school experience. Game play helps instill a sense of control that can transfer to a real-world scenario and also helps the young person put thoughts and feelings into words. Playing with the therapist is a great picture of working together and that the child is not alone. Gaming produces a sense of mastery and control and provides a context for the young person to be aware of the sense of control that is possible in their real world.

Adapted from Hull, K. B. (2015). Technology in the playroom. In K. J. O'Conner, C. Schaefer & L. D. Braverman (Eds.), *Handbook of play therapy* (2nd Ed.) (pp. 613–627). John Wiley and Sons.

Touch and Learn – Emotions

Author: Jennifer Taylor, LCSW, RPT-S
Hardware: Phone or tablet
Software: Touch and Learn – Emotions app, no Wi-Fi required

Population: Preschool and elementary school aged children and/or children diagnosed with autism spectrum disorder or other developmental delays

Instructions: A basic goal of many mental health treatment plans is to correctly name feelings words and be able to understand and recognize the facial cues of others. After downloading this Touch and Learn Emotions app, the user is shown four high-quality images of real people making over 30 different feelings faces or emotions. The four images are equal if size and can all be seen at one time easily on a regular phone. The voice in the app names a feeling (for example, sad, proud, excited, etc.) and the user touches the corresponding picture that matches the feeling. If the user correctly identifies the feeling, the app responds with positive praise like "Good job!" or "You got it". If the user chooses incorrectly, then they hear a buzzing sound and can continue to try again until they do choose correctly. Users are not scored or graded and can continue with new prompts for as long as they desire. The faces shown for each face represent people of diverse cultural backgrounds and all ages (birth through old age).

As an assessment tool, this app is a quick and easy way to learn how well children can identify feelings based on visual cues (looking at real people's faces). Although the app does not have any scoring or game-style features, the clinician can simply keep a tally mark on a sheet of paper as the client works through a sample set of pictures. As a baseline, a clinician might notice how many feelings are correctly identified out of a set of ten choices. If a child is able to correctly identify the majority of faces, this may be an indication that they have some basic skills in identifying emotions. Clinicians can also notice if the child does well on basic emotions (happy, sad, mad) but lacks the richness of emotional expression for other feelings (proud, frustrated, excited).

When working with a child that has a limited vocabulary of feeling faces, has difficulty identifying her own emotions, or has deficits in recognizing and understanding the facial cues of others, this app can be helpful. As an ongoing tool, the clinician and child then practice making the feelings faces for each other, can discuss any errors in identification (for example, confusing, mad, and worried) and note the child's progress over time.

Rationale: This app shows high-quality photographs of a diverse group of people (ethnicity, age, gender) that allows the child an opportunity to mimic the expressions observed by the variety of people that may be encountered in their daily life. Because there is no scoring or gaming component, the child can practice as few or as many faces as they can tolerate without any pressure to outperform anyone else. The app doesn't collect any personal data or retain any information so it can be used repeatedly throughout the day without any concern for handling protected health information.

YouTube as a Means to Foster Communication

Author: Rachel Altvater, Psy. D., RPT-S
Hardware: Computer, tablet, or smartphone
Software: Website or YouTube app and the internet
Population: All ages
Rationale: Leisurely play has transmuted in the past decade. YouTube is presently one of the most popular websites and smartphone/tablet applications (apps) amongst youth. It features a plethora of video content for entertainment and educational purposes. Children and adolescents are infatuated with and spend a noteworthy amount of time watching the wide variety of videos readily available on the site. Popular YouTube stars and videos become trendy topics and are met with millions of views and channel subscriptions.

Videos can be incorporated into play sessions for assessment and intervention purposes. YouTube content that children and adolescents absorb for hours will give a substantial amount of insight into their internal and external experiences. What draws this child to this video? What needs or desires are being met? Children often choose to spend their unrestricted time engaging in play with something which or someone who provides a deep level of satisfaction, enjoyment, mastery, connection, control, and purpose. Play therapy assessment focuses on the same concepts. Translating this assessment from traditional toys to digital toys greatly abets modern children who only know a world surrounding by technological screens. These videos can also be utilized to process presenting concerns, provide directive interventions, and offer psychoeducation for a wide range of presenting concerns.

Use

Child-led: Children and adolescents can be invited to choose whichever video(s) they choose to watch and share in the session, without further directives or suggestions. It is important to remember that application of traditional play therapy techniques (e.g., tracking, reflection of content, reflection of feeling) still applies to digital interventions. Inquisition about the choice and content of the video allows the child or adolescent to invite the clinician further into their world. Clinicians are encouraged to ask themselves what they notice about the video. Are there any parallels to this video and something the child thinks, feels, or has experienced? Externalization and projection are essential components to the play therapy process to provide a safe enough distance to process psychological material. The individuals on the screen hold the same role as a traditional, tangible toy in this regard. Of note, if an inappropriate video is chosen, the clinician is invited to further explore the video components with the child, teach appropriate boundaries, and set necessary limits. Children sometimes watch videos without direct parental supervision, so they might become exposed to content that they are unaware is inappropriate.

Clinician-led: Clinicians research YouTube content before or during the play session to provide a directive play therapy intervention. For example, if a child is struggling with self-esteem difficulties, a clinician might choose to show the child an empowering video or music video about self-love and appreciation. If a child is struggling with anxiety and panic attacks, a clinician might choose to play a guided imagery or progressive muscle relaxation video. Clinicians are encouraged to implement digital creativity in finding relevant videos. Search engines (e.g., Google) can be helpful for finding an abundance of ideas. Video choice is dependent upon clinician comfort, relevance to presenting concerns, and developmental appropriateness for the child.

PowerPoint Journeys

Author: Theresa Fraser CYC-P, CPT-S, RPT, MA, RCT
Hardware: Computer/Mac/PC with microphone
Software: PowerPoint
Population: Children/adolescents
Intervention: After child or adolescent (builder) builds a world in the sandtray, a photo is taken and the world is given a title by the builder. The therapist copies the photo and places it in a PowerPoint template. Each PowerPoint slide depicts the photo of one sandtray. The title of the world is added to the slide as sessions progress in the therapeutic process. As the therapeutic termination stage approaches, the therapist invites the builder to review the PowerPoint and reflect on the sandtray journeys they have shared. The discussion can include identification of themes that have shown up, special images (miniatures) that have been chosen, images that may have only been used once or in multiple trays, and perhaps how themes have impacted life outside of the tray or how themes have related to the treatment goals identified for therapy.

If the children or adolescent is comfortable, she/she/they can use the PowerPoint program to record the narration of their sandtray journey. The therapist should practice in advance using the narration tool by choosing the slide show tab to click the record slide show button. They then can support the child/adolescent in doing the same. The PowerPoint can be given to the builder as well as shared with caregivers in the closing session if the builder agrees.

Emotional Texting

Author: Sueann Kenney-Noziska, MSW, LCSW, RPT-S
Hardware: Phone or tablet
Software: No additional software needed.
Population: Adolescents; individual work

Instructions: This technique uses the numbers and corresponding letters on a cellphone keypad as a medium to identify and process various emotions. During the activity, the therapist and client take turns spelling out different feelings using the numbers on the phone keypad while the other person tries to decode the emotion. Each feeling is processed.

At the beginning of the session, the importance of identifying and processing emotions is discussed. Part of this discussion should focus on the dynamic of ignoring distressing feelings instead of dealing with them. Even though this may seem effective, the feelings still exist and continue to bother the person until the emotions are brought out into the open and addressed.

In this game, feeling words are spelled out using the numbers on the cell phone keypad, thereby giving a "code" that the other person must decipher. Once the emotion is decoded, it is processed. For example, "sad" would be coded as "723", "scared" would be "722733", and "confused" would be "26638733". Since this intervention requires decoding via the process of elimination, the activity is best suited for adolescents who have the cognitive sophistication to decode the emotions.

At the end of the game, the following processing questions can be asked:

1. What was the easiest feeling to discuss?
2. What was the hardest feeling to discuss?
3. Who is the easiest person in your life for you to talk with about your feelings?
4. Who is the hardest person for you to communicate your feelings to?
5. What can be done to make it easier to express your emotions?

Rationale: Therapy provides a unique forum for facilitating the development of healthy emotional expression and regulation. This intervention targets emotional identification and processing using the letters on the keypad of the cell phone. For clients who avoid discussing feelings, particularly distressing ones, this technique can provide the foundation for overall emotional regulation.

As feelings are chosen for the intervention, the therapist can prescriptively select emotions according to presenting problems, issues, and/or treatment goals. The emotions identified and processed can be common emotions to support general emotional expression or can be feelings geared toward a specific topic such as divorce, death, or abuse.

Throughout the activity, the therapist has the opportunity to normalize and validate emotions. As an additional component, coping skills to manage emotional distress can be identified and discussed.

Meet Them Where They're at

Author: Tammy Pawlak, MMFT, ACAS, BCCS

Hardware: iOS (Apple iPad)

Software: Virtual Sandtray app
Population: Children, adolescents individual and families
Instructions: "Meet them where they're at". This is a common phrase used in the community of therapeutic clinicians. Some children and adolescents, especially those who are on the autism spectrum or have sensory difficulties, find it difficult to enjoy or even participate in interventions done within a physical sand tray. Furthermore, many children and adolescents who enter therapy services are not doing so willingly, and as an adolescent, who wants to play in the sand? In a society that is technology-driven, meeting a client or family where they are might include the use of technology and electronic devices. In the same aspect, parents may express or complain that they do not understand why their child spends so much time using technology, thus sometimes creating a lack of cohesion between parent/child. This Virtual Sandtray app intervention not only helps a clinician to meet the client where they are at, but it can also help a parent to meet their child where they are at.

The clinician will review with the child and parent the use of the Virtual Sandtray app, reminding them there is no good or bad, no wrong or right in either of their creations, and to let the clinician know when each person is finished. The clinician will invite the child to either create one sand tray for child and parent to use together or divide the tray any way of their choosing and designate which portion of the tray the parent will use. The child, parent and clinician can sit anywhere in the office space while parent and child both view and use the iPad that has the Virtual Sandtray app loaded onto it. The clinician will give a directive or prompt to the family the same way they would if using a physical sand tray such as, "Create a tray with your favorite things".

When the child and parent inform the clinician that they are finished with their tray, the clinician will ask each one to share their creation with the clinician and with one another, usually beginning with the parent. The clinician will invite the parent to identify strengths they observed of the child while creating the tray; identify similarities of the trays; identify strengths of the child/parent relationship.

Rationale: Children and adolescents may find it difficult to express their likes/dislikes, needs/wants, emotions/feelings verbally or in a physical sand tray with a clinician or parent. These tasks can be accomplished through the use of a device and app that piques their interest and assists with expressing themselves. This intervention can assist a clinician to build rapport with a client in order to meet them where they are at in their treatment needs. This intervention will also facilitate parent and child working together while allowing the parent to experience and better understand their child through a virtual and technological world.

Console

Super Mario Party – Social Skills Group

Author: Michael Ehrig, M.S., AMFT

Hardware: Nintendo Switch, additional controllers; optional: television, HDMI cable, Nintendo Switch dock

Software: Super Mario Party is a Nintendo Switch (Console) game

Rationale: The social skill deficits for children that can be treated with the use of this intervention are basic communication skills, developing empathy, building rapport, problem-solving skills, how to work together, waiting for their turn, and regulation of emotions, to name a few. Each child will have the opportunity to experience these social skills through unique situations within the game. Additionally, individual symptoms of depression or anxiety can be secondary symptoms treated within the group separate from the regulation of emotions that arise from gameplay. Each child may experience an increase in self-esteem and positive emotions through task mastery of individual mini-games within the gameplay.

Principles: The game layout is very similar to a traditional game board. Each player in the group chooses their character. The players get to choose how big of a board they would like to play on (the bigger the board, the longer it takes for the game to end with a winner). Every player is given their own turn to roll a dice to move spaces on the board. After every player has had a chance to roll their dice and move on the board, a mini-game is triggered. These mini-games can be one player versus the other three players, two players teamed up together to play against the other two players, or all players together on the same team trying to beat the computer-controlled character. Depending on the layout of the mini-game such as one versus three, two versus two, or everyone on the same team, the winner or winners will gain stars. The stars are the currency for who is the current leader and eventual overall winner at the end of the board.

Application: The role of the therapist for this particular intervention is quite simple in that the players will run the game itself. In order to enhance the experience therapeutically, the therapist can utilize the pause button. The pause button allows the therapist to stop and process after each mini game. After the mini-game, players can discuss what feelings or experiences they felt within the game and the therapist can make the connection to the social skill being enacted within the activity. For example, a mini-game will drop four types of sport balls down to players one by one and it is up to the player to pass it to the correct player to insert the ball into the correct bucket in order to get a completion score for everyone to get a star. The therapist will be able to process problem solving, communication, working together as a team, and waiting for their turn among others.

Mario Kart 8 Deluxe – Family

Author: Michael Ehrig, M.S., AMFT

Hardware: Nintendo Switch with additional controllers as needed, optional: additional television, Nintendo Switch Dock

Software: Mario Kart 8 Deluxe is a Nintendo Switch (console) game. The game allows for up to 12 players, which is perfect for small or big families. Additional controllers will be needed to support up to 12 players. Additionally, a big television would provide a better experience as the game divides each player's character into a small box on the screen. The more the players, the smaller the character box for each player to see. The Nintendo Switch connects easily to a television screen through a provided HDMI cable when purchasing the Nintendo Switch Console or with the dock.

Rationale: The Mario Kart 8 Deluxe game provides a non-threatening environment for families to be able to work on broken relationships. The relationships among family members may have deteriorated over time because of arguments or conflict, causing members of the family to feel that every interaction in the present and future will be negative. Through gameplay, symptoms of communication, frustration tolerance, stress management, self -regulation, and positive emotions can be experienced. Individual symptoms of depression and anxiety can be secondary treatment goals through positive interactions among family members.

Principles: This game allows for each family member to choose their own character and vehicle. Each character and vehicle have their own strengths and weaknesses within the race. Small characters are quick but can be easily bumped off and around the track, while bigger characters are slower but do not budge when bumping others off or around the track. Specific vehicles also provide strength and weaknesses such as increased speed but lack of control, increased control but slower speed, or an overall average but not good or great car. The races can be team-based (family versus computer) or specific family members on opposing teams. On the track, players are able to gain items to help them, such as being able to plant a banana peel to cause others to spin out of control if they run over it or items that can slow other racers' progression through the level.

Application: For the context of this intervention, the therapist can utilize the team-based option to have the family members work together on the same team. Each member of the team wants to finish as quickly as possible within the game to gain a score which encourages the family support each other to do well because it is an overall score and not an individual. Through the various items that help players individually, the therapist can equate those items to supportive acts for the family to practice in their daily interactions. For example, a player can lay a banana peel and state an affirmation about another person or things they are grateful that another family member does. As the family is able to have more positive interactions, symptoms of communication, frustration tolerance, stress management, and self-regulation will start to mend broken relationships. The family will have experience working together in a fun way to achieve a greater goal similar to their family goals in life.

Smash Brothers – Individual

Author: Michael Ehrig, M.S., AMFT

Hardware: Nintendo Switch

Software: Super Smash Brothers Ultimate is a Nintendo Switch console game that allows up to 8 players to play at once. No additional controllers are required for the individual gameplay utilized in this intervention. Additionally, a television is not needed either as the client can play on the gamepad with the joy-con controllers attached or use the console as a television screen and detach the joy-con controllers.

Rationale: The gameplay allows for people to utilize self-expression, self-regulation, stress management, frustration tolerance, and exploration of coping skills. An individual who finds themselves dealing with depression with heavy irritability or difficulties processing anger in effective ways can benefit from the gameplay. Super Smash Brothers Ultimate allows for players to control their environment and express anger without harm or consequences to those around them.

Principles: The client is allowed to choose their character and each character has their own special abilities. There are different modes such as one versus seven or team-based matches in which the client can work together with computer allies. Throughout the match, items are dropped from the sky onto the fighting grounds that can aid players in winning. The goal is to knock out each opposing player three or more times until the last player or team is left standing. As each player is hit more and more by opposing players, the percentage of that player rises. When a player gets to a high percentage, it becomes easier to knock that player off of the map.

Application: Therapists can utilize the various different aspects of this game to education, reflect, and bring awareness of a client's anger manifestation. Therapists can educate clients to help them understand as stressful or frustrating experiences happen without processing, the percentage of our anger rises. After the anger gets to a certain percentage, it takes one small tap similar to the game for the player to express their anger in an unhealthy way. The items dropped in the game can be utilized to bring awareness to a client's coping skills in real life. For example, if a player eats a fruit in the game, the percentage will go down. Therapists can help clients make connections on what coping skills (fruit) can they utilize to help bring their percentage down. Also, being able to reflect on a client's experiences while expressing anger within the gameplay can bring additional awareness from the therapist to the client.

Rock Band 4 – Family

Author: Michael Ehrig, M.S., AMFT

Hardware: Xbox One console, HDMI cable, Rock Band instrument set

Software: Rock Band 4 is a multiplayer game on the Xbox One console. The game has different types of music instruments that can be purchased for gameplay. For the family intervention, it is best to have a guitar, drum set, and microphone for the best experience. There are bundles that can be purchased with the game and three musical instruments together. The console connects to a television screen through a HDMI cable.

Rationale: Families struggling with communication, clear understanding of familial roles, and negative interactions can benefit from this intervention. Individual symptoms of concentration, depression, and anxiety can be secondary benefits to the intervention. As each member is able to gain confidence from mastery and positive interactions, the negative symptoms may decrease.

Principles: The game has 1,500 songs, ranging in difficulty from easy to hard. It has individual solo pieces within the overall song that must be completed by the different instruments. The game takes a good amount of concentration and focus to be able to properly hit all the notes to play a complete song. Each player has to choose their instrument such as the guitar, drum, and singing. Players can also make their own songs together as a family.

Application: The therapist can utilize the clear role definition and appreciation of each role similar to a family system. Each player in the game has a significant role for an overall goal of completing the song together. This allows for families to work together and encourage each other to do the best they can and be there for support if one is struggling. The connections between the family dynamics in the game are similar to the family dynamics in life. Also, the gameplay allows for family members to practice effective communication in a safe activity and environment. After the family is able to gain some experience working together, the therapist can have them create their own song, similar to creating their own goals (song) for the family outside of the game.

Overcooked – Family/Couples

Author: Michael Ehrig, M.S., AMFT

Hardware: Nintendo Switch console; optional: television, HDMI, additional controllers, dock

Software: Overcooked is a Nintendo Switch console game. It is a multiplayer game that allows up to four players. It can be played on a television screen with a HDMI cable connection. Additional controllers are required if four players are playing at one time.

Rationale: In the context of couples, the symptoms of depression, anxiety, and communication can be improved through gameplay. The game is fast-paced and will elicit communication styles between couples when under distress and timed tasks. The game requires a great amount of concentration, focus, and teamwork.

Principles: Each player is placed within the kitchen and given a set of orders to cook for hungry customers. There are different roles within the kitchen that each player must quickly adapt to. If the orders are not created in time or are not up to perfection by customer's standards, then players will lose the game. It has a variety of modes based on different competitive challenge levels, meant to push each person in the kitchen to their limits.

Application: Therapists can use this game to assess the couple's communication levels from a base level and when adversity hits. The therapist can identify dysfunctional communication styles and see who shuts down and who overpowers the conversation in a non-threatening environment of gameplay. A very good benefit to this intervention is that it is providing a profound experience for the couple to remember and draw upon after therapy. Simply providing strategies to fix communication in traditional talk therapy may be difficult for the couple to learn anything new since it is repeating the same communication from home. When utilizing this intervention, couples may find themselves having better communication in a fun and learning environment that will be easier to recall in the future.

Virtual Reality

Tilting in Therapy

Author: John Burr, LCSW, RPT-S
Population: Adolescent (12+), adult. Individual
Hardware: Oculus Quest (n.d., also available on other virtual reality platforms)
Software: Google Tilt Brush
Instructions: The use of virtual reality is gaining in popularity among adolescent and young adults. Using the language of technology with our current generation provides a pathway to their inner world that has previously been unavailable.

Before implementing this intervention, the practitioner should seek permission from the parents about their adolescent's use of VR. I explain to the parents that the application I use is an art program and that it is no different than their child being asked to draw, paint, use clay, or other expressive arts, except this is done in a 3D manner.

I use an Oculus Quest all-in-one mobile VR headset in my psychotherapeutic practice. Because it is an all-in-one system there are no wires or computer needed. The portability allows me to use the system anywhere I want. The application used with the Oculus Quest is Google Tilt Brush. Tilt Brush is a 3D painting program that is easy to use and requires no artistic skills. The app has a variety of brushes that have animated effects and sounds. Brushes include fire, stars, electricity, snow, petals, diamonds, wiggles, and more. The application also allows you to insert images that are preinstalled or to access a website and upload from a list of thousands of free images available.

Before using this intervention, the practitioner needs to have experience using Tilt Brush so he/she can help the client use the tools available. The first time a client uses Tilt Brush, a great deal of the time will be spent becoming familiar with the application and the use of the hand controllers. My clients easily learn how to use this app and can create amazing art where they are completely immersed in their creation.

Tilt Brush allows you to "cast" what is being done in VR to your phone. An Oculus app will need to be installed on your phone. The "casting" allows the practitioner to be a witness and to have an active part of the creative process.

The practitioner can use a directive or non-directive approach. A non-directive approach would be done by asking the client to create whatever they feel prompted to make with no direction or expectation of what to create. A directive approach might include asking your client to create their hopes, desires, anxiety, depression, or fear. An example would be if a client drew their depression, the practitioner could prompt them to literally go inside the depression and to experience it from the inside out, which can only be done three-dimensionally. You can transport away from what was created or be above or below it. You can easily increase or decrease the art allowing the client to create different experiences using size. This allows the client to gain perspective and insights and to experience their inner world through VR.

Rationale: My clients often say they are "blown away" when they use the Oculus Quest and the Tilt Brush application. They tell me it's cool, creative, and fun. One of the benefits of using VR art in therapy is your client being able to literally go inside their art. Using VR is using the language of our youth today. It takes painting in therapy to a whole new level. The app is fully interactive and involves the use of the body, sound, color, images, space and more. Your client is limited only by their imagination. The canvas in unlimited, so clients can create as much art as they desire. Using VR art in therapy increases the possibility to express feelings, emotions, and to facilitate a change of perspective.

I have been using expressive arts for 34 years and for me this has been a game-changer when working with my clients, especially teenagers. I must admit that, when I have free time at work, I can be found creating my own world of imagination.

Wander VR Journeys

Author: Theresa Fraser CYC-P, CPT-S, RPT, MA, RCT
Hardware: Oculus Quest, Oculus Go

Software: Wander
Other: Internet is required, as the program utilizes the Google Street view program
Population: Children/adolescents/families
Intervention: Children and youth in the care of a child welfare agency often experience multiple placement changes. "This means that each time a child is moved, they lose not only their current caregivers but also the relationships they have with other siblings (foster/adoptive/full/step/kin), peer relationships, and school relationships".

(Fraser, 2014, p. 27)

Sometimes the treatment goal is to support the child/youth to create a 2D Life Book that chronicles the experiences they have had, the relationships they have shared, and places they have been. Life Book work beginnings are linked in the 1960's to Mary R. Horn of the Children's Bureau of Los Angeles. Ms. Horn identified that a Life Book can include a scrapbook or photo album with ticket stubs, report cards, or photos (Aust, 1981). This 2D tool serves as an overall artifact of their life experiences.

When photographs have been lost or unavailable, Google images or Google street view can provide necessary resources. This is especially valuable for children/youth who have immigrated to a new country or have who lost all that they have owned because of house fires or moves.

Life story work uses the Life Book as a therapeutic tool to help the child understand the events as they were experienced. The predisposing, precipitating, and perpetuating factors surrounding each event are explored to create the story or understanding that accompanies an artifact. Therefore, though Life Books provide details of the child's history, they may not provide information that helps the child have an understanding of his or her history. This is important so that the feelings of loss are connected to specific events rather than transferred to new experiences.

(Fraser, 2014, p. 30)

A 3D or immersive life story work experience can be achieved with VR tools and programs such as Wander.

In his paper "The Ultimate Display", Ivan Sutherland (1965) introduced immersion in a simulated world. He stated that VR is more than just interacting with 3D worlds; it provides the opportunity for the traveler to interact in remote real worlds, computer-generated worlds, or a combination of these (Sutherland, 1965; Gobbetti & Scateni, 1998). Using the Oculus headset, the participant both sees and hears things in the virtual environment. The system paired with the program Wander can help children not only see previous environments but also visit/experience these as the Wander program paired with Google street view.

Consideration

The therapist needs to ensure that both therapeutic alliance and safety have been created with the child/adolescent/family as sensory experiences can be a powerful reminder of the past. Hence, the therapist needs to also be skilled at holding such experiences, especially if they have also not experienced the virtual environment. The therapist also needs to prepare the child/youth's caregivers so that they also can hold the power of the experience in between VR sessions.

Familial Adaptation

Supporting a child to revisit early spaces can assist the child/youth to link past to present. If current caregivers are provided the same opportunity, they can gain insight into the spaces where the child has had to survive. This can assist foster/adoptive parents to gain empathy, which can help the child develop an increased sense of safety and permanency in order to increase attunement and promote attachment (Reese, 2009). This process can further assist caregivers to acknowledge issues of grief and loss.

Other Applications

The VR experience can be also valuable for:

- Children/youth/families who have immigrated to a new country and did not have adequate time to say goodbye to their place of origin, especially if the stored Google street view posts a pre-war view.
- Children/youth/families have lost all that they have owned because of house fires or eviction.
- Children who have lost family members in other towns, states, countries and did not get to say goodbye.

Ultimately, the goal of utilizing this tool is support the child/youth/family in adapting to the life experiences and transitions that have often been forced upon them. "Transitions permeate our lives. The capacity to successfully transition from one place to another, one activity to another, one internal state to another is fundamentally related to the capacity to self-regulate" (Perry, 2013, p. 698).

BreathePeace World

Author: Ryan Kelly, PhD
Hardware: HTC Vive Pro, two Vive controllers, two 1.0 base stations, 8 by 8 feet or more of VR space, Vive wireless adapter (optional), Bluetooth heart-rate monitor (optional)
Software: BreathePeace World

Population: Young children (4–10 years) working on emotional or stress regulation

Instructions: Before the session, interview the parents to identify the ABC's of the child's anxiety or emotional dysregulation. Introduce them to the techniques you will be working on with the child, including the VR medium and the BreathePeace World program. You should encourage the parents to purchase the Aya book to read to their child before the session to foster interest and conceptualization. The next session should be with the child, and proceed as follows:

1) Give age-appropriate psychoeducation on whatever is causing the dys-regulation (e.g., anxiety, anger) and why deep breathing, muscle relaxation, and mindfulness helps. This should include a discussion on what our body does when we feel powerful feelings (e.g., higher heartrate, breathing, tense muscles, etc.).

2) Demonstrate how to use the skills, such as square or diaphragmatic breathing and muscle relaxation.

3) Begin the VR application. The program requires minimal experience (can be seated or standing); however, many children are new to VR, which means you may need to start off with the basics (e.g., the Home area). This is also a great way to further develop rapport. At this point, if you have not done so, I recommend getting their resting heart rate (if not using a monitor, have them count their heartbeat for ten seconds and multiply by six).

4) Begin the BreathePeace World app. They will meet Aya the baby panda bear in the first part and will continue in the second part to do deep, calm breathing with her in a snowy forest. In this app, as Aya breathes in, magical colors come into her chest and the trees all rise up. The opposite happens as she breathes out. Make sure to point this out (or have them point this out) to foster a conceptual understanding of what to do and how it works.

5) As the child practices the breathing with Aya, introduce some mindful-ness techniques by having them focus on the snowflakes, the rise of the trees, the changing of the colors, and gradually draw their focus into their physical state (e.g., heart rate, muscles, etc.). Remark on how calm Aya seems – saying or prompting them to discover that every muscle in her body looks relaxed – and have them imagine hundreds of tight rubber bands in their arms and legs loosening all at once, leaving their limbs soft and heavy. Continue this for a few moments.

6) Take the child's heartrate again, pointing out the likely decrease, and have them describe their state of calm and relaxation (e.g., how their body feels). A feeling wheel may be helpful here, too. Together, consider when and how they can use this skill at home or school, making sure to use examples that are likely to occur based upon past events.

7) Have the child's parents purchase download the app on their mobile device to practice at home, especially when the child is experiencing

feelings like anxiety or anger. Continue using Aya and the peaceful imagery to help the child develop their understanding and use of these therapeutic skills. Parents should prompt their upset child with the *choice* of practicing "Aya's breathing", which should be paired with verbal praise and possibly positive reinforcement within a token economy.

Rationale: We are all equipped with a necessary stress response system. It houses the uncomfortable neurological process that has protected our species for thousands of years. For some, it provides a keen awareness and healthy avoidance of legitimate threats, while serving as a strong intrinsic motivator to thrive. However, for others, it can elicit an unhealthy over-reactivity to such "threats" or cause a hypervigilance of *perceived* dangers that significantly interferes with one's life. When executive functioning fails to regulate these processes automatically, the individual must proactively engage the behavioral response areas of the brain to inhibit the stress response through parasympathetic activation – a fancy way of saying that they need to practice deep breathing, muscle relaxation and mindfulness to preventatively and acutely treat stress and/or emotional dysregulation. Young children often struggle to develop these skills because of difficulty conceptualizing what anxiety is and how biofeedback can alleviate it. By increasing immersion and providing a fun common language and imagery, therapists can more effectively help young children enjoy, learn, and use these skills to improve their social, emotional, and behavioral functioning.

Conclusion

Clinicians who work from numerous different theoretical perspectives find value in the use of digital tools in play therapy. The use can vary from play therapist to play therapist. The importance in hearing how different people use these therapeutic tools is to understand how very differently or similarly the tools can be used to achieve therapeutic outcomes. No matter how large or small the software or hardware, the impact is immeasurable.

Note

1. Adapted from the intervention Social Media from Grant, R. J. (2017). *Play-based interventions for Autism spectrum disorders and other developmental disabilities.* New York, NY: Routledge.

References

Aust, P. H. (1981). Using the life storybook in treatment of children in placement. *Child Welfare, 60*(8), 535–536, 553–560.

Fraser, T. (2014). Home should be where your story begins. *Relational Child and Youth Care Journal, 28*(2), 27–33.

Gobbetti, E., & Scateni, R. (1998). Virtual reality: Past, present and future. In G. Riva, B. K. Wiederhold, & E. Molinari (Eds.), *Studies in health technology and informatics,*

Vol. 58: Virtual environments in clinical psychology and neuroscience: Methods and techniques in advanced patient-therapist interaction. Amsterdam, Netherlands: IOS Press.

Jamerson, J. (2019, March). *Digital media arts: Therapeutic interventions for adolescents and others.* Workshop presented at Expressive Therapies Summit: Creativity & The Arts in Healing, Los Angeles, CA.

Oculus (n.d.). *Compare headsets.* www.oculus.com/compare/

Perry, B. D., F.M. (2013). *Brief: Reflections on childhood, trauma and society* [E-Reader Version]. https://itunes.apple.com/us/book/brief/id668004730?mt=11

Reese, J. (2009). *Life story books for adopted children: A family.* London, UK: Jessica Kingsley Publishers.

Sutherland, I. E. (1965). *The ultimate display.* http://worrydream.com/refs/Sutherland%20-%20The%20Ultimate%20Display.pdf

13 Jen, Jack, and Tyler
Detailed Case Examples

Case examples are invaluable to highlight and illustrate the concepts discussed in any clinical book, research, or training. Hearing how concepts come together in a clinical way with clients allows the mind to envision and integrate the concepts. The following case examples are meant to provide such illustrations and details intended to expand on concepts that contribute to the case formulation and treatment plan. To ensure confidentiality, all identifying information has been altered. Each case example will highlight the use of a different type of digital hardware: tablet, console, and virtual reality.

iPad Pro, 12.9" Tablet

Virtual Sandtray®©

Jennifer (Jen) is a seven-year-old second grade student who presented for play therapy services with her mother. Jen's mother was concerned about her daughter's difficulties in social situations, sibling interactions, and her self-esteem. Jen lives with both of her biological parents and three siblings. She is the third-born child.

Jen and her siblings have all been found to be within the gifted range intellectually, through formal psychological assessments. This is an important aspect to recognize as it is a common experience for gifted people to have some social difficulties. Being gifted is fundamentally about thinking differently than most other people. The gifted person's frequent depth and breadth of thought often contributes to difficulties in situations in which the gifted person(s) and non-gifted person(s) do not understand why the other does not understand, formulate, or discuss things in the same or similar way. It can be as though the parties are speaking different languages, and in some ways, they are (Stone, 2018, 2019; Daniels & Piechowski, 2009).

Giftedness also impacts the play therapy experience. This impact manifests as behaviors, needs, and interests which may not be presented in the same way as their similar-aged peers. One reason for these differences is asynchronous development (Stone, 2019; Silverman, 1997). It is very common for gifted people to develop at significantly different rates in certain areas as compared to their peers. Three of the common areas are: physical, emotional, and intellectual. A seven-year-old gifted person could present with the physical development (size, stature, coordination, motor, etc.) of a four-year-old, the emotional development of a five-year-old, and the intellectual development of a 14-year-old. This is only one example and the configurations can be quite varied.

This asynchrony can be a little startling to a play therapist, as the presentation is different for each category and out of the range of expectation at times. For instance, if the client has an intellectual developmental level of a 14-year-old but throws a temper tantrum of a five-year-old when s/he loses while playing Uno, it can be startling to witness. The 14-year-old intellect playing the game is impressive. The therapist can be pleasantly surprised by the advanced strategies and game play, the planning ahead, and the like, and then alerted (and possibly confused) by the young behavior and lack of expected exhibited social skills, frustration tolerance, and coping skills during the tantrum.

Jen exhibited asynchronous behaviors frequently as reported by her mother and teacher, and as witnessed in sessions. She had a significant amount of confusion when the asynchronicity arose as she did not understand why her behaviors were so different than others (she could recognize this when she was not in the middle of a situation) or why people responded to her negatively. She was experiencing a whole host of incongruencies in which what she expected either of herself or others, and/or what others expected of her, did not match up. This led to a tremendous amount of frustration and confusion for all involved.

Since Jen's emotional development was a bit delayed compared with her intellectual development, her response to this confusion and frustration often was behaviors that were unacceptable to others. She would get in trouble or have negative peer interactions, which would lead to self-questioning her abilities, her position, and activate her perfectionism. Frequently Jen would employ methods she hoped would allow her to regain control, which would, in turn, help her to feel safe but also would repel and upset others.

With an ability and propensity for non-stop thinking (a very busy mind) in great breadth and depth, this is a child who was questioning herself, others, and her position in the world almost constantly. She was exhausted and feeling rejected by those who were frequently either tired of her, unable to find ways to improve the situation, or both. People who interacted with her frequently felt like she would act superior and controlling and Jen often felt alone.

Often, Jen interacted with others who do not understand her. At the young age of seven, she already expects this will be the norm. The play therapist who can speak her language and coordinate the mental health care in a customized way, such as prescriptive play therapy, has a distinct advantage. If her complexities are respected, understood, and incorporated into the treatment, the therapeutic interactions will not only be successful, but will model important differences for her compared to what she typically experiences.

Sessions

Jen began her play therapy treatment with sessions full of exploration. She initially wanted to know all the rules and boundaries of the playroom. These is certainly different for each play therapist. In this office, the rules are few and include the following: 1) this is a place where we respect each other; 2) respect the play room: be careful with the items in the play room; and 3) more respect for the play room: we clean up an activity together before moving on to the next one. The first one, respecting each other, is something that is congruent with who this therapist is as a person. Respect is highly regarded, as is communication. Over time mutual respect grows along with rapport and results in a typically harmonious therapeutic relationship. Even when topics are difficult or two people do not agree, an underlying respect for one another improves the interactions. Age does not dictate the level of respect in the playroom, therefore, the emphasis is on mutuality. The first and third playroom rules were somewhat confusing for Jen initially, and became second nature as time went on.

The concept of mutual respect can be confusing for many children as often adults expect respect from the child in a hierarchical manner and do not afford the respect in return. The conceptualization of the nature of the relationship is one of: "I am the adult and you will respect my position, opinions, and requests/demands and you are the child who is not in a position of receiving respect". In the playroom, this dynamic is altered to include mutuality for both people (or each in a family). The client (any age) and the therapist both bring his/her own life expertise and experience to the session and together this is used toward the goal of life improvement. For many, this is a new experience and the reality of it will be reinforced through the many interactions within the playroom in both verbal and non-verbal ways.

Jen met with the therapist weekly and the treatment spanned 26 weeks. She attended regularly and sessions were rescheduled as needed to maintain the momentum of treatment. Meetings with the parents were offered on an as-needed basis per their discretion and they scheduled one appointment between sessions ten and 11 to discuss some at-home interactions and receive some parenting information. The therapist scheduled three appointments with the parents; one between sessions five and six to discuss what had been understood to date about Jen's personality, styles, and needs and discuss any questions brought up by the parents; one between sessions 14 and 15 to ask some questions of the parents, fill in missing information, and answer questions which had arisen; and finally one before session 26 to discuss the treatment to date, how the work had integrated into day-to-day life, and the termination process.

It is understood that rescheduling sessions so they are not missed is not possible in all situations, either for the therapist or client because of scheduling; however, maintaining consistency in the sessions is desirable. If a session is 45 minutes in length with consistent weekly attendance, then the first five to ten minutes are spent reconnecting and, if verbal interaction is a part of the session, informing of the week's happenings. Reconnection can be done in many ways and with many play activities and certainly do not require verbalizations. The next 30 minutes are the "meat" of the session, with activities and interactions that move the treatment forward in some way. The remaining time is used for closure; a beginning and an end to the time together and a desired reduction in the chance that the client will return to day-to-day life in a prematurely more open, more vulnerable position. If the client misses sessions or the sessions have to be scheduled further apart, the connection/reconnection process could take much longer, the meat time may be reduced, and the closure process could be more difficult. These are generalities and would potentially be different depending on the particular client, environment, and treatment plan.

Jen initially spent most of her time playing board games. She particularly enjoyed games which involve strategy, such as Mancala, MasterMind, and Stratego. These games yielded a wealth of information about Jen's approach to her world. She is the strategist. Jen really enjoyed and received an enormous amount of reinforcement in her life, for her ability to evaluate a defined situation and create ways to successfully maneuver through it. She was able to define her goal and, through incorporation of environment details, be successful in that goal. For the therapist, watching her work through this with such ease while playing a board game brought the question, "Why she was unable to apply these skills to her social interactions?", to the forefront. It was important to understand more about Jen.

The board games are very helpful to assess and understand areas such as level of mastery, frustration tolerance, coping skills, strategic abilities, rough IQ estimate, social interaction abilities/styles, competitiveness, norm compliance level, level of rapport, and development (Stone, 2016). For Jen, the predetermined structure to the board games allowed her initially to gain confidence and mastery and assisted with establishing a solid rapport. For some children, board game play therapy (Stone, 2016) is helpful throughout the treatment; however, for Jen it became a way to stay in her comfort zone. In line with prescriptive play therapy, it was decided that a new activity would be introduced to help Jen "drop down" to a more emotionally driven arena. "Drop down" is a term used to refer to approaching things from an intellectualized place (brain) to an emotionally driven place (heart).

Traditional sandtray was introduced to Jen and she was shown the tray, sand, and shelves of miniature figures. She ever-so-briefly touched the sand and decided she did not want to touch it. She discussed everything from the feel of the sand to the germs it must harbor, and she wanted no part. The process of, and information gleaned from, the sandtray process was really desired so Jen was given a few options: art materials, Virtual Sandtray on an iPad, and/or sensory materials. She chose the Virtual Sandtray. She was excited about the use of the iPad and the description of the process. Jen was able to create a world without having to touch the sand.

Jen was offered a quick tutorial run-through of the basic features, such as digging in the sand, building up the sand, painting the sand, and placing the 3D models. She listened intently for a few minutes and then began touching the iPad in quick, purposeful movements. It was merely moments before she had created a scene which included green grass, lava, barriers of sand, and holes dug deep to a liquid layer. She began searching through the models to find just the right buildings, fences, and animals. She was encouraged to ask for help but opted not to, even when it would have benefitted her. The therapist would then recognize when Jen was struggling a bit and offered assistance, either subtly or by directly stating, quickly and succinctly, how to do something such as resize an animal. She was most receptive to an excited statement such as, "Oh, did you see that you can make that animal bigger? If you want to do that, long press here and make it bigger". It was not done for her by the therapist; rather, it was an instruction through pointing at the screen components.

Over time Jen created many sandtrays. Some sessions she would create a brand-new tray and work on it for the majority of the session time. Other sessions she opted to return to a previously saved tray. In these instances, the amended tray was saved within the app under a different file name. For instance, if the original file was named "flowers" then the next one could be named "flowersb" to distinguish it from any others. This allows the therapist to go back to each, compare and contrast, and see how the changes made corroborated with the historical and current information. Each client has an individual, confidential login in the Virtual Sandtray App (VSA), so when Jen logged in, she had all her trays available to her.

The recurring undercurrent themes of Jen's trays were chaos and exclusion. Her trays were packed full of items. It appeared as though she were depicting what it felt like in her mind: busy and full, with so many things going on that it was hard to know where to focus. If one looked closely, it could be seen that within the apparent chaos were pockets of separation and detail. In one area there were 15 dragons of all types and sizes amongst the trees and interacting with others in some way. In the sand, partially buried and on its side, was a small dragon separate from all the others. Each of Jen's complex and chock-full trays had these elements scattered about. It was difficult to determine if it were a test for the therapist, "Can you figure out what I am trying to tell you? Are you capable of understanding me, because most people are not", or if Jen herself was unaware of what she was portraying. Either way, the recurrence of the themes was significant and had elements that were corroborated by her history.

Different sandtray therapy theories approach, witness, and process the sandtray intervention differently. A fantastic feature of the VSA is that it can be utilized in whatever way the therapist desires. It is a tool which invites the therapist to utilize his or her own theoretical foundation. In the sessions with Jen, approaching this from a prescriptive perspective, allowed the process and interaction to unfold as was determined by the therapist and client.

At times Jen worked within her state of flow. She was completely silent or would murmur quietly to herself. She would finish a tray and sit back and look at it or change the angles so she could inspect specific portions. She would rotate the tray, zoom in, and take screenshots of what she felt was important. Other times Jen was more directly interactive with the therapist. She asked questions which would range from how to accomplish something in the tray to soliciting the opinion of the therapist. At times there was a story upon completion of the tray or finishing for the session and other times there was not.

In one session she asked the therapist what she thought of the creation. This was her third session using the VSA. Responses by the therapist were focused on understanding, as much as possible, what Jen really wanted to know, what she sought by asking the question(s). For instance, was she seeking approval? Did she have a more logistic need? Did she want the therapist to join in the story or process or give guidance? Was she stuck? The underlying intention or need of the question was really important.

Since the theme of exclusion was so prevalent in her life outside the play therapy room and in her trays, when Jen asked the therapist what the little dragon could do (the half-buried one mentioned earlier), it appeared to be a query based in a need for interaction and guidance. The therapist responded with questions to better understand how Jen conceptualized the scenario. This was the therapist's attempt to avoid assumptions. The interaction about this little excluded dragon started out very vague and ambiguous and became more specific as more was understood about Jen's view of the tray's dynamic.

Jen revealed that the dragon was stuck. She knew she needed to get out of the sand soon or she may never get uncovered. There were so many other dragons around and she had no idea how to dig herself out. The other dragons were not even paying attention to her and she had been there a long, long time. Jen had revisited this saved tray a number of times and ended up with files ranging in names from "Dragons" to "Dragons 7". She was correct, this little dragon really had been there a long, long time. It was clear she was stuck. A discussion about the identification and role of a supportive helper started during "Dragons 5". How does one identify a helper? How does one vet the helper to determine trustworthiness? How does one ask for help?

These concepts were very frightening for Jen. They created insecure and unsafe feelings for her, and she would typically avoid these situations at all costs. Fortunately, the rapport between the therapist and client had been established well and when the therapist requested of Jen to extend her comfort zone, she was a cautious participant. Jen was able to assign a colorful dragon whose arms were on her hips in the role of helper. This dragon had proven her trustworthiness and therefore could help the little dragon.

When the little dragon was unburied in "Dragons 7", the process was long and comparatively drawn out. The little dragon, now named "Fire", was too weak to pull herself out of the sand; she needed the colorful dragon's help. The colorful dragon swished the sand away from Fire as she hummed a reassuring tune. Finally, Fire was free. She thanked the colorful dragon and asked if they could remain friends. The colorful dragon began to fly away, then she turned back toward Fire. "Maybe", she said, and she flew away. Fire had mixed feelings about this. She was happy the colorful dragon saved her and sad that she went away without knowing if they could become friends. "Sometimes you just don't know", Jen said.

In future VSA trays, Jen introduced helpers on her own. She frequently depicted helpers as not being initially trustworthy, and some situation would happen to show the helper's true character. Once the true character was clear, the central figure in the story would opt to trust him/her. Ultimately Jen had five 3D models she used repeatedly as helpers in her tray worlds. Her parents reported that Jen's interactions at home and school had improved drastically. Some behaviors and patterns to look for to determine if/when Jen needed to return to play therapy after the conclusion session were given to the parents.

There were many therapeutic powers of play and core agents of change employed within the use of the VSA for Jen. All four of the therapeutic powers of play quadrants were activated: facilitates communication, fosters emotional wellness, increases personal strengths, and enhances social relationships. Within those quadrants the following core agents of change were identified: self-expression, access to the unconscious, direct and indirect teaching, catharsis, abreaction, positive emotions, stress management, creative problem solving, self-regulation and self-esteem, therapeutic relationship, attachment, social competence, and empathy. The conversation with Jen's parents included these core agents as concepts we addressed and the progress she had made with each. The discussion was incredibly informative for all due to the use of the core agents of change. The structure provided language to understand the processes and dynamics of the play therapy sessions. The VSA was the tool and the play therapy process produced the forward movement and growth.

After approximately 18 months, Jen requested a follow-up session through her parents. She spent the session investigating the playroom for any changes and pointing them out. In addition, she excitedly updated the therapist about her involvement in a hip-hop dance team and how she was enjoying fourth grade. She discussed how she was frequently bored academically and together Jen and the therapist spoke with her mother about pursuing acceleration and/or enrichment. Overall, the concerns that Jen and her family initially brought to the play therapy process had been resolved toward a much healthier balance.

Consoles

Nintendo Switch

Jack was an eight-year-old, third-grade student who presented for play therapy treatment with his mother. It was reported that Jack was experiencing a significant amount of anxiety regarding social communication, particularly at school and afterschool activities. He would shut down, turn away, and hide under furniture when he had to verbally interact with other children. He attended a small school which accepted and accommodated his needs in this area, however, in third grade group projects and assignments became a frequent requirement. The first few years of school, the hope was that Jack would become more comfortable with the environment, teachers, and peers as well as reach new levels of maturity and increase his willingness to verbally interact.

Initially, Jack did not want to come to the playroom without his mother. The reluctance to interact with the therapist was unexpected, as adults were not listed in his areas of difficulty. He sat close to his mother and avoided eye contact with the therapist. Therefore, for the first two sessions, she attended with Jack. He participated in the activities and his anxiety appeared to lessen as he felt more safe and secure in the environment and interactions. He began sitting further away from his mother and his posture relaxed noticeably. It was agreed by all that he would come into the next session without his mother.

This session was the first with Jack and the therapist alone. The gains he had made during the weeks before seemed to vanish and he sat uncomfortably in the corner on a Hugibo pillow. The process of being in the playroom was repeated to remind Jack of his options. He was free to explore the room and choose what he would like to do. Since he was not choosing an activity and, based on his non-verbal behavior, his anxiety appeared to be worsening, the therapist opted for a parallel play route and started to play with the magnet tiles. The therapist narrated the play in hopes that Jack would become interested. His posture and stance did not change.

After quite some time of building and rebuilding, the therapist put the magnet tiles away and brought the Nintendo Switch off the shelf. Zelda BOW was the chosen game and the therapist removed the joy con controllers and placed the screen on a flat surface, propped up and facing the direction where Jack was sitting. The therapist could see that Jack's eyes were now watching the therapist and her activities. The verbalizations of the therapist included some details of the game play and some frustration at not being able to find all the components to complete the current quest. The therapist said to Jack directly, "usually kids in here use this left-hand controller and we play together. I am not very good at the left-hand controls so if you decide you want to help, I would be very grateful". After saying this, the game was resumed. Jack spent the next ten minutes inching closer and closer, until he said, "Hey, I know where that item is. I saw it on a YouTube video". Without making eye contact or verbalizing anything that acknowledged his involvement, the therapist passed over the left-hand controller.

The Nintendo Switch is unique in that the controllers can be used independently. Each controller is used for different functions, for instance, the left controller has the ability to make the character, Link, walk and change directions. However, the left controller cannot change the viewpoint, so if two different people have a controller, they must work together to accomplish simple tasks, including not walking off a cliff. Everything from accomplishing goals to self-preservation relies on the communication between the two players. If this gameplay was important enough for Jack, he would have motivation to sit closer to the screen and the therapist by default and to speak to the therapist to coordinate movements and efforts.

The interest shown by Jack in the use of Zelda and the Nintendo Switch let the therapist know that this was going to be a highly motivating activity. He had watched a lot of YouTube videos of people playing Zelda but had never played it himself. He was initially a little frustrated by the one-controller-per-person arrangement, but the desire to play helped him to move past the frustration.

There were quite a few instances when Jack did not communicate his needs or desires within the game. This lack of communication led to a variety of events. When exploring the different areas, Link, the main character of the game, can encounter a variety of dangers including trolls called bokoblins, skeleton-like creatures called stalkoblins, flying keese, and more. Link was attacked multiple times by these creatures without a good way to defend the character due to the lack of communication between the therapist and client. Link also fell off a cliff and missed out on catching a horse. A brief pause in the game allowed time for the therapist and Jack to regroup and discuss goals and tactics. A new approach was devised which included non-verbal communication regarding the direction Link would travel in and therefore need to look. A discussion about how the music changed when danger was close by resulted in one person specifically listening for the music and alerting the other person. Ways to work together to battle enemies were also discussed. The game was un-paused, and the play continued with much greater success.

Jack soon became aware of the benefits of communicating with an identified person about what he wanted out of an interaction. Jack became quite verbal about what he thought should happen in the game at any given moment. Once he was confidently coming into the playroom, getting out the switch, and giving the right-hand joy con controller to the therapist, it was time to work on the next level skills of teamwork and communication. A solid level of comfort was desired so the potential backslide, as experienced in the first solo session, would be minimized before challenging him.

The therapist reflected what it was like to have Jack demand certain things of the therapist, not work as a true team, and not have space for the goals of *both* people playing. The therapist pondered whether or not any of what the she was experiencing with Jack happens in other situations. Does Jack remain quiet until he is motivated to engage and then tries to take over and control the situation? Once Jack tries to control the situation do his peers reject him? What was that rejection like for Jack? Certainly, most humans do not like rejection; however, Jack's experience of this appeared to exacerbate some of what Jack was already understanding about his place in the world: he felt he was not acceptable as a withdrawn person nor was he acceptable as an outspoken person. It was difficult for him to recognize his own contribution to the dynamic or that moderation of his responses could result in a more satisfactory outcome. Jack and the therapist explored this further.

It was identified that Jack had difficulty moderating his responses to uncomfortable situations. If he felt "less than" in some way with an interaction, then he felt he would need to respond in a way that represented one of the two ends of the spectrum: all-in, with a need to control the situation so he did not feel too vulnerable, or all-out, so he could feel (relatively) unaffected by the situation. Neither felt sufficient to him, as he had a strong desire to be accepted by his peers and included in activities.

Soon Jack was requesting to play other games in sessions. Board games became a common request. It quickly became apparent that Jack continued a similar response pattern: withdraw or control. This game play included a significant amount of mirroring, modeling, and processing to assist Jack with an increased level of self-awareness. Once he truly understood the patterns of his interactions and his part in them, he could choose to alter his responses. If he did not choose to change his responses, then an exploration into what he desired would be important. If he chose not to change his responses, it would indicate that his need for something else was stronger than his need for the improved social interactions and the treatment plan/goals would need to be altered. If you can identify the motivation and need in a situation, and address it, the drive for change is exponentially increased.

Some exciting information was generated from the Zelda game play. In reviewing the treatment to this point, Jack was able to engage in play activities with the therapist first with his mother present and then again when his mother was not, after a readjustment period. The Nintendo Switch was a highly motivating digital tool and the Zelda game allowed the game play components to reveal and highlight some of Jack's social difficulties. Board game play also revealed the same response patterns. The consistency gave strength to the hypotheses. Both Zelda and board game play continued throughout the remainder of the treatment. Jack was encouraged to tolerate the gray areas between the black and white polar ends. Slowly the safety and trust of the relationship allowed Jack to experiment with the gray. For example, instead of attempting to gain full control of the interactions, Jack worked on reciprocal interactions. In Zelda, what did the two players want to accomplish as a team? What might they want separately, and how could that be supported by the other and integrated into the general game play? The more successes he experienced, the more motivation he had to continue. The more motivation he had, the more progress he made. The more progress he made, the more confidence he had to attempt these new skills outside of the play therapy room.

The therapeutic powers of play core agents that were activated in these sessions included the following: facilitates communication – self-expression, direct and indirect teaching; fosters emotional wellness – positive emotion, counterconditioning fears, stress inoculation, and stress management; increases personal strengths – creative problem solving, resiliency, moral development, self-regulation, and self-esteem; and enhances social relationships – therapeutic relationship, attachment, social competence, and empathy. The activities were very well-suited for his needs and desires. The high motivation he felt toward playing the activities increased his personal resilience and kept him moving forward in his self-awareness and growth.

A meeting with Jack's mother revealed that he had been attempting different social responses and interactions during his afterschool activities. This was most likely due to the nature of the interactions: periodic (not daily like school), structured around an activity, and time-limited. The few remaining sessions were focused on these attempts and the important generalization to his school interactions. A phone meeting with Jack's teacher informed her of the work to date and the teacher and therapist collaborated regarding appropriate support for Jack to experience success in school. After the conclusion of play therapy, a brief email from his mom included positive updates regarding Jack's greatly improved social interactions and participation in required and non-required group activities.

Virtual Reality

Beat Saber

Tyler was a ten-year-old boy who lived with family members because of the death of his father and because of his mother's inability to care for him. Tyler presented as an empathic young man who experiences his perceptions of many things very deeply. He had become quite proficient in allowing others to see a relatively happy young boy, but the pain of trauma, loss, and grief were quite close to the surface.

His caregivers brought him to play therapy to provide additional support for this child who had already experienced so much pain in life. In addition, some difficult behaviors had emerged and, although they had great insight into the etiologies of the behavior, they 1) did not want an increase in the behaviors and 2) felt the current level was quite disruptive to their household. Tyler lived with the two adult family members and their two biological children, ages four and 12.

Tyler was seen in play therapy for approximately two years. The initial presenting issues included angry verbal and non-verbal outbursts, hitting the younger child in the house, enuresis, poor sleep cycles, and food hoarding. The trauma and loss in his life resulted in the formation of an extremely cautious and distrusting world view. Adults were not to be trusted and, even if he extended the boundaries to trust an adult, that adult could leave even if s/he did not want to. The foundation of trust, safety, and reliability were paramount for Tyler and for the play therapy work.

This situation required a large amount of "front loading". Front loading is the process of discussing, informing, and preparing the parents, caregivers, collateral contacts, and so on for the process and/or interventions that the upcoming sessions may or will include. This includes the description of any interventions and the rationale behind such interventions. At times, particularly in instances of introducing new tools such as digital ones, frontloading includes having the adult(s) try the intervention. It is important that the caregivers understand the therapeutic underpinnings of the use of the tool. This is true with any play therapy intervention.

From a caregiver's perspective, it can be very confusing how playing a game of HORSE (a basketball game), or working with shaving cream, puppets, board games, or digital tools can be helpful in therapy. "I am paying you *how much* to *play x* with my child?" can be a common theme. This speaks to the importance of front loading and therapist competence and comfort. If the play therapist has a solid theoretical foundation, applies the therapeutic powers of play, understands the core agents of change, and communicates these effectively to the caregivers and/or collateral contacts, the initial understanding of the play therapy process will improve dramatically. In addition, follow-up check-in appointments with the caregivers will improve. The subsequent conversations with the caregivers will build on the information and education given before the course of treatment and/or intervention(s).

Tyler began his time in play therapy with a consistent focus on Legos® and Playmobil®. He built and destroyed again and again. He depicted unsafe worlds and interactions repeatedly. When support and helpers were introduced, they were swiftly rejected. Involvement by the play therapist was not accepted for quite some time. As the rapport was established, the therapist was invited into the play bit by bit. Tyler's verbal and non-verbal interactions with the therapist were indicating an increasing level of comfort and safety.

He further explored the items in the play therapy room as his comfort increased. Over the next year, he expanded to playing board games, drawing, and even writing a book together all about him, his family, and his history. It was reported by home and school that his aggressive behaviors had been predominantly extinguished. His enuresis had stopped. Tyler was doing quite well. He would have expected spikes in difficulties around certain anniversaries. The family and therapist would discuss these in advance and prepare by discussing how to best support him.

Academically, Tyler had amazing strengths in reading and writing. He devoured books and enjoyed writing short stories and graphic novels. He had some difficulties in math and with attending to details. Teachers and his caregivers had attempted to show him the importance of learning how to pay attention to details in different settings. His caregivers modeled how they accomplished this in their day-to-day tasks. Tyler was not integrating it into his life, and the adults in his life were increasingly worried that this perceived inability (on Tyler's part) was affecting his self-esteem.

Some part-to-whole and detail identification activities were introduced to Tyler within the play therapy sessions. He would participate to a point. It did not appear that the activities were highly motivating enough to keep him engaged to the point of recognizing either: the value in the effort required to attend to details or the value in the effort required to integrate the skills into his activities. The challenge was to find something he really wanted to do that would include identification, practice, and integration of attention to detail skills. After a front loading conversation with the caregivers, it was decided to use the virtual reality game, *Beat Saber*, in session. The adults were able to use the headset for a demonstration session (the demo version) and the therapeutic powers of play agents were discussed.

The gameplay is a pretty simple concept that can become more complicated when/if one chooses increased levels of difficulty. Each time one plays Beat Saber, they are to choose a song and level of difficulty. With the head-mounted VR display headset in place, the player stands oriented to a hallway and his/her hands are seen as two different colored light sabers. The haptic response within the handheld controllers has the mind believing the light sabers exist, and even touching the "blades" together yields sparks and tension. The music starts and cubes that correspond to the light saber colors begin to come toward the player. Each cube has either an arrow or a dot on it. The arrow indicated the direction in which the cube must be sliced in half. A dot on the cube indicates that it can be sliced in any direction. For instance, if a blue cube with an arrow pointing to the right comes into view, then the player knows they must use the hand with the blue light saber to swing to the right and cut the cube in half. The pieces fall down into the abyss below and the player then attend to whatever cubes come forward next. Sometimes they appear quickly in succession, sometimes they are slower; sometimes one appears at a time and other times both colors appear at once dictating that both hands will slice at once.

As the music plays, the cubes present in ways that predominantly correlate with the beat. A movement rhythm can be found as one slices the cubes with the light sabers. The game includes settings which can be altered depending on the client's needs. As an example, the arrows can be removed from the cubes so the person can slice in any direction, thereby reducing the incidence of frustration and allowing for the practice of purely color responsiveness. As the confidence and mastery skills increase, the settings can be changed. There is a lot going on in Beat Saber. There are music, colors, scenery, and arrows/ direction, as well as a goal of not missing any cues and receiving a high score; however, it is coordinated, and the level of difficulty can be customized. The music and game play are fun, upbeat, and highly motivating. The cubes arrive in front of you and it is fun and active to slice them in half. The songs are time-limited and a score is given at the end. A choice is then given to restart the same level or begin a new one.

Because of the combination of the highly motivating activity and the focus on attending to details, Beat Saber seemed the preferred choice for Tyler. He was very excited to try anything in virtual reality. He was acclimated to the VR experience through the use of theBlu and NatureTreks programs before moving on to Beat Saber. This allowed Tyler to better understand the overall experience of VR, the controllers, and his own body in the VR space before having the added tasks included in Beat Saber. He did not report any simulation sickness.

After completing the tutorial, Tyler set out to play a level higher than his ability. The therapist attempted to steer him toward starting at the "easy" level and working his way into harder levels as he became more acclimated. He opted to begin at a more difficult level and was told it was simple to change the level if he decided it was desired. Once he realized for himself that the level he chose was too advanced, he quickly navigated to an easier level. Tyler had a lot of fun slicing the cubes and repeated levels over and over to increase his score. When he first began using the program, he missed quite a few of the cubes in general and also made mistakes with both the cube color cues and the directional cues. Once he understood the task, he exhibited great perseverance as he worked through the levels and increased his score.

Tyler had been involved in the family meeting wherein the use of VR and *Beat Saber* was discussed. He heard the connection with his tendency to miss cues and details. He started to declare, during the play, "Look at all these details I am slicing!". He was very proud of himself as his scores steadily increased. After the session, the process of beginning at a level that was too advanced, the perseverance and attention to detail that was necessary to improve his score, and the sense of pride and accomplishment, was verbalized by both Tyler and the therapist. The fun, active energy in the room was palpable.

The hope was, as he understood the process he went through with *Beat Saber* to feel successful, that this would guide him toward generalizing what he had learned and experienced. The application of the following concepts started to have value for him: 1) choose a task that is at or below your perceived ability level to acclimate to the task, 2) progress as confidence grows, 3) keep practicing until the task feels more achievable, and 4) attention to details and cues helps one feel more successful in the task at hand. His caregivers were asked to 1) reinforce when they witnessed him or heard of him (i.e., from a teacher) successfully attending to cues and/or details and 2) prompt him in non-stressful situations to attend to cues and/or details. The non-game play practice in the time between sessions would assist him with integrating his newly identified abilities into his day-to-day life.

Tyler continued to play Beat Saber for many weeks and ultimately achieved levels much higher than the therapist ever reached. His confidence grew by leaps and bounds within and between sessions, and his family was recognizing the difference. The therapeutic powers of play activated within the use of Beat Saber include the following: fosters emotional wellness with positive emotions, stress inoculation, and management; enhance social relationship with therapeutic relationship and social competence; increases personal strengths with resiliency, creative problem solving, self-regulation, and self-esteem; and facilitates communication with self-expression and direct and indirect teaching. The use of VR and the *Beat Saber* game in play therapy facilitated understanding and change that the other items in the playroom could not.

Conclusion

The inclusion of each of these therapeutic digital tool interventions allowed a path and process of change which might not have happened. Jen, Jack, and Tyler each chose software and hardware that spoke to them in some way and allowed them to express what they needed to in a way that was engaging, fun, and highly motivating. Having DPT tools available for clients to choose, along with a knowledgeable play therapist, enhances the play therapy process.

References

Daniels, S., & Piechowski, M. (2009). *Living with intensity*. Great Potential Press.
Silverman, L. (1997). The construct of asynchronous development. *Peabody Journal of Education, 72*(3&4), 36–58.

Stone, J. (2016). Board games in play therapy. In K. J. O'Connor, C. E. Schaefer, & L. D. Braverman (Eds.), *Handbook of play therapy* (2nd ed., pp. 309–326). Wiley.

Stone, J. (2018). *Working with gifted children in play therapy, part 1.* https://jentaylorplaytherapy.com/working-gifted-children-part-1/

Stone, J. (2019). Connecting gifted people: Utilizing technology in mental health to speak an intellectually gifted person's language. In J. Stone (Ed.), *Integrating technology into modern therapies* (pp. 149–165). Abingdon, UK: Routledge.

14 Conclusion

Hope

It is my sincere hope that you found some gems in this book that will enhance and expand your play therapy practice. Gems we find in books can open minds and change worlds. The intention for this book was not to be all-encompassing, but to assure the play therapist's mind regarding technology use in play therapy. There is therapeutic value in the discussion of your client's interests, in the knowledge of such interests, entering their world and culture, and the inclusion of digital tools in play therapy. Digital play therapy is not about jumping on some trendy bandwagon; it is about appropriately incorporating cultural shifts and having a foundation for such inclusion.

Digital Play Therapy

Digital play therapy is a modality that utilizes highly motivating, immersive activities to incorporate areas of client interest into the play therapy process to deepen relationships, gather information, implement interventions, and advance the treatment plan forward.

Digital play therapy incorporates a variety of techniques to enter the client's world and connect within their culture. For those clients who have interest in digital programs, games, and hardware, DPT allows the space and utilization of their interests in a therapeutic environment. The inclusion of such tools honors parts of the client which might be marginalized in other arenas and emphasizes the acceptance of all parts of the client. Accessibility for all is a goal, and DPT expands the possibilities for those who are unable to access traditional methods, for a multitude of reasons. Play therapists are in a unique and privileged role to be invited into another's sacred world. It is important that we join hands and find value in current cultures as a profession.

4 Cs

The 4 Cs therapist incorporates competency, comfort, culture, and the aspiration to capability into their day-to-day work. We all strive for these goals for the benefit of our clients and of our own personal and professional integrity. We can take pride in knowing we are working toward betterment throughout our careers. There is no finishing line; these are lifelong aspirations for the play therapist. Consultation, supervision, education, research, and experience will propel the play therapist forward in their 4 C quests.

Prescriptive

Prescriptive play therapists tailor the treatment conceptualization and interventions to the client and their needs. This one-size-does-*not*-fit-all approach allows for the customization in pairing not only the play therapy tools with the client needs, but also the connection, interactions, interpretations, and interventions within the play therapy. Human beings tend to have many commonalities along with many differences. Prescriptive play therapy honors and attends to such differences. A play therapist is best equipped when they know the foundation of many different theories and approaches and apply them as deem appropriate with their 4 C principles.

Modalities

Play therapy modalities have been defined by Kaduson & Schaefer for our exploration and application. How these modalities are incorporated into your practice may change over time depending on your clientele and the cultural needs they encompass. These modality categories might look different throughout your career, but the fundamental concept is to acknowledge and utilize modalities which meet your client's needs and activate the therapeutic powers of play.

Understanding Research

Research is a daunting subject for many, and the purpose of its inclusion in the book is to provide some basic information while sparking an interest in the necessary process of critical review of the information we encounter. Hopefully you have an increased grasp, or a bit of a reminder, of the concerns regarding confirmation bias, research methodology, pitfalls in data handling, and how conclusions are reached in research. The future could bring some much-needed shifts in the transparency of research design, collection, and therefore the conclusions drawn, so we might have more solid foundations for programs and policies that affect us all. These are exciting times.

Folk Devils and Moral Panic

Folk devils and moral panic have been fed by fear for as long as humans have interacted with anything. We are wired for flight–fight–freeze acute stress responses through our hypothalamus. These responses are here to keep us safe from perilous situations. There is a cycle to these processes whereby the acute stress response is activated, there is a lot of expressed concern, followed by other perspectives, and landing in adjustment to attain a sense of balance once again. It is critical in any of these situations to breathe, find one's center, and assess what the scenario is truly bringing. If the situation has negative aspects, learn more; discover more; understand more. Find ways to bring it into balance. Chicken Little believed the sky was falling and the world was ending while stirring everyone into a panic and leading them all straight to the fox and therefore to their demise. Versions of this story date back thousands of years and continue the messages: do not believe everything you are told, slow down and evaluate a situation, and be brave.

Hardware and Software

The types of hardware and software will change dramatically over the years while this book is on the shelves, but the basics will remain. The importance of discovering which systems and programs meet the needs of one's clients is paramount. The journey a play therapist takes in discovering this need-to-tool fit will be career long. DPT is not about incorporating all types of programs, games, and systems. Some things will not be a good fit for the therapist who has attended to the 4 Cs and others will yield therapeutic results that will strike excitement in all who are involved. A balance of 4 C exploration and attainment along with congruency and self-awareness will serve the profession well.

Video Game Genres

The many different video game genres are not all-inclusive or indicative of an issue-free categorization system, but they do provide us some direction when searching through the thousands of available programs. The genres give play therapists a place to start, or from which to continue, the journey of finding therapeutic value within the use of DPT. Different types, and different games within each type, will have certain similarities and differences so it is important to realize that one size does not fit all and that even programs within a category are not all the same. The genres are not mutually exclusive. There will be a lot of overlap with other genres being represented within many gaming programs.

Digital Citizenship

Digital citizenship focuses on the important aspects of education, protection, and respect when utilizing digital tools. Understanding and navigating through the important guidelines that digital citizenship provides allows the play therapist, clients, and families to incorporate healthy online behavior into their day-to-day lives. Co-play interactions benefit the therapist–client relationship as well as peer and familial intergenerational relationships. The digital native, immigrant, technoskeptic, technophobe, and technoneccessist each have a place in the DPT world. Teaching, guiding, and reinforcing digital citizenship will enhance the experience of all involved and the citizenship may very well generalize to other day-to-day interactions.

Interventions

Numerous esteemed colleagues contributed their tried and true, beloved DPT interventions for your review. Although reading a single author's opinions and experiences can be valuable, the importance of gathering information from multiple clinicians cannot be discounted. Therefore the interventions in this section represent clinicians from around the world and multiple theoretical foundations. I am certain you will have your own discoveries and uses to add to this type of list. Perhaps we can include them in the next edition of this book.

Case Examples

Case examples are frequently my favorite part of any mental health–focused book. After reading the concepts and gems provided by the author, the case examples are a fantastic way to read and envision how the concepts look in action. Perhaps the clinician proceeded differently than you would have, but the concepts are illustrated in a way that hopefully allows the reader to formulate how it would look within their own 4 C construct. This is one of the beautiful aspects of DPT: it is not a theory, it is a modality, and it can be adopted and adapted within one's existing structure to form a congruent experience for the client and the therapist.

The Future

The future of DPT, play therapy in general, and society are certainly unknown to me, but I predict that play therapists will come to own this portion of play within mental health. We know play. We understand the therapeutic powers of play as no other discipline does or will. New generations of digital-native clients and therapists are here, and they continue to quickly usher in. The questions will shift from "why would we include these tools" to "why are we not/ would we not including/include these tools?"

The future will hopefully bring some significant shifts in the way research is formulated, conducted, analyzed, conceptualized, and shared. Transparency is going to be fundamental in our ability to formulate future societal decisions and recommendations. Professional and personal directions are informed by the understandings gleaned from research and we must have solid ground beneath our feet to move forward. Folk devils and moral panic only serve us to the point of awareness, so that we are aware that there is something to explore further. Past that point they can become counterproductive.

I will continue to speak, write, supervise, practice, and learn about the many facets of the digital world and DPT. I have experienced the power of joining with my clients when they feel heard, seen, understood, and accepted and DPT is a very powerful modality in this regard. I have watched parallels of numerous life concepts displayed and worked through during the use of digital tools. I have witnessed and been told of the generalization of skills and understandings being incorporated into a client's day-to-day life and interactions.

Thank You

Thank you for your time and attention to the words printed in this book, the concepts presented, and the incorporation of the important advancements in the play therapy field. As a play therapist, mother, psychologist, business owner, perfectionist, and a continual 4 C pursuant, I can assure you that more revelations will come over time. My hope is that many of you will join the ever-growing numbers of mental health and medical practitioners who have embraced the incorporation of digital tools into their work.

The more we understand about the various components involved in our societal shift to a technologically driven world, the inter- and intra-play between and within the components, and the effects each have on our personal and professional lives, the better-equipped we all will be to navigate. I raise a virtual glass to you as a toast for what has been and what is to become. May you expand on these concepts and uses in ways not yet discovered.

Index